SCIENTISTS: Their Lives and Works

SCIENTISTS. Their Lives and Works

Marie C. Ellavich, Editor

VOLUME 4

**Helen Plum Library
Lombard, IL**

DETROIT • NEW YORK • TORONTO • LONDON

AN IMPRINT OF GALE

Scientists: Their Lives and Works

Edited by Marie C. Ellavich

Staff

Sonia Benson, *U•X•L Senior Editor*
Carol DeKane Nagel, *U•X•L Managing Editor*
Thomas L. Romig, *U•X•L Publisher*

Shanna P. Heilveil, *Production Associate*
Evi Seoud, *Assistant Production Manager*
Mary Beth Trimper, *Production Director*

Margaret Chamberlain, *Permissions Specialist*

Tracey Rowens, *Art Director*
Cynthia Baldwin, *Product Design Manager*
Linda Mahoney, *Typesetter*

Library of Congress Cataloging-in-Publication Data

Scientists : Their lives and works

   edited by Marie C. Ellavich.
      p. cm.
     Includes bibliographical references and index.
     Contents: v. 4. A-Z
     ISBN 0-7876-1874-8
     1. Physical Scientists—Biography. 2. Social scientists—Biography.
Q141.S3717 1997
509'.2'2—dc20
[B]
                                         96-25579
                                       CIP

Contents

Nicolaus Copernicus

Scientists by Field of Specialization ix

Reader's Guide xxv

Timeline of Scientific Breakthroughs xxvii

Words to Know xxxi

VOLUME 4

Joy Adamson 1

Jöns Jacob Berzelius 7
    Carl Gustaf Mosander (box) 12

Vilhelm Bjerknes 15
    Jacob Bjerknes (box) 19

Wernher von Braun 22
    Alan Shepard (box) 29

Benjamin Carson 33

Kenneth B. Clark 40

Nicolaus Copernicus 48
   Jean-Bernard-Léon Foucault (box) 52

Patricia S. Cowings 55

Seymour Cray 59

Raymond A. Dart 66
   Robert Broom (box) 71

Alice Evans 74
   David Bruce (box) 78

Henry Ford 80
   Gottlieb Daimler (box) 87

Dian Fossey 92
   Biruté Galdikas (box) 97

Galileo Galilei 100
   Simon Stevin (box) 106

Alice Hamilton 110

Frédéric Joliot-Curie and Irène Joliot-Curie 117
   Georg von Hevesy (box) 123

Johannes Kepler 126
   Giovanni Domenico Cassini (box) 132

Har Gobind Khorana 133
   Robert W. Holley (box) 138

Flemmie Pansy Kittrell 141

Lewis H. Latimer 145

Rita Levi-Montalcini 150
   Stanley Cohen (box) 154

Carolus Linnaeus 157
   Georges Cuvier (box) 161

Wangari Maathai 164

Maria Mitchell 170
   Jan Oort (box) 174

Isaac Newton 176
   Robert Hooke (box) 181

Ida Tacke Noddack 185
    Emilio Segrè (box) 188

David Powless 190

Julia Robinson 194

Carl Sagan 198

Helen Brooke Taussig 208
    Alfred Blalock (box) 213

Valentina Tereshkova 215
    Sally Ride (box) 218

J. J. Thomson 220
    William Crookes (box) 225

Alan Turing 228

Picture Credits 235

Index 237

Scientists by Field of Specialization

Includes *Scientists,* volumes 1-4.
Italic type indicates volume numbers.

Valentina Tereshkova

Aeronautical Engineering
Wernher von Braun *4:* 22
Orville Wright *3:* 987
Wilbur Wright *3:* 987

Agriculture
Norman Borlaug *1:* 105
George Washington Carver *1:* 144
Sally Fox *1:* 298
Charles Townshend *3:* 911

Anatomy
Florence R. Sabin *3:* 822
Berta Scharrer *3:* 847

Anthropology
Raymond A. Dart *4:* 66
Irene Diggs *1:* 229

Thor Heyerdahl *2:* 448
Donald Johanson *2:* 515
Louis S. B. Leakey *2:* 575
Mary Leakey *2:* 575
Richard Leakey *2:* 575
Margaret Mead *2:* 633
Arthur C. Parker *3:* 717

Archaeology
George Bass *1:* 53
Louis S. B. Leakey *2:* 575
Mary Leakey *2:* 575
Richard Leakey *2:* 575

Astronomy and Space
Jocelyn Bell Burnell *1:* 69
Wernher von Braun *4:* 22
Annie Jump Cannon *1:* 131
Nicolaus Copernicus *4:* 48
Patricia S. Cowings *4:* 55
Sandra M. Faber *1:* 270
Galileo Galilei *4:* 100
Margaret Geller *2:* 380
Stephen Hawking *2:* 432
William Herschel *2:* 441
Edwin Hubble *2:* 487
Johannes Kepler *4:* 126
Maria Mitchell *4:* 170
Carl Sagan *4:* 198
Valentina Tereshkova *4:* 215
James Van Allen *3:* 917

Astrophysics
E. Margaret Burbidge *1:* 117
Geoffrey Burbidge *1:* 117
Subrahmanyan Chandrasekhar *1:* 150

Atomic/Nuclear Physics
Luis Alvarez *1:* 7
Fred Begay *1:* 58

Niels Bohr *1:* 98
Enrico Fermi *1:* 285
Maria Goeppert-Mayer 2: 399
Shirley Ann Jackson 2: 498
Tsung-Dao Lee *3:* 1012
Lise Meitner 2: 639
Ida Tacke Noddack *4:* 185
J. Robert Oppenheimer 2: 680
Max Planck *3:* 759
Ernest Rutherford *3:* 805
Abdus Salam *3:* 832
J. J. Thomson *4:* 220
James S. Williamson *3:* 964
Chien-Shiung Wu *3:* 999
Chen Ning Yang 3: 1012

Bacteriology

Alice Evans *4:* 74
Alexander Fleming *1:* 292
William Augustus Hinton *2:* 463

Biochemistry

Bruce N. Ames *1:* 19
Paul Berg *1:* 75
Elizabeth H. Blackburn *1:* 88
Carl Ferdinand Cori *1:* 161
Gerty T. Cori *1:* 161
Gertrude Belle Elion 2: 468
George H. Hitchings 2: 468
Har Gobind Khorana *4:* 133
Florence Seibert *3:* 855
Maxine Singer *3:* 870

Biology

Francisco Dallmeier *1:* 192
Charles Darwin *1:* 203
Paul R. Ehrlich *1:* 254
Sally Fox *1:* 298

Stephen Jay Gould *2:* 415
Ernest Everett Just *2:* 543
Ruth Patrick *3:* 733
Berta Scharrer *3:* 847
Edward O. Wilson *3:* 969

Biomedical Engineering
Godfrey Hounsfield *2:* 483
Robert K. Jarvik *2:* 502
James E. Lovelock *2:* 596

Biophysics
Edith H. Quimby *3:* 776

Botany
Luther Burbank *1:* 112
George Washington Carver *1:* 144
Sylvia A. Earle *1:* 239
Carolus Linnaeus *4:* 157
Ruth Patrick *3:* 733
Mark Plotkin *3:* 766

Cardiology
Helen Brooke Taussig *4:* 208

Chemistry
Svante Arrhenius *1:* 30
Jöns Jacob Berzelius *4:* 7
Katharine Burr Blodgett *1:* 92
Marie Curie *1:* 181
Pierre Curie *1:* 181
John Dalton *1:* 197
Humphry Davy *1:* 211
Michael Faraday *1:* 275
Lloyd A. Hall *2:* 427
Dorothy Hodgkin *2:* 474
Frédéric Joliot-Curie *4:* 117
Irène Joliot-Curie *4:* 117

Percy L. Julian 2: 529
Antoine Lavoisier 2: 568
Dmitry Mendeleev 2: 654
Alfred Nobel 2: 670
Ida Tacke Noddack 4: 185
Louis Pasteur 3: 723
Linus Pauling 3: 738
Joseph Priestley 3: 772

Climatology
James E. Lovelock 2: 596

Computer Science
Charles Babbage 1: 37
Lynn Conway 1: 158
Seymour Cray 4: 59
Bill Gates 2: 363
Godfrey Hounsfield 2: 483
Steven Jobs 2: 508
Jaron Lanier 2: 562
Marvin Minsky 2: 665
Robert Noyce 2: 674
Alan Turing 4: 228
An Wang 3: 923

Cosmology
Stephen Hawking 2: 432
William Herschel 2: 441
Edwin Hubble 2: 487

Crystallography
Dorothy Hodgkin 2: 474

Ecology
Rachel Carson 1: 137
Francisco Dallmeier 1: 192
Paul R. Ehrlich 1: 254
Ruth Patrick 3: 733
Edward O. Wilson 3: 969

Electrical Engineering

Seymour Cray *4:* 59
Lee De Forest *1:* 217
Thomas Alva Edison *1:* 244
Lewis H. Latimer *4:* 145
Guglielmo Marconi *2:* 607
William Shockley *3:* 862
Nikola Tesla *3:* 889
Vladimir Zworykin *3:* 1017

Engineering

Lynn Conway *1:* 158
Lee De Forest *1:* 217
Rudolf Diesel *1:* 224
Thomas Alva Edison *1:* 244
R. Buckminster Fuller *1:* 333
Meredith Gourdine *2:* 422
Godfrey Hounsfield *2:* 483
Steven Jobs *2:* 508
Elijah McCoy *2:* 628
James Watt *3:* 945
Granville T. Woods *3:* 980

Entomology

Edward O. Wilson *3:* 969

Environmentalism

Joy Adamson *4:* 1
Jacques Cousteau *1:* 168
Richard Leakey *2:* 575
Wangari Maathai *4:* 164

Environmental Science

Bruce N. Ames *1:* 19
Helen Caldicott *1:* 124
Paul R. Ehrlich *1:* 254
James E. Lovelock *2:* 596
Mark Plotkin *3:* 766

David Powless *4:* 190
Edward O. Wilson *3:* 969

Epidemiology
Helene D. Gayle *2:* 376

Ethnobotany
Mark Plotkin *3:* 766

Ethology
Karl von Frisch *1:* 320
Jane Goodall *2:* 405
Konrad Lorenz *2:* 588

Evolutionary Biology
Raymond A. Dart *4:* 66
Charles Darwin *1:* 203
Jane Goodall *2:* 405
Stephen Jay Gould *2:* 415

Genetics
Bruce N. Ames *1:* 19
Paul Berg *1:* 75
Norman Borlaug *1:* 105
Francis Crick *1:* 174
Rosalind Franklin *1:* 302
Walter Gilbert *2:* 384
Har Gobind Khorana *4:* 133
Barbara McClintock *2:* 622
Gregor Mendel *2:* 648
Maxine Singer *3:* 870
James D. Watson *3:* 933

Geology
Keiiti Aki *1:* 1
Robert D. Ballard *1:* 48
Stephen Jay Gould *2:* 415
Charles F. Richter *3:* 780

Geophysics

Keiiti Aki *1:* 1
Vilhelm Bjerknes *4:* 15
Alfred Wegener *3:* 951

History of Science

Stephen Jay Gould 2: 415

Horticulture

Luther Burbank *1:* 112

Immunology

Anthony S. Fauci *1:* 280
William Augustus Hinton *2:* 463

Industrial Engineering

Henry Ford *4:* 80
David Powless *4:* 190

Industrial Medicine

Alice Hamilton *4:* 110

Invention

Richard Arkwright *1:* 24
Alexander Graham Bell *1:* 62
Henry Bessemer *1:* 82
Jacques Cousteau *1:* 168
Humphry Davy *1:* 211
Henry Ford *4:* 80
Lee De Forest *1:* 217
Rudolf Diesel *1:* 224
Thomas Alva Edison *1:* 244
Michael Faraday *1:* 275
R. Buckminster Fuller *1:* 333
Meredith Gourdine 2: 422
Robert K. Jarvik 2: 502
Edwin H. Land 2: 556
Lewis H. Latimer *4:* 145

James E. Lovelock *2:* 596
Theodore Maiman *2:* 601
Guglielmo Marconi *2:* 607
Elijah McCoy *2:* 628
Alfred Nobel *2:* 670
Robert Noyce *2:* 674
Auguste Piccard *3:* 753
Jacques Piccard *3:* 753
William Shockley *3:* 862
Nikola Tesla *3:* 889
Robert Watson-Watt *3:* 939
James Watt *3:* 945
Granville T. Woods *3:* 980
Orville Wright *3:* 987
Wilbur Wright *3:* 987
Vladimir Zworykin *3:* 1017

Limnology
Ruth Patrick *3:* 733

Logic
Bertrand Russell *3:* 794

Marine Biology
Angeles Alvariño *1:* 15
Rachel Carson *1:* 137
Sylvia A. Earle *1:* 239
Ernest Everett Just *2:* 543

Mathematics
Charles Babbage *1:* 37
Subrahmanyan Chandrasekhar *1:* 150
Karl Friedrich Gauss *2:* 371
David Hilbert *2:* 454
Isaac Newton *4:* 176
Julia Robinson *4:* 194
Bertrand Russell *3:* 794
William Thomson, Lord Kelvin *3:* 905

Alan Turing *4:* 228
Norbert Wiener *3:* 959
James S. Williamson *3:* 964

Medicine
Helen Caldicott *1:* 124
Benjamin Carson *4:* 33
Charles Richard Drew *1:* 233
Anthony S. Fauci *1:* 280
Helene D. Gayle *2:* 376
Alice Hamilton *4:* 110
Robert K. Jarvik *2:* 502
Louis Keith *2:* 549
Oliver Wolf Sacks *3:* 827
Jonas Salk *3:* 838
Patrick Steptoe *3:* 882
Helen Brooke Taussig *4:* 208
Vivien Thomas *3:* 897
Levi Watkins Jr. *3:* 929
Rosalyn Sussman Yalow *3:* 1004

Metallurgy
Henry Bessemer *1:* 82

Meteorology
Vilhem Bjerknes *4:* 15
Tetsuya Theodore Fujita *1:* 326
Auguste Piccard *3:* 753
Alfred Wegener *3:* 951

Microbiology
Alexander Fleming *1:* 292
Charlotte Friend *1:* 316
Louis Pasteur *3:* 723
Jonas Salk *3:* 838

Microscopy
Albert Baez *1:* 44
Vladimir Zworykin *3:* 1017

Molecular Biology

Bruce N. Ames *1:* 19
Elizabeth H. Blackburn *1:* 88
Francis Crick *1:* 174
Rosalind Franklin *1:* 302
Walter Gilbert *2:* 384
Linus Pauling *3:* 738
James D. Watson *3:* 933

Natural History

Raymond A. Dart *4:* 66
Charles Darwin 1: 203
Stephen Jay Gould 2: 415

Neurobiology

Rita Levi-Montalcini *4:* 150

Neuroendocrinology

Berta Scharrer *3:* 847

Neurology

Sigmund Freud *1:* 308
Karl Menninger *2:* 660
Oliver Wolf Sacks *3:* 827

Neurosurgery

Benjamin Carson *4:* 33

Nutrition

Flemmie Pansy Kittrell *4:* 141

Oceanography

Angeles Alvariño *1:* 150
Robert D. Ballard *1:* 48
Jacques Cousteau *1:* 168
Sylvia A. Earle *1:* 239
Auguste Piccard *3:* 753
Jacques Piccard *3:* 753

Organic Chemistry
Percy L. Julian *2:* 529

Paleontology
Raymond A. Dart *4:* 66
Stephen Jay Gould *2:* 415
Donald Johanson *2:* 515
Louis S. B. Leakey *2:* 575
Mary Leakey *2:* 575
Richard Leakey *2:* 575

Pathology
Norman Borlaug *1:* 105

Pediatric Medicine
Benjamin Carson *4:* 33
Helen Brooke Taussig *4:* 208

Pharmacology
Gertrude Belle Elion *2:* 468
George H. Hitchings *2:* 468
Mark Plotkin *3:* 766

Philosophy of Science
Galileo Galilei *4:* 100
Max Planck *3:* 759
Bertrand Russell *3:* 794

Physical Chemistry
Svante Arrhenius *1:* 30

Physics
Luis Alvarez *1:* 7
Svante Arrhenius *1:* 30
Albert Baez *1:* 44
Fred Begay *1:* 58
Niels Bohr *1:* 98
Marie Curie *1:* 181

Pierre Curie *1:* 181
Albert Einstein *1:* 260
Michael Faraday *1:* 275
Enrico Fermi *1:* 285
Galileo Galilei *4:* 100
Robert H. Goddard *2:* 392
Maria Goeppert-Mayer *2:* 399
Stephen Hawking *2:* 432
Shirley Ann Jackson *2:* 498
Frédéric Joliot-Curie *4:* 117
Irène Joliot-Curie *4:* 117
James Prescott Joule *2:* 524
Antoine Lavoisier *2:* 568
Tsung-Dao Lee *3:* 1012
Theodore Maiman *2:* 601
Guglielmo Marconi *2:* 607
James Clerk Maxwell *2:* 616
Lise Meitner *2:* 639
Isaac Newton *4:* 176
Robert Noyce *2:* 674
J. Robert Oppenheimer *2:* 680
Max Planck *3:* 759
Edith H. Quimby *3:* 776
Wilhelm Röntgen *3:* 787
Ernest Rutherford *3:* 805
Abdus Salam *3:* 832
William Shockley *3:* 862
J. J. Thomson *4:* 220
William Thomson, Lord Kelvin *3:* 905
James Van Allen *3:* 917
Robert Watson-Watt *3:* 939
Chien-Shiung Wu *3:* 999
Rosalyn Sussman Yalow *3:* 1004
Chen Ning Yang *3:* 1012
Vladimir Zworykin *3:* 1017

Physiology

Ivan Pavlov *3:* 746

Primatology

Dian Fossey *4:* 92
Jane Goodall *2:* 405

Psychiatry

C. G. Jung *2:* 536
Karl Menninger *2:* 660

Psychology

Kenneth B. Clark *4:* 40
Patricia S. Cowings *4:* 55
Sigmund Freud *1:* 308
C. G. Jung *2:* 536
Ivan Pavlov *3:* 746
B. F. Skinner *3:* 876

Psychophysiology

Patricia S. Cowings *4:* 55

Radiology

Edith H. Quimby *3:* 776

Rocket Science

Wernher von Braun *4:* 22
Robert H. Goddard *2:* 392
James Van Allen *3:* 917

Seismology

Keiiti Aki *1:* 1
Charles F. Richter *3:* 780

Sociobiology

Edward O. Wilson *3:* 969

Social Science

Kenneth B. Clark *4:* 40

Surgery

Benjamin Carson *4:* 33
Charles Richard Drew *1:* 233
Robert K. Jarvik *2:* 502
Vivien Thomas *3:* 897
Levi Watkins Jr. *3:* 929

Virology

Charlotte Friend *1:* 316
Dorothy Horstmann *2:* 480
Albert Sabin *3:* 814

Wildlife Conservation

Joy Adamson *4:* 1
Dian Fossey *4:* 92
Jane Goodall *2:* 405

Zoology

Karl von Frisch *1:* 320
Ernest Everett Just *2:* 543
Carolus Linnaeus *4:* 157
Konrad Lorenz *2:* 588
Edward O. Wilson *3:* 969

Reader's Guide

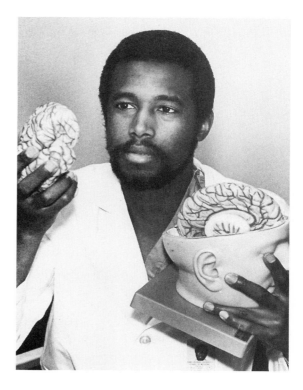

Benjamin Carson

Budding scientists and those entering the fascinating world of science for fun or study will find inspiration in this fourth volume of *Scientists.* The series presents detailed biographies of the women and men whose theories, discoveries, and inventions have revolutionized science and society. From Nicolaus Copernicus to Bill Gates and Elijah McCoy to Margaret Mead, *Scientists* explores the pioneers and their innovations that students most want to learn about.

Scientists from around the world and from all times are featured, in fields such as astronomy, ecology, oceanography, physics, and more.

In *Scientists,* volume 4, students will find:

- Thirty-three scientist biographies, each focusing on the scientist's early life, formative experiences, and inspirations—details that keep students reading

- "Impact" boxes that draw out important information and sum up why each scientist's work is indeed revolutionary

- Nineteen biographical boxes that highlight individuals who influenced the work of the featured scientist or who conducted similar research

- Sources for further reading so students know where to delve even deeper

- More than fifty black-and-white portraits and additional photographs that give students a better understanding of the people and inventions discussed

Scientists, volume 4, begins with a list of the scientists in all four volumes, categorized by fields ranging from aeronautical engineering to zoology; a timeline of major scientific breakthroughs; and a glossary of scientific terms used in the text. Cross references, appearing in bold in the text, direct the student to related entries throughout the four-volume set. The volume concludes with a cumulative subject index for the series so students can easily find the people, inventions, and theories discussed throughout *Scientists.*

Suggestions

We welcome any comments on this work and suggestions for individuals to feature in future editions of *Scientists.* Please write: Editors, *Scientists,* U• X• L, Gale Research, 835 Penobscot Bldg., Detroit, Michigan 48226-4094; call toll-free: 800-877-4253; or fax to: 313-961-6348.

Timeline of Scientific Breakthroughs

Isaac Newton

1507 **Nicolaus Copernicus** presents his revolutionary theory that the Sun, not Earth, is the center of the solar system.

1607 **Johannes Kepler** discovers his first two laws of planetary motion: a planet orbits the Sun in an ellipse, and it moves faster when near the Sun and slower when farther away.

1613 **Galileo Galilei** presents evidence for the Copernican model of the solar system with the Sun at its center.

1687 **Isaac Newton** establishes the law of universal gravitation.

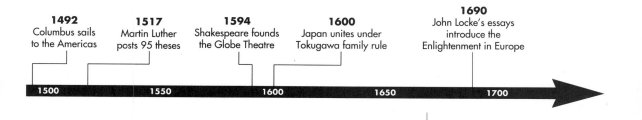

1492
Columbus sails
to the Americas

1517
Martin Luther
posts 95 theses

1594
Shakespeare founds
the Globe Theatre

1600
Japan unites under
Tokugawa family rule

1690
John Locke's essays
introduce the
Enlightenment in Europe

1500   1550   1600   1650   1700

1735   **Carolus Linnaeus** publishes the first edition of *Systema Naturae,* in which he outlines his new system for classifying and naming plants and animals.

1807–17 **Jöns Jacob Berzelius** analyzes over 2,000 compounds of 43 elements in preparing to publish the most accurate list of atomic weights of his time.

1847   **Maria Mitchell** discovers a comet; she will later become the first woman professional astronomer.

1882   **Lewis H. Latimer** invents an improved carbon filament for electric lighting that lasts longer than Thomas Edison's.

1897   **J. J. Thomson** discovers that all atoms have charged subatomic particles called electrons.

1908   The Ford Motor Company comes out with the Model T, fulfilling **Henry Ford**'s dream of producing a reliable, affordable car for the average American.

1911   **Alice Hamilton** becomes a special investigator for the U.S. Bureau of Labor after presenting a paper on occupational diseases.

1918   The West Bergen (Norway) Weather Service begins issuing detailed weather reports for the government and military, putting into practice **Vilhelm Bjerknes**'s new meteorological techniques.

1924   **Raymond A. Dart** examines the fossils of a creature found in Africa that he believes to be the "missing link."

1930   Due to the efforts of **Alice Evans,** U.S. public health officials recognize the need to pasteurize milk in order to prevent the disease brucellosis.

1934   **Irène Joliot-Curie** and **Frédéric Joliot-Curie** announce that they have created artifical radioactivity.

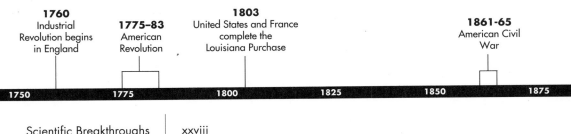

1760
Industrial Revolution begins in England

1775–83
American Revolution

1803
United States and France complete the Louisiana Purchase

1861-65
American Civil War

1750   1775   1800   1825   1850   1875

1934 **Ida Tacke Noddack** suggests a theory of nuclear fission, the process in which the nucleus of a uranium atom is split. Her concept is ignored for several years until proven accurate in 1939.

1936 **Alan Turing**'s paper "On Computable Numbers" describes a machine that serves as the model for the first working computers.

1944 The Blalock-Taussig shunt is first used on a human infant as a cure for "blue baby" syndrome. **Helen Brooke Taussig** identified the cause of blue baby syndrome and came up with the idea for this surgical cure.

1948 **Julia Robinson** begins what will become twenty-two years of work on the tenth problem on the list of twenty-three unsolved problems drawn up by German mathematician David Hilbert.

1952 **Rita Levi-Montalcini**'s tissue culture experiments prove to her the existence of nerve growth factor, a protein that stimulates the growth of nerve cells.

1954 **Kenneth B. Clark**'s report on the negative effects of segregated schools on black children becomes the basis of the landmark Supreme Court Case decision on segregation in *Brown v. Board of Education*.

1960 **Joy Adamson**'s book *Born Free: A Lioness of Two Worlds* draws worldwide attention to the cause of wildlife preservation.

1963 **Valentina Tereshkova** becomes the first woman to fly in space on the Soviet *Vostok 6* rocket.

1963 **Flemmie Pansy Kittrell**'s school of human ecology at Howard University provides a model for the the Head Start program, which is created by the U.S. government to help poor, pre-kindergarten-aged children.

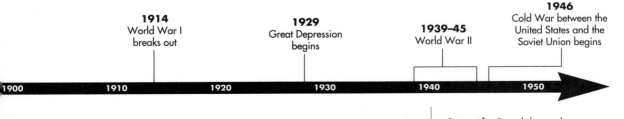

1914
World War I
breaks out

1929
Great Depression
begins

1939–45
World War II

1946
Cold War between the
United States and the
Soviet Union begins

1900   1910   1920   1930   1940   1950

1964 **Seymour Cray** develops the CDC 6600, the most powerful computer of its day and considered by many to be the first supercomputer.

1969–71 The Saturn family of rockets, designed by **Wernher von Braun** and his team, launches the first American spacecraft to land on the Moon's surface.

1970 **Har Gobind Khorana** synthesizes the first artificial gene.

1976 **David Powless** forms a company that develops and markets a recycling method for the hazardous wastes generated by steel mills.

1977 **Wangari Maathai** turns her idea of paying poor people in Kenya to plant trees and shrubs into a nationwide environmental organization known as the Green Belt Movement.

1980 *Cosmos,* a popular series examining the wonders of science and the universe, airs on public television. **Carl Sagan** is the show's co-writer and narrator.

1983 **Dian Fossey** publishes *Gorillas in the Mist,* calling attention to the plight of the mountain gorilla.

1987 **Benjamin Carson** leads a team of seventy medical personnel in separating a pair of Siamese twins joined at the backs of their heads.

1992 During the eight-day flight of the space shuttle *Endeavour,* **Patricia S. Cowing**'s biofeedback techniques to combat motion sickness are successfully put into use.

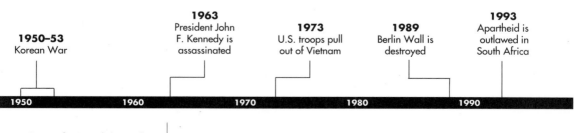

1963
President John F. Kennedy is assassinated

1973
U.S. troops pull out of Vietnam

1989
Berlin Wall is destroyed

1993
Apartheid is outlawed in South Africa

1950–53
Korean War

1950   1960   1970   1980   1990

Words to Know

A

Absolute zero: the theoretical point at which a substance has no heat and motion ceases; equivalent to -276°C or -459.67°F.

Algae: a diverse group of plant or plantlike organisms that grow mainly in water.

Alpha particle: a positively charged nuclear particle that consists of two protons and two electrons; it is ejected at a high speed from disintegrating radioactive materials.

Alternating current: the flow of electrons first in one direction and then in the other at regular intervals.

Amino acids: organic acids that are the chief components of proteins.

Anatomy: the study of the structure and form of biological organisms.

Anthropology: the science that deals with the study of human beings, especially their origin, development, divisions, and customs.

Aorta: the main artery of the human body that starts out at the left ventricle of the heart and carries blood from the heart to be distributed throughout the body.

Archaeology: the scientific study of material remains, such as fossils and relics, of past societies.

Artificial intelligence: the branch of science concerned with the development of machines having the ability to perform tasks normally thought to require human intelligence, such as problem solving, discriminating among single objects, and response to spoken commands.

Asteroid: one of thousands of small planets located in a belt between the orbits of Mars and Jupiter.

Astronomy: the study of the physical and chemical properties of objects and matter outside Earth's atmosphere.

Astrophysics: the branch of physics involving the study of the physical and chemical nature of celestial objects and events.

Atomic bomb: a weapon of mass destruction that derives its explosive energy from nuclear fission.

Atomic weight: the mass of one atom of an element.

B

Bacteria: a large, diverse group of mostly single-celled organisms that play a key role in the decay of organic matter and the cycling of nutrients.

Bacteriology: the scientific study of bacteria, their characteristics, and their activities as related to medicine, industry, and agriculture.

Bacteriophage: a virus that infects bacteria.

Ballistic missile: a self-propelled object (like a rocket) that is guided as it ascends into the air and usually falls freely.

Behaviorism: the school of psychology that holds that human and animal behavior is based not on independent will nor motivation but rather on response to reward and punishment.

Beta decay: process by which a neutron in an atomic nucleus breaks apart into a proton and an electron.

Big bang: in astronomy, the theory that the universe resulted from a cosmic explosion that occurred billions of years ago and then expanded over time.

Binary stars: a system of two stars revolving around each other under a mutual gravitation system.

Binary system: a system that uses the numbers 1 and 0 to correspond to the on or off states of electric current.

Biochemistry: the study of chemical compounds and processes occurring in living organisms.

Biodiversity: the number of different species of plants and animals in a specified region.

Biofeedback: a method of learning to gain some voluntary control over involuntary bodily functions like heartbeat or blood pressure.

Biology: the scientific study of living organisms.

Biophysics: the branch of biology in which the methods and principles of physics are applied to the study of living things.

Biosynthesis: the creation of a chemical compound in the body.

Biotechnology: use of biological organisms, systems, or processes to make or modify products.

Black holes: regions in space that exert an extremely intense gravitational force from which nothing, including light, can escape.

Botany: the branch of biology involving the study of plant life.

Byte: a group of binary digits (0 and 1) that a computer processes as a unit.

C

Carbon filament: a threadlike object in a lamp that glows when electricity passes through it.

Carburetor: the device that supplies an internal-combustion engine with a mixture of vaporized fuel and air that, when ignited, produces the engine's energy.

Carcinogen: a cancer-causing agent, such as a chemical or a virus.

Catalyst: a substance that enables a chemical reaction to take place either more quickly or under otherwise difficult conditions.

Cathode: a negatively charged electrode.

Cathode rays: electrons emitted by a cathode when heated.

Cerebrum: the uppermost part of the brain that, in higher mammals, covers the rest of the brain and is considered to be the seat of conscious mental processes.

Chemistry: the science of the nature, composition, and properties of material substances and their transformations.

Chromosome: threadlike structure in the nucleus of a cell that carries thousands of genes.

Circuit: the complete path of an electric current including the source of electric energy; an assemblage of electronic elements.

Classification: a system of naming and categorizing plants and animals in which they are grouped by the number of physical traits they have in common. The ranking system goes from general to specific: kingdom, phylum, class, order, family, genus, and species.

Climatology: the scientific study of climates and their phenomena.

Combustion: a rapid chemical process that produces heat and light.

Conductor: a substance able to carry an electrical current.

Conservation biology: the branch of biology that involves conserving rapidly vanishing wild animals, plants, and places.

Conservation laws: laws of physics that state that a particular property, mass, energy, momentum, or electrical charge is not lost during any change.

Cosmic rays: charged particles, mainly the nuclei of hydrogen and other atoms, that bombard Earth's upper atmosphere at velocities close to that of light.

Cosmology: the study of the structure and evolution of the universe.

Cross-fertilization: a method of fertilization in which the gametes (mature male or female cells) are produced by separate individuals or sometimes by individuals of different kinds.

Cryogenics: the branch of physics that involves the production and effects of very low temperatures.

Crystallography: the science that deals with the forms and structures of crystals.

Cytology: the branch of biology concerned with the study of cells.

D

Deforestation: the process of cutting down all the trees in a forest.

Desertification: the changing of productive land to desert, often by clearing the land of trees and other plant life.

Diffraction: the spreading and bending of light waves as they pass through a hole or slit.

Direct current: a regular flow of electrons, always in the same direction.

DNA (deoxyribonucleic acid): a long molecule composed of two chains of nucleotides (organic chemicals) that contain the genetic information carried from one generation to another.

E

Earthquake: an unpredictable event in which masses of rock shift below Earth's surface, releasing enormous amounts of energy and sending out shockwaves that sometimes cause the ground to shake dramatically.

Ecology: the branch of science dealing with the interrelationship of organisms and their environments.

Ecosystem: community of plants and animals and the physical environment with which they interact.

Electrocardiograph: an instrument that makes a graphic record of the heart's movements.

Electrochemistry: the branch of physical chemistry involving the relation of electricity to chemical changes.

Electrodes: conductors used to establish electrical contact with a nonmetallic part of a circuit.

Electromagnetism: the study of electric and magnetic fields and their interaction with electric charges and currents.

Electron: a negatively charged particle that orbits the nucleus of an atom.

Embryo: an animal in the early stages of development before birth.

Embryology: the study of embryos and their development.

Entomology: the branch of zoology dealing with the study of insects.

Environmentalism: the movement to preserve and improve the natural environment, and particularly to control pollution.

Enzyme: any of numerous complex proteins that are produced by living cells and spark specific biochemical reactions.

Epidemiology: the study of the causes, distribution, and control of disease in populations.

Equinox: the two times each year when the Sun crosses the plane of Earth's equator; at these times, day and night are of equal length everywhere on Earth.

Ethnobotany: the plant lore of a race of people.

Ethnology: science that deals with the division of human beings into races and their origin, distribution, relations, and characteristics.

Ethology: the scientific and objective study of the behavior of animals in the wild rather than in captivity.

Evolution: in the struggle for survival, the process by which successive generations of a species pass on to their offspring the characteristics that enable the species to survive.

Extinction: the total disappearance of a species or the disappearance of a species from a given area.

F

Flora: the plants of a particular region or environment.

Foramen magnum: the opening at the base of the skull through which the spinal cord enters the cranial cavity.

Fossils: the remains, traces, or impressions of living organisms that inhabited Earth more than ten thousand years ago.

Frontal systems: a weather term denoting the boundaries between air masses of different temperatures and humidities.

G

Gamma rays: short electromagnetic wavelengths that come from the nuclei of atoms during radioactive decay.

Game theory: the mathematics involved in determining the effect of a particular strategy in a competition, as in a game of chess, a military battle, or in selling products.

Gene: in classical genetics, a unit of hereditary information that is carried on chromosomes and determines observable characteristics; in molecular genetics, a special sequence of DNA or RNA located on the chromosome.

Genetic code: the means by which genetic information is translated into the chromosomes that make up living organisms.

Genetics: the study of inheritance in living organisms.

Genome: genetic material of a human being; the complete genetic structure of a species.

Geochemistry: the study of the chemistry of Earth (and other planets).

Geology: the study of the origin, history, and structure of Earth.

Geophysics: the physics of Earth, including studies of the atmosphere, earthquakes, volcanism, and oceans.

Global warming: the rise in Earth's temperature that is attributed to the buildup of carbon dioxide and other pollutants in the atmosphere.

Gravity: the force of attraction (causing free objects to accelerate toward each other) that exists between the surface of Earth (as well as other planets) and bodies at or near its surface.

Greenhouse effect: warming of Earth's atmosphere due to the absorption of heat by molecules of water vapor, carbon dioxide, methane, ozone, nitrous oxide, and chlorofluorocarbons.

H

Heliocentric: having the Sun as the center.

Herpetology: the branch of zoology that deals with reptiles and amphibians.

Histology: the study of microscopic plant and animal tissues.

Hominids: humanlike creatures.

Hormones: chemical messengers produced in living organisms that play significant roles in the body, such as affecting growth, metabolism, and digestion.

Horticulture: the science of growing fruits, vegetables, and ornamental plants.

Hybridization: cross-pollination of plants of different varieties to produce seed.

Hydraulics: the study of the forces of fluids as they apply to accomplishing mechanical or practical tasks.

Hydrodynamics: the study of the forces exerted by fluids in motion.

Hydrostatics: a branch of physics that studies fluids at rest and the forces they exert, particularly on submerged objects.

Hypothesis: an assumption made on the basis of scientific data that is an attempt to explain a principle in nature but remains tentative because of lack of solid evidence.

I

Immunology: the branch of medicine concerned with the body's ability to protect itself from disease.

Imprinting: the rapid learning process that takes place early in the life of a social animal and establishes a behavioral pattern, such as a recognition of and attraction to its own kind or a substitute.

In vitro fertilization: fertilization of eggs outside of the body.

Infrared radiation: electromagnetic rays released by hot objects; also known as a heat radiation.

Infertility: the inability to produce offspring for any reason.

Internal-combustion engine: an engine in which the combustion (burning) that generates the heat that powers it goes on inside the engine itself, rather than in a furnace.

Invertebrates: animals lacking a spinal column.

Ion: an atom or groups of atoms that carries an electrical charge—-either positive or negative—-as a result of losing or gaining one or more electrons.

Isomers: compound that have the same number of atoms of the same elements, but different properties because their atoms are arranged differently.

Isotope: one of two or more atoms of a chemical element that have the same structure but different physical properties.

L

Laser: acronym for light amplification by stimulated emission of radiation; a device that produces intense light with a precisely defined wavelength.

Light-year: in astronomy, the distance light travels in one year, about six trillion miles.

Limnology: the branch of biology concerning freshwater plants.

Logic: the science of the formal principles of reasoning.

Lunar eclipse: the passing of the Moon either wholly or partially into the shadow created by Earth's position in front of the Sun; that is, when the three bodies align thus: Moon—Earth—Sun.

M

Magnetic field: the space around an electric current or a magnet in which a magnetic force can be observed.

Maser: acronym for microwave amplification of stimulated emission of radiation; a device that produces radiation in short wavelengths.

Metabolism: the process by which living cells break down organic compounds to produce energy.

Metallurgy: the science and technology of metals.

Meteorology: the science that deals with the atmosphere and its phenomena and with weather and weather forecasting.

Microbiology: branch of biology dealing with microscopic forms of life.

Microwaves: electromagnetic radiation waves between one millimeter and one centimeter in length.

Molecular biology: the study of the structure and function of molecules that make up living organisms.

Molecule: the smallest particle of a substance that retains all the properties of the substance and is composed of one or more atoms.

Moving assembly line: a system in a plant or factory in which an item that is being made is carried past a series of workers who remain in their places. Each worker assembles a particular portion of the finished product and then repeats the same process with the next item.

Mutation: any permanent change in hereditary material, involving either a physical change in chromosome relations or a biochemical change in genes.

N

Natural selection: the natural process by which groups best adjusted to their environment survive and reproduce, thereby passing on to their offspring genetic qualities best suited to that environment.

Nebulae: large, cloudy bodies of dust in space.

Nerve Growth Factor (NGF): the nutrients that determine how nerve cells take on their specific roles in the nervous system.

Nervous system: the bodily system that in vertebrates is made up of the brain and spinal cord, nerves, ganglia, and other organs and that receives and interprets stimuli and transmits impulses to targeted organs.

Neurology: the scientific study of the nervous system, especially its structure, functions, and abnormalities.

Neurosecretion: the process of producing a secretion by nerve cells.

Neurosurgery: surgery on the nerves, brain, or spinal cord.

Neurosis: any emotional or mental disorder that affects only part of the personality, such as anxiety or mild depression, as a result of stress.

Neutron: an uncharged particle found in atomic nuclei.

Neutron star: a hypothetical dense celestial object that consists primarily of closely packed neutrons that results from the collapse of a much larger celestial body.

Nova: a star that suddenly increases in light output and then fades away to its former obscure state within a few months or years.

Nuclear fallout: the drifting of radioactive particles into the atmosphere as the result of nuclear explosions.

Nuclear fission: the process in which an atomic nucleus is split, resulting in the release of large amounts of energy.

Nuclear physics: physics that deals with the atomic nucleus, atomic energy, the atom bomb, or atomic power.

Nucleotides: compounds that form the basic stuctural units—the stairs on the spiral staircase—of DNA, and are arranged on the staircase in a pattern of heredity-carrying code "words."

Nutritionist: someone who studies the ways in which living organisms take in and make use of food.

O

Oceanography: the science that deals with the study of oceans and seas.

Optics: the study of light and vision.

Organic: of, relating to, or arising in a bodily organ

Ozone layer: the atmospheric layer of approximately twenty to thirty miles above Earth's surface that protects the lower atmosphere from harmful solar radiation.

P

Paleoanthropology: the branch of anthropology dealing with the study of mammal fossils.

Paleontology: the study of the life of past geological periods as known from fossil remains.

Particle physics: the branch of physics concerned with the study of the constitution, properties, and interactions of elementary particles.

Particles: the smallest building blocks of energy and matter.

Patent: a government grant giving an inventor the right to be the only person to sell an invention for a set length of time.

Pathology: the study of the essential nature of diseases, especially the structural and functional changes produced by them.

Pediatrics: a branch of medicine involving the development, care, and diseases of children.

Pendulum: an object that hangs freely from a fixed point and swings back and forth under the action of gravity, often used to regulate movement, as the pendulum in a clock.

Periodic table: a table of the elements in order of atomic number, arranged in rows and columns to show periodic similarities and trends in physical and chemical properties.

Pharmacology: the science dealing with the properties, reactions, and therapeutic values of drugs.

Phylum: the first division of the animal kingdom in the Linnaeus classification system. The ranking of the system is in order from the general to the specific—kingdom, phylum, class, order, family, genus, and species.

Physics: the science that explores the physical properties and composition of objects and the forces that affect them.

Physiology: the branch of biology that deals with the functions and actions of life or of living matter, such as organs, tissues, and cells.

Planetologist: a person who studies the physical bodies in the solar system, including planets and their satellites, comets, and meteorites.

Plankton: floating animal and plant life.

Plasma physics: the branch of physics involving the study of electrically charged, extremely hot gases.

Primate: any order of mammals composed of humans, apes, or monkeys.

Projectile motion: the movement of an object thrust forward by an external force—for example, a cannonball shot out of a cannon.

Protein: large molecules found in all living organisms that are essential to the structure and functioning of all living cells.

Proton: a positively charged particle found in atomic nuclei.

Psychiatry: the branch of medicine that deals with mental, emotional, and behavioral disorders.

Psychoanalysis: the method of analyzing psychic phenomenon and treating emotional disorders that involves treatment sessions during which the patient is encouraged to talk freely about personal experiences, especially about early childhood and dreams.

Psychophysiology: a branch of psychology that focuses on combined mental and bodily processes.

Psychology: the study of human and animal behavior.

Psychotic: a person with severe emotional or mental disorders that cause a loss of contact with reality.

Q

Quantum: any of the very small increments or parcels into which many forms of energy are subdivided.

Quasar: celestial object more distant than stars that emits excessive amounts of radiation.

R

Radar: acronym for radio detection and ranging; the process of using radio waves to detect objects.

Radiation: energy emitted in the form of waves or particles.

Radio waves: electromagnetic radiation.

Radioactive fallout: the radioactive particles resulting from a nuclear explosion.

Radioactivity: the property possessed by some elements (as uranium) or isotopes (as carbon 14) of spontaneously emitting energetic particles (as electrons or alpha particles) by disintegration of their atomic nuclei.

Radiology: the branch of medicine that uses X rays and radium (an intensely radioactive metallic element) to diagnose and treat disease.

Redshift: the increase in the wavelength of all light received from a celestial object (or wave source), usually because the object is moving away from the observer.

RNA (ribonucleic acid): any of various nucleic acids that are associated with the control of cellular chemical activities.

S

Scientific method: collecting evidence meticulously and theorizing from it.

Seismograph: a device that records vibrations of the ground and within Earth.

Seismology: the study and measurement of earthquakes.

Semiconductor: substances whose ability to carry electrical current is lower than that of a conductor (like metal) and higher than that of insulators (like rubber).

Shortwave: a radio wave having a wavelength between ten and one hundred meters.

Slide rule: a calculating device that, in its simplest form, consists of a ruler and a sliding attachment that are graduated with logarithm tables.

Social science: the study of human society and individual relationships within it, including the fields of sociology, anthropology, economics, political sicence, and history.

Sociobiology: the systematic study of the biological basis for all social behavior.

Soil erosion: the loss of usable topsoil, often due to clearing trees and other plant life from the land.

Solid state: using semiconductor devices rather than electron tubes.

Spectrum: the range of colors produced by individual elements within a light source.

Statics: a branch of physics that explores the forces of equilibrium, or balance.

Steady-state theory: a theory that proposes that the universe has neither a beginning nor an end.

Stellar spectra: the distinctive mix of radiation emitted by every star.

Stellar spectroscopy: the process that breaks a star's light into component colors so that the various elements of the star can be observed.

Sterilization: boiling or heating of instruments and food to prevent proliferation of microorganisms.

Supernova: a catastrophic explosion in which a large portion of a star's mass is blown out into space, or the star is entirely destroyed.

T

Theorem: in mathematics, a formula, proposition, or statement.

Theory: an assumption drawn from scientific evidence that provides a plausible explanation for the principle or principles behind a natural phenomenon. (A *theory* generally has more evidence behind it and finds more acceptance in the scientific community than a *hypothesis*.)

Thermodynamics: the branch of physics that deals with the mechanical action or relations of heat.

Trace element: a chemical element present in minute quantities.

Transistor: a solid-state electronic device that is used to control the flow of electricity in electronic equipment and consists of a small block of semiconductor with at least three electrodes.

V

Vaccine: a preparation administered to increase immunity to polio.

Vacuum tube: an electric tube from which all matter has been removed.

Variable stars: stars whose light output varies because of internal fluctuations or because they are eclipsed by another star.

Variation: in genetics, differences in traits of a particular species.

Vertebrate: an animal that has a spinal column.

Virology: the study of viruses.

Virtual reality: an artificial computer-created environment that seeks to mimic reality.

Virus: a microscopic agent of infection.

Voltaic pile: a basic form of battery that was the first source of continuous and controllable electric current.

W

Wavelength: the distance between one peak of a wave of light, heat, or energy and the next corresponding peak.

X

X ray: a form of electromagnetic radiation with an extremely short wavelength that is produced by bombarding a metallic target with electrons in a vacuum.

Z

Zoology: the branch of biology concerned with the study of animal life.

Zooplankton: small drifting animal life in the ocean.

SCIENTISTS: Their Lives and Works

Joy Adamson

*Born January 20, 1910
Toppau, Silesia (now Opava,
Czech Republic)*

*Died January 3, 1980
Near Nairobi, Kenya*

oy Adamson became known around the world for her book *Born Free: A Lioness of Two Worlds* (1960), the story of an orphaned lion cub that Adamson raised and later returned to the wild in East Africa. The book was also the basis of a 1964 film and an American television series. In an interview with Roy Newquist, Adamson observed that the enormous sales of *Born Free* "proves the hunger of people to return . . . to a world of genuine proportion, a world in which our balance and basic values have not been destroyed. All this shows how important it is to preserve the animal life we have left." Both a naturalist and an artist, Adamson produced approximately 400 paintings of wildflowers, 80 pictures of coral fish, and 570 images of African tribes. For illustrating seven books on the flora (regional plant life) of East Africa, she received the Gold Grenfall Medal from the Royal Horticultural Society in 1947.

Christened Friederike Viktoria Gessner, Adamson was born on January 20, 1910, in Troppau, Silesia (now Opava in

Joy Adamson's books about her work with orphaned animals popularized the issue of wildlife conservation.

IMPACT

Joy and George Adamson are considered pioneers in the environmental movement because of their work to protect animals in their natural habitats. Joy Adamson's book, *Born Free,* documents her experience raising—and eventually returning to the wild—an orphaned lion cub in East Africa. The book became a best-seller and drew worldwide attention to the cause of wildlife preservation. Adamson used her fame as a writer and naturalist (someone who studies nature scientifically) to raise funds for conservation efforts and to organize boycotts against products made from endangered animals. (A boycott is a form of protest in which a group of people publicly refuse to do business with a company, industry, or government.) Her tactics continue to be used by environmental activists.

the Czech Republic). Her parents were Viktor Gessner, an architect, urban planner, and civil servant; and Traute (Greipel) Gessner, who came from a family of wealthy paper manufacturers. Adamson's parents divorced when she was twelve. She attended school in Vienna, where she studied music, metalwork, woodsculpting, art history, dressmaking, and design; she then began preparations for a medical career. In 1935, Adamson married the Austrian businessman Viktor von Klarwill.

Immigrates to Africa

Adamson traveled to Kenya in 1937 to explore the possibility of establishing a home in East Africa. Her marriage to Von Klarwill ended in divorce at this time, and Adamson remained in Africa. In 1938, Adamson married Peter Bally, a botanist (a scientist who studies the biology of plant life) with the Nairobi Museum, whom she had met on her voyage to Africa. It was Bally who gave Adamson the name "Joy." The couple spent their honeymoon on a scientific expedition to the Chyullu Mountains on the border of Kenya and Tanzania. A painter of flowers himself, Bally encouraged Adamson to paint the plants he collected in his work. Adamson gradually expanded her range of subjects to include tribal life, landscapes, and animals. Adamson and Bally were divorced in 1942. In 1943, she married George Adamson, a warden with Kenya's Game Department. Adamson continued her work painting flowers during these years and contributed samples of native plant life to the Royal Botanical Gardens, also known as Kew Gardens, near London, England.

Raises lion cub

In 1956, George Adamson shot a lioness that attacked him when he accidentally approached her cubs. He brought the lioness's three cubs home to Adamson, who had already raised many animals. Although Adamson wanted to raise all of the cubs, her husband insisted that the three lions would require too much care. On his orders, two cubs were sent to the Rotterdam Zoo in the Netherlands. The departure of the two cubs focused Adamson's attention on the fate of young animals that were orphaned or wounded in the wild. She began a national animal orphanage that, after more than half a century, continues to operate in Nairobi.

The smallest of the cubs, Elsa, remained with the Adamsons. The challenges and rewards of raising the female cub became the basis of *Born Free*. In the book, Adamson conveyed the emotional attachment that developed between the lion and her human caretakers. Adamson indicated to Roy Newquist that she developed an "utterly genuine and simple and natural" relationship with this lion, who "could understand my thoughts and act according to them.... I know that she was not merely responding [to] my mood or from physical signals. Elsa opened, for me, so many completely new and staggering insights into animal psychology."

Returns lion to the wild

Despite her close relationship with the lion cub, Adamson resolved not to turn Elsa into a pet, and she accepted an offer from the warden of the Maasai Mara Reserve—a wildlife reserve in southern Kenya—to provide Elsa with a permanent home. The attempt at establishing Elsa in the wild, however, failed. Born in the high altitudes and dry climate of northern Kenya, Elsa fell ill in the hotter and lusher conditions 350 miles to the south. In addition, George Adamson could find no way to persuade local prides (family groups of lions) to accept Elsa.

After the poor results at Maasai Mara Reserve, a second site was identified for Elsa's reintroduction to the wild. The district commissioner at Meru in Northern Tanzania, close to

Adamson with Elsa the lioness

where Elsa was born, offered to provide a home for the lion. At two and a half years, Elsa should have been able to find her own food, join a pride, and mate; but because she was raised by humans, she wasn't as good at these things as other lions. George Adamson provided Elsa with some training and looked for ways to help her join the local prides. When it was clear that Elsa had mated, the Adamsons left Elsa on her own. After the birth of her cubs, Elsa disappeared for six weeks. At the end of this period, the lioness paid the Adamsons the first of many visits with her cubs.

Assists second generation of lions

When Elsa was five, she died of a tick infection, and a local lioness drove the cubs out of the territory. After a long search, George Adamson found the cubs and transported them to the Serengeti National Park in Northern Tanzania, where they were set free. Adamson told the cubs' story in her best-selling books *Living Free* and *Forever Free;* a film based on the books was released in 1971.

Establishes wildlife preservation fund

Adamson's books, films, and lectures, as noted in the *New York Times* on January 5, 1980, "brought a new awareness of relations between man and animal to millions of people." In order to encourage people to donate money to efforts in wildlife conservation, Adamson established the Elsa Wild Animal Appeal fund in the United Kingdom in 1961, in the United States in 1969, and in Canada in 1971. Adamson donated most of the proceeds from her books and films to this fund. In addition, she was a pioneer in efforts to protect endangered species by boycotting products made from fur and other animal parts. Increasingly she preferred wild animals to people, and Adamson began living by herself in 1971 at a lakeside estate outside of Nairobi.

During these years, Adamson achieved unique success in raising a cheetah. She wrote two books about the cat, *The Spotted Sphinx* and *Pippa's Challenge*. Surprisingly little was known about cheetahs when Adamson began her studies. In 1976, Adamson embarked on her last major enterprise. She was given a leopard cub, which she named Penny, to raise. Primarily a solitary and secretive animal, Penny nevertheless brought Adamson to see her cubs when they were only a few days old. The story of finding a suitable natural location for reintroducing Penny to the wild is described in Adamson's book *Queen of Shaba*.

Honored for wildlife conservation work

Adamson received many awards for her wildlife preservation work, and her paintings were exhibited around the world. On January 3, 1980, at age seventy, Adamson was murdered by a Turkana servant she had dismissed. On August 20, 1989, at age eighty-three, George Adamson was shot while driving to the rescue of a German woman being attacked by Somali thieves. Adrian House, in *The Great Safari: The Lives of George and Joy Adamson,* described the two as prophets—the people who first spread the ideas of the green movement (a trend of increased environmental activism). Through their work they stimulated concern for animals and for the planet that humans and animals share.

Further Reading

Adamson, George, *My Pride and Joy,* Collins Harvill, 1986.

Adamson, Joy, *Born Free: A Lioness of Two Worlds,* Pantheon, 1960.

Adamson, Joy, *Forever Free,* Harcourt, 1962.

Adamson, Joy, *Living Free,* Harcourt, 1961.

Adamson, Joy, *Pippa's Challenge,* Harcourt, 1972.

Adamson, Joy, *Queen of Shaba: The Story of an African Leopard,* Harcourt, 1980.

Adamson, Joy, *The Searching Spirit: An Autobiography,* Collins Harvill, 1978, Harcourt, 1979.

Adamson, Joy, *The Spotted Sphinx,* Harcourt, 1969.

Cass, Carolyn, *Joy Adamson: Behind the Mask,* Weidenfeld and Nicholson, 1992.

House, Adrian, *The Great Safari: The Lives of George and Joy Adamson,* William Morrow, 1993.

Major Twentieth Century Writers, Gale, 1991.

Newquist, Roy, *Counterpoint,* Rand McNally, 1964.

New York Times, January 5, 1980, p. 1.

Jöns Jacob Berzelius

Born August 20, 1779
Väversunda, Sweden

Died August 7, 1848
Stockholm, Sweden

Jöns Jacob Berzelius was a Swedish chemist who became the most respected scientist in his field in the early 1800s. He conducted research in a number of areas, and his findings have provided some of the basic knowledge at the heart of modern chemistry. It was largely due to Berzelius's support of the atomic theory (model developed to explain the properties and behaviors of atoms) of English chemist **John Dalton** (1766-1844; for more information see volume 1, pp. 197-202) and his work determining the atomic weight of various elements that the scientific world eventually accepted the idea that all matter is composed of atoms. Berzelius's system of chemical notation that uses letters to identify different elements became a standard that is still used today. He also developed the ideas of catalysts (substances that enable chemical reactions to occur either more quickly or under otherwise adverse conditions) and isomers (compounds that contain the same number of atoms of the same elements but have different properties because their atoms are arranged differently).

Jöns Jacob Berzelius's various contributions to the field of chemistry include the system of chemical notation and the determination of atomic weights.

7

Berzelius also discovered a number of new elements and wrote a chemistry textbook that shaped the work of generations of scientists. Highly suspicious of new ideas in his later years, he was a man both respected and feared as the ultimate authority in chemistry in his day.

Berzelius was born in Väversunda, Sweden, on August 20, 1779. His father, Samuel, was a clergyman and schoolmaster who died when Berzelius was four years old. His mother, Elizabeth Dorothea, was remarried two years later to Anders Ekmarck, a pastor who had five children of his own. Then, in 1788, Berzelius's mother died. After two years, his stepfather remarried and Berzelius and his sister were sent to live with the family of their mother's brother, Magnus Sjösteen. Berzelius had begun his education at the home of Ekmarck, where all the children of the household were instructed by Ekmarck and private tutors. After moving to the house of his uncle, he entered the local school in Linköping. But Berzelius did not find life with his uncle's family enjoyable; he and his cousins did not get along and they argued a great deal. In 1794, Berzelius took a position as a tutor on a local farm in order to escape the conflicts at his uncle's house.

Natural world inspires studies

Berzelius had planned on becoming a clergyman, like his father and stepfather had been. But while tutoring at the farm, he became interested in collecting and identifying the flowers and insects he found there. He decided to pursue his new fascination with natural science and entered the medical school in Uppsala, Sweden, where he received his degree in 1802.

Reads first chemistry book

While a student at Uppsala, Berzelius was exposed to a number of scientific thoughts, both inside and outside the classroom, that would shape the path of his life's work. During this time, he was introduced to the study of chemistry by his oldest stepbrother. The two read through a chemistry textbook by themselves and carried out some experiments together. Another important experience for Berzelius was reading about the invention of the voltaic pile, a basic form of battery that was the first source of continuous and controllable electric current. After reading about the voltaic pile, Berzelius built one himself using zinc disks and copper coins. With this tool, he conducted research on the effects of electricity on various medical disorders. In this research, which was the subject of his 1802 doctoral dissertation, Berzelius did not find that electricity had any effect on the condition of patients. But this early work did establish his lifelong interest in electrical phenomena.

Conducts experiments with Hisinger

After leaving Uppsala, Berzelius took a position as assistant to the professor of medicine and pharmacy at the College of Medicine in Stockholm, Sweden. The position paid no salary, but it allowed Berzelius to pursue his interest in chemistry. There Berzelius met the wealthy mine owner Wilhelm Hisinger (1766-1852), who had a strong interest in chemistry and mineralogy. The two men began a series of experiments that grew out of Berzelius's interest in electrical effects. They studied the effects of electrical current on a number of saltwater solutions. They found that salts could be decomposed, or broken down into their basic elements, by an electrical current, with hydrogen and metals collecting at the negative electrode and oxygen at the positive electrode. These experiments were later improved upon and extended by the chemist **Sir Humphry Davy** (1778-1829; for more

IMPACT

Jöns Jacob Berzelius provided many of the tools and concepts that are now standards in the field of chemistry. In his search for convenient and efficient ways to conduct chemical research and document findings, he designed laboratory equipment and devised a method of representing chemical elements with letters rather than names or pictures—innovations that were quickly accepted and imitated by other scientists. He was one of the first people to work with English chemist John Dalton's atomic theory. By determining the atomic weight of numerous elements (atomic weight is the mass of one atom of an element), Berzelius proved that atoms of different elements did in fact have different properties, convincing other scientists that Dalton's ideas were correct. Along with Berzelius's scientific accomplishments, his widely popular chemistry textbooks and reviews, and his strong personality as a leader of the Swedish Academy of Science made him a major influence in the development of the field of chemistry in the early 1800s.

information, see volume 1, pp. 211-216) in England. The mutual interest of Davy and Berzelius in this topic led to a long-term friendship between the two scientists.

Develops electrochemical theory

Based upon the results of his research, Berzelius arrived at a theory of the composition of compounds, which are substances formed from two or more united parts or elements. He asserted that all compounds consist of both electrically positive atoms and electrically negative atoms. A compound such as potassium oxide was produced, he thought, by the combination of positive potassium atoms and negative oxygen atoms. In his view, some atoms had both a positive and a negative tendency, displaying their positive characteristic when combined with a negative atom and their negative characteristic when combined with a positive atom. Berzelius's dualistic or electrochemical theory became popular, especially in the field of mineralogy.

In 1807, he was appointed to the position of professor of medicine and pharmacy at the College of Medicine. This position provided Berzelius with a salary as well as a laboratory in which to work. He turned his interest to organic chemistry (the study of the carbon compounds of living things) and began analyzing a number of animal substances such as blood, fat, and milk. However, he was not able to adapt his electrochemical theory to organic compounds, and he eventually abandoned his studies in this area. Because of the limitations of the electrochemical theory, it eventually fell out of favor with chemists.

Becomes a leader in chemistry

Berzelius was elected a member of the Swedish Academy of Science in 1808. He would play a leading role in that institution for the rest of his life. In 1810 he became president of the Academy, and in 1818 he was appointed secretary of the organization. By 1832 he had chosen to devote all of his energies to the Academy, resigning his post at the College of Medicine.

Berzelius was widely recognized as one of the great scientific researchers of his era. He discovered two new elements, selenium (1818) and thorium (1829), and students working with him discovered lithium, valadium, and a number of rare earth elements. He and Hisinger had also discovered cerium in 1803, shortly after German chemist Martin Klaproth (1743-1817) had announced the same discovery.

Determines atomic weights

One of Berzelius's greatest accomplishments involved his work on atomic weights. Upon learning of the atomic theory of English chemist John Dalton, he became an immediate and enthusiastic supporter of the concept. Dalton had proposed that all forms of matter, whether solid, liquid, or gas, consist of tiny particles called atoms. Atoms are the smallest unit of any element, and the atoms of each element are unique. An atom of gold, for example, would have different characteristics than an atom of hydrogen. One of the unique properties of every type of atom, Dalton noted, was weight. Berzelius saw the importance of determining the atomic weights of the elements as accurately as possible.

Over the decade from 1807 to 1817, Berzelius conducted careful analyses of more than 2,000 compounds of 43 elements. In order to complete these analyses, he frequently had to invent new instruments or develop new techniques of analysis. His research eventually allowed him to publish a list of atomic weights that was by far the most accurate of its time.

Names isomers and catalysts

Berzelius also played an important role in organizing the science of chemistry. In 1831, for example, he studied the problem of chemical compounds that have the same chemical formula but different physical and chemical properties. He suggested that such compounds be called isomers, meaning "compound of equal parts." Similarly, in 1840 he proposed that all elements with more than one set of properties be

Carl Gustaf Mosander, Swedish Chemist

A large share of the credit for unraveling the complex nature of the rare earth elements (the elements with atomics numbers 58 through 71) goes to Carl Gustaf Mosander (1797-1858). Mosander was an assistant of Jöns Jacob Berzelius at the Stockholm Academy of Sciences, where he eventually became curator of minerals and the Permanent Secretary. Mosander became interested in the rare earth elements in the late 1830s. Fifty years earlier, a Swedish army officer, Carl Axel Arrhenius, had discovered a new mineral that he named ytterite near the small town of Ytterby. Chemists spent much of the next century trying to separate the mineral into its many chemically-similar parts.

The first breakthrough in this effort occurred in 1794 when Finnish chemist Johan Gadolin (1760-1852) showed that ytterite contained a large fraction of a totally new oxide (a compound composed of oxygen and an element or a charged combination of elements), which he called yttria. A decade later, German chemist Martin Klaproth (1743-1817), Berzelius, and Berzelius's collaborator Wilhelm Hisinger (1766-1852) showed that ytterite also contained a second oxide, which they called ceria. Mosander first concentrated his efforts on the ceria part of ytterite. In 1839, he found that the ceria contained a new element that he named lanthanum (for "hidden"). Mosander did not publish his results immediately, however, because he was convinced that more discoveries were yet to be made.

He was not disappointed in these hopes. In 1841, he identified a second new component of ceria. He named the component didymium, for "twin," because it was so closely related to lanthanum. Later research showed that didymium was not itself an element, but a complex mixture of other rare earth elements. In 1843, Mosander turned his attention to the yttria portion of ytterite. He was able to show that yttria consisted of at least three components. He kept the name yttria for one and called the other two erbia and terbia (now known as erbium and terbium). While the compounds originally called ceria and yttria were proven to be composed of a number of elements by Mosander, the discovery of the elements cerium and yttrium are credited to those who first identified the compounds. Mosander himself is given credit for the discovery of the elements lanthanum, erbium, and terbium, and he is recognized as a key figure in solving the mysteries of the rare earth elements.

termed allotropes. Berzelius also studied substances that alter the rate of chemical reactions without being altered by the reactions themselves. He proposed the name catalyst for such substances.

Creates system of chemical notation

The one area that students are most likely to associate with Berzelius is that of chemical symbols. Before Dalton's time, chemists had used pictographs (picture-like drawings) to represent the elements. Dalton had tried to improve this practice by specifying certain pictographs for the atoms of each element, a system which seemed clumsy and illogical to Berzelius. He proposed instead that each chemical element be represented by a single letter or a pair of letters taken from the Latin name for the element. Thus, he assigned the letter O as the chemical symbol for oxygen, H for hydrogen, N for nitrogen, Au for gold (aurum), Pb for lead (plumbum), and so on. This system is still used in chemistry today.

Writings influence scientific world

Berzelius's impact on chemistry resulted not only from his own research and theorizing, but also from his skills as an educator, writer, and administrator. In 1803 he published the first edition of his chemistry textbook, which eventually went through six editions in six languages. For the next fifty years, the book was regarded as the final authority in the field of chemistry. Berzelius also published an annual review of chemical research each year between 1821 and 1849. Known as the leading authority in chemistry in the world by 1830, Berzelius exchanged ideas with many of the other great scientists of his day in letters and in his extensive travels in Europe.

Challenges new ideas

Through such means as his textbook and annual reviews, Berzelius dominated European chemistry until his death in 1848. This influence was not always positive. As he grew older, he fell into poor health and became very conservative and disagreeable. Once an innovator in science himself, he was quick to condemn any new ideas presented by other scientists in his later years. He was held in such esteem that any idea that did not meet with his approval often went no further in the scientific community.

In 1835, at the age of 56, Berzelius married Elisabeth Poppius. As a wedding gift, Swedish King Charles XIV made Berzelius a baron of the realm. In 1836, the chemist received the Copley Medal from the Royal Society of London for his work in the classification of minerals. Berzelius died in Stockholm on August 7, 1848.

Further Reading

"Berzelius, Jöns Jacob," *Dictionary of Scientific Biography,* Volume III, Scribner's, 1970, pp. 90-97.

Jorpes, J. Erik, *Jac. Berzelius: His Life and Work,* [Stockholm], 1966.

Vilhelm Bjerknes

Born March 14, 1862
Oslo, Norway
Died April 9, 1951
Oslo, Norway

Vilhelm Bjerknes is considered the father of modern meteorology, which is the science of the weather and the structure of Earth's atmosphere. Bjerknes applied the principles of hydrodynamics, the study of the forces exerted by fluids in motion, and thermodynamics, the study of the behavior of heat, to explain the movement of air masses in the atmosphere. This movement is largely responsible for the weather patterns on Earth. By analyzing the weather with scientific and mathematical principles, Bjerknes laid the groundwork for using weather observations and mathematics to create accurate, long-term weather forecasts. He put his ideas, commonly known as the Bergen School of meteorology, into practice at his Geophysical Institute and Weather Service in Bergen, Norway. For his important contributions to physics and geophysics (the science concerned with the physical properties of Earth, which includes the studies of weather, earthquakes, volcanoes, oceans, radioactivity, and other fields), Bjerknes was awarded many honors and was inducted as a foreign member

Vilhelm Bjerknes is considered the father of modern meteorology.

Vilhelm Bjerknes (surname pronounced B'yerk-niss) laid the groundwork for today's field of meteorology with his research into the movement of the air in Earth's atmosphere. By understanding the relationship of movement in the atmosphere to weather conditions, meteorologists are able to calculate long-term patterns in the weather and provide more accurate forecasts. To support the wide scope of his new meteorological system, Bjerknes stressed the importance of having a worldwide system to collect weather data, both on the ground and in the atmosphere, using tools such as weather balloons. The field of meteorology, once an inexact practice based on local observations, was elevated by Bjerknes to a respected scientific system.

of the Royal Society of London and the National Academy of Science.

Assists in father's research

Vilhelm Frimann Koren Bjerknes was born on March 14, 1862, to Carl Anton Bjerknes and Aletta Koren in Kristiania (now Oslo), Norway. His father, educated as a mining engineer, became a well-regarded teacher of physics and researcher in hydrodynamics. The younger Bjerknes began working with his father at an early age and maintained an interest in his father's research problems for the rest of his life. Beginning his formal studies in mathematics and physics at the University of Kristiania in 1880, Bjerknes focused his research on hydrodynamics until 1887, when he decided to set an independent course as he moved on to complete his master of science degree, which he received in 1888. His understanding of the need for creativity and independent thinking in scientific research would later make Bjerknes an ideal partner for younger scientists.

After receiving his degree, Bjerknes received a state fellowship that allowed him to study in Paris. There he became acquainted with the work of well-known scientists such as German physicist Heinrich Hertz (1857-1894) and French mathematician and physicist Jules Henri Poincaré (1854-1912), both of whom were working in the field of electrodynamics, the study of electrical currents. Bjerknes obtained a position in which he worked with Hertz, and he conducted research in electrodynamics that helped to verify some of Hertz's ideas and experiments.

Bjerknes then returned to Norway and school, focusing on electrodynamics, and completed his doctoral degree in

1892. After obtaining a job lecturing at Stockholm's School of Engineering in 1893, he secured a position as professor of applied mechanics and mathematical physics at the University of Stockholm in 1895. He married Honoria Bonnevie that same year. Their son, Jacob Bjerknes, was born in 1897. Jacob would become a famous meteorologist in his own right and one of his father's most important collaborators. While at Stockholm, Bjerknes discontinued active research in electrodynamics in favor of returning to his father's hydrodynamic studies. He identified and corrected some errors in his father's ideas and presented the revised conclusions in a two-volume work that was finished in 1902.

Lays foundations of a new meteorology

When he returned to his research in hydrodynamics, Bjerknes decided to investigate the physical movements of nature's largest fluid systems, the atmosphere and the oceans. (Air is considered a fluid). It was through this course of study that he formulated the theory of physical hydrodynamics. Bjerknes realized that while the atmosphere had some qualities of a fluid system, its motion was also affected by heat. He noted that the Sun's heat is converted to motion in the atmosphere. In addition, atmospheric motion itself generates heat through friction (the rubbing of one piece of matter against another), which in turn causes motion. Bjerknes realized that atmospheric motion therefore can be properly understood and predicted only in a framework that uses both hydrodynamics and thermodynamics, the study of heat.

Since atmospheric motion creates weather patterns, Bjerknes's work held great promise for meteorological forecasting. Although observation of the progression of weather systems had already become important as a means of weather forecasting, predictions at that time were not very reliable, particularly in the longer term. Bjerknes's theory offered a scientific method that promised to enable meteorologists to forecast weather accurately, even in the longer term, by scientifically approaching the different aspects of atmospheric conditions.

Lectures on new system

Bjerknes visited the United States in 1905 to present his meteorology program in lectures at the Massachusetts Institute of Technology and to seek funding for continued research. He was rewarded with a research associateship at the Carnegie Institute in Washington, D.C., and an annual stipend (a sum of money that is usually not large enough to be called a salary) from the Carnegie Foundation, which he continued to receive until 1941. In 1909 he began lecturing to gain support from the world meteorological community for his intensive analysis and forecasting techniques. During this time he also spoke out on the importance of upper-air wind observations with the relatively new pilot balloon and theodolite tracking technique (a tool for mapping the surface of the Earth).

Bjerknes moved to the University of Kristiania as professor of applied mechanics and mathematical physics in 1907. His most significant collaborations began shortly afterwards. With his new assistant, Johann Wilhelm Sandström, he wrote the first volume of *Dynamic Meteorology and Hydrography,* dealing with the static (being at rest) state of the atmosphere and fluids, in 1910. The second volume, which deals with the kinematic or massless movement of the atmosphere and fluids (considering movement without reference to the mass and force of objects), was published the following year in collaboration with his new assistants, Theodor Hesselberg and Olav M. Devik. The final volume was written entirely by Bjerknes's collaborators and was not published until 1951. Among his other collaborators were fellow Norwegian geophysicist Harald Ulrik Sverdrup, who joined Bjerknes in 1911.

In 1912, Bjerknes's geophysical work was made more visible with his acceptance of a professorship of geophysics at the University of Leipzig in Germany. He also became chair of its new geophysical institute and soon brought Hesselberg, Sverdrup, Halvor Solberg, and his son, Jacob Bjerknes, to work with him. Several years later, however, World War I (1914-18) made research conditions increasingly difficult at Leipzig. Therefore, when his friend, the zoologist and arctic explorer Fridtjof Nansen, presented Bjerknes with the oppor-

Jacob Bjerknes, Norwegian Meteorologist

Jacob Bjerknes (1897-1975), following in the family tradition, spent his career refining the scientific ideas of his father, the geophysicist Vilhelm Bjerknes (who had continued research begun by his father). Working with other colleagues at the Bergen Weather Service founded by Vilhelm Bjerknes, Jacob translated his father's mathematical models of atmospheric movement into practical physical models. The symbols that appear on weather maps and charts that indicate air masses and frontal systems (the boundaries between air masses of different temperatures and humidities) are a direct result of Jacob Bjerknes's work.

Bjerknes recognized that the air masses described by his father had their own life cycles. Warm air masses build up and then break down as they move. When a cold front meets a warm front, the warm air is forced upward, creating a line of unstable air that can produce precipitation (water that reaches the ground in forms such as rain, snow, and ice). With his fellow meteorologist Halvor Solberg, he also observed that the turbulent air in this line of instability—known as a squall line—and the air mass that follows it can generate small groups or "families" of cyclones, or low pressure systems with counterclockwise winds and upward motion.

Later in his career, Bjerknes came to work in the United States, where he became one of the first people to use weather photographs from rockets and weather satellites. Beginning in 1959, he focused on the interrelationship of the atmosphere and the temperature of the oceans. This work helped explain differences in world climates as well as the ocean warming effect known as "El Niño." With this practical application of his father's ideas, Jacob Bjerknes had developed the basic tools of modern meteorology.

tunity to found his own geophysical institute at the new University of Bergen in Norway in 1917, the scientist accepted. The move to Bergen initiated the most productive period of Bjerknes's career.

Founds Geophysical Institute and Weather Service

Initially, the new geophysical institute was housed in rather cramped quarters in the Bergen Museum's Meteorological Observatory. Nevertheless, Bjerknes started a wide program of research that included work on the dynamic theory of atmospheric movement, systematic daily observation of basic meteorological conditions, intensive calculation of predictions and graphic representation of meteorological change, and timely weather forecasts. Using telegraph and telephone networks, the weather center was able to develop a unified weather picture over a large geographic area. This ability to obtain widespread information over a short period of time allowed the detection of new weather patterns.

By July 26, 1918, with the study of new analytical techniques still in progress, the experimental Western Bergen Weather Service, manned by Bjerknes, his son, and Solberg, was issuing detailed reports for the benefit of the government and military. The center for their work had been moved to the attic of a large home donated to Bjerknes for use as headquarters for the meteorology division of the Bergen Geophysical Institute. Eventually, the weather service became a useful source of sophisticated local forecasts that were made available to fishermen, farmers, and the budding commercial aviation industry.

Develops Bergen cyclone model

One of the major advances in meteorology resulting from Bjerknes's work was the recognition of the presence of air masses that were constantly in motion in the atmosphere. This became known as the Bergen cyclone model. It was demonstrated that these air masses were cyclonic (winds that move counterclockwise and upward) and consisted of a tongue of warm air, lying parallel to the ground, bounded on two sides by cold air. The temperature contrast at the edges of the air mass was dramatic and could be defined by a line. The forward line was called the steering line. The rear line, which coincided with the leading edge of most storms, was called the squall line. In 1921, Jacob Bjerknes and Helvor Solberg renamed these lines as warm fronts and cold fronts—the terms used in weather forecasting today. For the first time, the recognition of air mass patterns made it possible to mathematically calculate what the weather would do over coming days and made weather predictions more reliable.

Bjerknes continued to publish a great deal of material. His most comprehensive work, *On the Dynamics of the Circular Vortex with Applications to the Atmosphere and to Atmospheric Vortex and Wave Motion,* appeared in 1921; and *Physical Hydrodynamics,* written with his son, Solberg, and Bergeron, came out in 1933. Bjerknes's many enthusiastic collaborators popularized the Bergen meteorological approach among scientists when they lectured and taught in many different western countries, particularly the United States.

In 1926 Bjerknes left the Geophysical Institute of Bergen in the hands of Sverdrup, his son, and other scientists he had trained, in order to accept a position as professor of mechanics and mathematical physics at the University of Oslo. He began teaching theoretical physics and planned a series of textbooks on the subject. The first of these, on vector analysis and kinematics, was published in 1929. He also returned to his father's "hydromagnetic" theories with meteorologist Einar Høiland for the projected second textbook in the series; he was, however, unable to solve a number of difficulties in his father's theories. At the same time, he remained a forceful spokesman for modern meteorology as both a practical and theoretical science, even after his retirement from the University of Oslo in 1932. Bjerknes died of heart failure at Oslo on April 9, 1951.

Further Reading

Friedman, Robert Marc, *Appropriating the Weather: Vilhelm Bjerknes and the Construction of a Modern Meteorology,* Cornell University Press, 1989.

Gillispie, Charles Coulston, editor, *Dictionary of Scientific Biography,* Volume 15, Supplement I, Scribner's, 1978, pp.167-69.

Wernher von Braun

Born March 23, 1912
Wirsitz, Germany
(now Wyrzysk, Poland)
Died June 16, 1977
Alexandria, Virginia

Wernher von Braun developed many of the rockets that launched the early spacecraft of the American space program.

Wernher von Braun was the most famous rocket engineer of his time and a well-known promoter of spaceflight. Teams under his direction designed the V-2 (a rocket built for the Nazis during World War II to deliver bombs), Redstone, Jupiter, and Pershing missiles, as well as the Jupiter C, Juno, and Saturn launch vehicles that carried most of the early U.S. satellites and spacecraft beyond Earth's atmosphere and ultimately to the Moon. He became a celebrity and a national hero in the United States, winning numerous awards, including the first Robert H. Goddard Memorial Trophy in 1958, the Distinguished Federal Civilian Service Award (presented by President Dwight D. Eisenhower) in 1959, and the National Medal of Science in 1977. As President Jimmy Carter stated at the time of his death: "To millions of Americans, [his] name was inextricably linked to our exploration of space and to the creative application of technology. He was not only a skillful engineer but also a man of bold vision; his inspirational leadership helped mobilize and maintain the effort we needed to reach the Moon and beyond."

Early interest in rockets and space

Wernher Magnus Maximilian von Braun was born on March 23, 1912, in the east German town of Wirsitz (now Wyrzysk, Poland). He was the second of the three sons of Baron Magnus Alexander Maximilian von Braun—then the principal magistrate (*Landrat*) of the governmental district. In 1932 and 1933, Baron von Braun served as the minister of nutrition and agriculture in the last two governments of the Weimar Republic before Nazi leader Adolf Hitler rose to power in Germany. The Baron's wife, Emmy (von Quistorp) von Braun, was a well-educated woman from the Swedish-German aristocracy with a strong interest in biology and astronomy. She inspired her son's interest in spaceflight by supplying him with the science fiction works of Jules Verne and H. G. Wells and by giving him a telescope—instead of the customary watch or camera—as a gift upon his confirmation into the Lutheran church in his early teens.

Despite these influences, the young von Braun was initially a weak student and was held back one year in secondary school because of his poor grades in math and physics. But he was very interested in astronomy and rockets. He obtained a copy of space pioneer Hermann Oberth's book *Die Rakete zu den Planeträumen* ("Rockets to Planetary Space") in 1925. Disturbed by the fact that he could not understand the book's complicated mathematical formulas, he decided to master his two weakest subjects. Upon completion of secondary school, von Braun entered the Berlin-Charlottenburg Institute of Technology, where he earned a bachelor of science degree in mechanical engineering and aircraft construction in 1932.

Begins career in rocketry

In the spring of 1930, von Braun found time to work as part of the German Society for Space Travel—a group founded in part by Hermann Oberth—that experimented with small, liquid-fueled rockets. Although Oberth returned to a teaching position in his native Romania, von Braun continued working with the society. When the group ran short of funds

Aerospace engineer Wernher von Braun played a key role in making the early American space program a success. Of the powerful rockets he designed, the most famous were the Saturn line, which were used to launch the Apollo spacecraft in the 1960s and 1970s. The Apollo missions were the first to send American astronauts into orbit around the moon and ultimately to land them on the moon's surface. Von Braun was known as an expert in spaceflight, and his frequent appearances and statements in the media helped to convince Americans of the importance of supporting a space program.

during the troubled economic period of the Depression in the early 1930s, von Braun, then twenty, reluctantly accepted the sponsorship of the German military. In 1932, as the Nazis were consolidating their influence over many aspects of German society, including the military, von Braun went to work for the German army's ordnance (combat equipment and supplies) department at Kummersdorf near Berlin, where he continued to develop liquid-fueled rockets. Entering the University of Berlin about the same time, he used his work at Kummersdorf as the basis for his doctoral dissertation and received his Ph.D. in physics in 1934.

Von Braun's staff at Kummersdorf eventually grew to some eighty people, and in early 1937— after the Nazis had seized power and were enacting ever harsher "racial purity" laws against Jews— the group moved to Peenemünde, a town on the Baltic coast where the German army and air force had constructed new facilities. Before the move, engineers at Kummersdorf had begun developing ever larger rockets, and in 1936 they completed the preliminary design for the A-4, better known as the V-2. This was a very ambitious undertaking, since the missile was to be 45 feet long, deliver a 1-ton warhead (bomb) to a target 160 miles away, and employ a rocket motor that could deliver a 25-ton thrust (an upward push) for 60 seconds, compared to the 1.5 tons of thrust supplied by the largest liquid-fueled rocket motors then available.

Perfects the V-2 rocket

Von Braun's team encountered numerous difficulties— perfecting the injection system for the propellants (fuel), mastering the aerodynamic properties of the missile (so it flies with less drag through the air), and especially developing its guidance system (so the course of the missile can be controlled during the flight). Even with the assistance of private industry and universities, the first successful launch of the A-4 did not occur at Peenemünde until October 3, 1942. Despite this success, failed launches continued to plague the project. As a result, the first fully operational V-2s were not fired until September 1944. Between then and the end of the war in 1945, approximately 6,000 rockets were manufactured at an underground production site named *Mittelwerk*. There, von Braun made use of slave labor obtained from Nazi death camps. Several thousand V-2s struck London, Antwerp, and other targets in the Allied nations (the countries fighting Germany in World War II). Von Braun's rockets were responsible for killing many people, but they were not strategically significant to the Nazi's war effort; the tide had already turned against Germany by that point in the war. The V-2, nonetheless, represented a great technological advance in rocketry.

Defends association with Nazis

The landmark development of the V-2 and von Braun's later importance in the American space program often overshadows the issue of his ethical responsibility for the suffering and loss of life associated with the V-2. Although the youthful, blond-haired, blue-eyed von Braun always gave credit to his whole team for the technical success of the V-2 and other programs, he clearly played a key role in the development of the missile. While he had no direct responsibility for production at *Mittelwerk*, von Braun was aware of conditions in the concentration camp that provided the factory's slave labor. Moreover, he had joined the Nazi party on May 1, 1937, and had become an officer in the elite Schutzstaffel, or SS, military and intelligence force on May 1, 1940.

Certain American records support von Braun's claim that he had joined both organizations only to further his work on rocketry. He also stated that his motivation in building missiles for the Nazis was to develop them for use in space travel and scientific endeavors; he cited his brief arrest by the Nazis in 1944 as proof that his concern was for the future of rocketry and that he lacked interest in the immediate wartime use of the V-2. All of this makes von Braun's ethical responsibility a difficult issue to resolve.

Moves to the United States

As World War II drew to a close in Europe in the early months of 1945, von Braun organized the move of hundreds of German military personnel from Peenemünde to Bavaria so they could surrender to the Americans rather than the army of the Soviet Union. After their surrender, about 120 of the rocket team members went to Fort Bliss near El Paso, Texas, as part of a military operation called Project Paperclip, through which many former Nazis—including outright war criminals like Klaus Barbie—were employed by the American military. There they worked on rocket development and used V-2s that had been captured from the Germans for high altitude research at the nearby White Sands Proving Ground in New Mexico. In the midst of these efforts, von Braun returned to Germany to marry his second cousin, Maria Louise von Quistorp, on March 1, 1947, returning with her to Texas after the wedding.

Develops Redstone and Jupiter missiles

In 1950, the von Braun team transferred to the Redstone Arsenal near Huntsville, Alabama, where between April 1950 and February 1956 it developed the Redstone medium-range ballistic missile (a self-propelled missile that is guided as it ascends) under his technical direction. Put into use in 1958, the Redstone was basically an offshoot of the V-2 but featured several modifications including an improved guidance system. The Redstone also served as a launch vehicle for space capsules, placing the first two U.S. astronauts into suborbital flight: Alan B. Shepard in May 1961 and Virgil I. "Gus" Grissom in July 1961. In February 1956 von Braun became the director of the development operations division of the newly established Army Ballistic Missile Agency (ABMA) in Huntsville. While located there, he and his wife raised three children—Iris Careen (born in 1948), Margrit Cecile (1952), and Peter Constantine (1960). Von Braun became a U.S. citizen on April 14, 1955.

The next missile designed by von Braun and his team was the Jupiter intermediate–range ballistic missile. Unlike the

Wernher von Braun with a model of the Jupiter-C rocket, 1958; James Van Allen looks on

Redstone and the V-2, which used liquid oxygen and an alcohol-water mixture as propellants, the Jupiter employed liquid oxygen and kerosene. Following its development, it was assigned to the Air Force for use after 1958. In the meantime, von Braun's engineers had developed the Jupiter C, which consisted of three parts or "stages." Its first stage was a modified Redstone missile, while the second and third stages were derived from the Sergeant missile, initially developed by the Jet Propulsion Laboratory. In its third launch on August 8, 1957, the Jupiter C carried a nose cone that became the first man-made object to be recovered from outer space. It also successfully used a new technique to carry off the excessive heat produced by friction (the rubbing of one piece of matter against another) upon the nose cone of a missile or spacecraft during re-entry into the atmosphere. In addition, the von Braun team developed the Pershing—a two-stage, solid-fuel ballistic missile that had its first test launch in February 1960.

Another group of rockets developed under von Braun was the Juno series. Juno I, a four-stage version of Jupiter C, launched America's first satellite, *Explorer I*, on January 31, 1958. Juno II, using the Jupiter missile as its first stage and Jupiter C upper stages, launched a number of satellites in the Pioneer and Explorer series of spacecraft, including the *Pioneer IV* that went past the Moon and entered an orbit around the Sun following its launch on March 3, 1959.

Transfers to NASA

Undoubtedly the greatest claim to fame of von Braun and his team was the powerful Saturn family of rockets, which propelled Americans into orbit around the Moon and landed 12 of them on the lunar surface between July of 1969 and January of 1971. Development of these launch vehicles began at ABMA and was completed in the 1960s under the management of the National Aeronautics and Space Administration (NASA), after von Braun and more than 4,000 ABMA employees transferred to NASA on July 1, 1960 to form the George C. Marshall Space Flight Center. Von Braun directed the Space Flight Center until February of 1970. The Saturn I

Alan Shepard, American Astronaut

The Mercury program was the first U.S. effort to accomplish manned spaceflight, and former navy test pilot Alan Shepard was the first American to venture into space. On May 5, 1961, Shepard was thrust into space aboard the Mercury capsule *Freedom 7* by a Redstone rocket to a height of 113 miles above Earth's surface. In flight, the capsule traveled at a speed of 5,180 miles per hour. After only 15 minutes and 22 seconds, during which time it traveled a distance of 2,300 miles, the capsule with Shepard aboard splashed down in the Atlantic Ocean. The textbook-perfect launch and flight of *Freedom 7* earned NASA's space program the support of the U.S. government and people around the world.

A hearing disorder grounded Shepard from further spaceflights for a number of years. But after a successful ear operation, he was named mission commander of *Apollo 14,* the fourth scheduled mission to the Moon. A Saturn V rocket launched the capsule on January 31, 1971. *Apollo 14* entered lunar orbit on February 4. The next day, Shepard and fellow astronaut Edgar Mitchell left the command module and descended in the lunar lander to the Moon's surface. Shepard became the fifth man to walk on the Moon. After conducting scientific experiments, the astronauts returned to Earth, splashing down in the Pacific Ocean on February 9. Shepard's leadership in the space program has been recognized with a number of honors, including the Medal of Honor, awarded by President Jimmy Carter in 1979.

and Ib were developmental rockets leading to the massive Saturn V that actually launched the astronauts of the Apollo program, the space program that attempted to send astronauts to the Moon. Propelled by liquid oxygen and kerosene in its first stage and liquid oxygen and liquid hydrogen for the two upper stages, the Saturn V stood 363 feet high, six stories above the top of the Statue of Liberty. Its first stage was made of the largest aluminum cylinder ever produced; its valves were as large as barrels, its fuel pumps were larger than refrigerators.

As von Braun repeatedly insisted, he and his team were not the only people responsible for the success of the Saturn and Apollo programs. In fact, the engineers at Marshall often urged more cautious solutions to problems than NASA ultimately adopted. One example involved the debate over "all-up" versus "step-by-step" testing of Saturn V. Having experienced numerous rocket system failures going back to the V-2 and beyond, the German engineers favored testing each stage of the complicated rocket individually to make sure they were operating properly. At NASA headquarters, however, administrator George Mueller preferred the Air Force approach, which relied much more heavily on ground testing. He therefore insisted upon testing Saturn V all at once in order to meet President John F. Kennedy's ambitious goal of landing an American on the Moon before the end of the decade. Von Braun hesitated but finally concurred in the ultimately successful procedure.

Promotes space exploration

Beyond his role as an engineer, scientist, and project manager, von Braun was also an important advocate for spaceflight, publishing numerous books and magazine articles, serving as a consultant for television programs and films, and testifying before Congress. Perhaps most important in this regard were his contributions, with others, to a series of *Colliers* magazine articles from 1952 to 1953 and to a Walt Disney television series produced by Ward Kimball from 1955 to 1957. Both series were enormously influential and, along with the fears of Americans that the Soviets were winning the space race, his work helped to strengthen American efforts to conquer space. As von Braun said to Kimball in late 1968 after the Apollo 8 orbit of the Moon: "Well, Ward, it looks like they're following our script."

In March 1970, NASA transferred von Braun to its headquarters in Washington, D.C., where he became Deputy Associate Administrator. He had hoped to renew interest in the space program, but a much smaller NASA budget, as he said, "reduced my function in Washington eventually to one of describing programs which I knew could not be funded for the next 10 years anyway." As a result, he resigned from the agency on July 1, 1972, to become vice president for engineering and development with Fairchild Industries of Germantown, Maryland. Besides his work for that aerospace firm, he continued his efforts to promote human spaceflight, helping to found the National Space Institute in 1975 and serving as its first president.

During his life, von Braun displayed a wide range of accomplishments beyond his remarkable role as a space pioneer. A musician who played the piano and cello, he loved the music of Mozart, Chopin, and Puccini. At the same time, he was an ardent outdoorsman who enjoyed scuba diving, fishing, hunting, sailing, and piloting an airplane. He died of cancer on June 16, 1977, at a hospital in Alexandria, Virginia.

Further Readings

Biddle, Wayne, "Science, Morality and the V-2," *New York Times,* October 2, 1992, p. A31.

Braun, Wernher von, with J. Kaplan and others, *Across the Space Frontier,* Viking, 1952.

Braun, Wernher von, with Cornelius Ryan, "Baby Space Station," *Colliers,* June 27, 1953, pp. 33-40.

Braun, Wernher von, with Cornelius Ryan, "Can We Get to Mars?" *Colliers,* April 30, 1954, pp. 22-28.

Braun, Wernher von, with Willy Ley, *Exploration of Mars,* Viking, 1956.

Braun, Wernher von, "Man on the Moon—The Journey," *Colliers,* October 18, 1952, pp. 52-60.

Braun, Wernher von, *Man on the Moon,* Sidgwick and Jackson, 1953.

Braun, Wernher von, *The Mars Project,* University of Illinois Press, 1953.

Braun, Wernher von, "The Redstone, Jupiter, and Juno," in *The History of Rocket Technology,* edited by Eugene M. Emme, Wayne State University Press, 1964, pp. 107-121.

Hunt, Linda, *Secret Agenda: The United States Government, Nazi Scientists, and Project Paperclip, 1945 to 1990,* St. Martin's Press, 1991.

Huzel, Dieter K., *Peenemünde to Canaveral,* Prentice-Hall, Inc., 1962.

Kennedy, Gregory P., *Vengeance Weapon 2: The V-2 Guided Missile,* Smithsonian Institution Press, 1983.

Neufeld, Michael J., "The Guided Missile and the Third Reich: Peenemünde and the Forging of a Technological Revolution," in *Science, Technology and National Socialism,* edited by Monika Renneberg and Mark Walker, Cambridge University Press, 1993.

Stuhlinger, Ernst and Frederick I. Ordway III, *Wernher von Braun: Crusader for Space,* Volume I, *A Biographical Memoir,* Krieger, 1994.

Wilford, John Noble, "Wernher von Braun, Space Pioneer, Dies," *New York Times,* June 18, 1977, pp. 16-18.

Benjamin Carson

Born September 18, 1951
Detroit, Michigan

Reader's Digest has called Benjamin Carson a miracle worker of modern medicine. As the director of pediatric neurosurgery (surgery on the nerves, the brain, or the spinal cord of children) at Johns Hopkins Hospital in Baltimore, Maryland, Carson has received recognition throughout the medical community for his surgical skills. He has undertaken many high-risk operations, primarily on children, involving complex and delicate neurosurgical procedures. In 1987, he gained international acclaim for leading a team of seventy medical personnel that separated a pair of Siamese twins (children who are born physically connected) who were joined at the backs of their heads.

Benjamin Carson is known for his success with high-risk brain surgeries, including the 1987 separation of a pair of Siamese twins joined at the head.

A childhood of fighting and poor grades

Carson was born on September 18, 1951, in Detroit, Michigan, to Robert and Sonya Carson. His parents divorced when he was eight years old, and he lived with his mother.

Although Carson dreamed of becoming a doctor, he was a poor student who had a tendency to get into a lot of fights. Whites taunted and threatened him because he was black. "He had no hope," his mother told *People*. "He just felt there was no way out, and so why should he try? He was just really at the point of no return."

When Carson was ten years old, his mother cut back his television viewing to three shows a week and forced him to read two books weekly and submit written book reports to her. Carson became an avid reader, and his grades steadily improved until he was near the top of his class. "Once I discovered that between the pages of those books . . . we could go anywhere and we could meet anybody and we could do anything, that's when it really started to hit me," he told *People*.

Faces racism

As his work at school began to improve, Carson ran into racial prejudice. Once he was confronted by a group of boys armed with sticks who threatened to kill him for going to school. When he joined a neighborhood football league, a group of white adults warned him to stay away; he did. His most humiliating experience took place in the eighth grade when a teacher scolded his white classmates for letting Carson, a black student, win the outstanding student award. These episodes inflamed his temper. He once opened a three-inch gash in the forehead of a schoolmate who teased him. He also broke the nose of another boy with a rock. And once he almost killed a friend in an argument; Carson tried to stab him in the stomach with a knife, but luckily the boy was wearing a heavy belt buckle that stopped the blade. Only fourteen at the time, Carson was shocked at what he had almost done, and he saw the direction his life could take. This experience drove him more deeply into his religion—he remains a Seventh-Day Adventist. (Adventism is a Christian denomination that espouses belief in the nearness of the second coming of Jesus Christ and of the end of the world.) His faith in God helped him control his temper.

After graduating third in his high school class, Carson

received offers from several prestigious universities. He accepted a scholarship to Yale University and went on to study medicine at the University of Michigan. His original intention was to become a psychotherapist, but after his first year of medical school, he discovered neurosurgery. "I loved dissecting things," Carson said in an *Ebony* interview. "And I always felt that I was very good with my hands. Neurosurgery was a natural for me."

Australia provides valuable experience

Carson did both his internship in general surgery (an internship is a period of training under the supervision of experienced doctors) and his residency in neurosurgery (residency is a period of advanced medical training) at Johns Hopkins Hospital, one of the top medical centers in the country. After graduating he became the hospital's first black neurosurgery resident. In 1983 he moved with his wife, Lacena (known as Candy), to Perth, Australia, to become the senior neurosurgery resident at Queen Elizabeth Medical Centre, one of that country's leading centers for brain surgery.

Due to a lack of qualified neurosurgeons in Australia and Carson's advanced medical skills, he quickly obtained valuable work experience. "I was operating so much," he told *Ebony*, "I was able to concentrate several years of experience into one year."

In 1984 Carson returned to Johns Hopkins and soon became one of the hospital's leading surgeons. He was promoted to director of pediatric neurosurgery within the year, becoming at the age of thirty-four the youngest director of a surgical division in the United States.

IMPACT

Because of the risks involved in operating on the brain, doctors often considered brain surgery a treatment of last resort (that is, something to consider only when all other methods have failed or been ruled out). Neurosurgeon Benjamin Carson, however, has had remarkable success with many of the most difficult brain surgeries. He has taken on cases that many other doctors would have labeled inoperable, particularly with young patients. His accomplishments have shown that certain conditions can be treated effectively with surgery, particularly in cases of brain tumors and seizures. In 1987 his skill drew international attention in a landmark operation in which Carson, with the support of a massive surgical team, separated a pair of Siamese twins joined at the back of their heads.

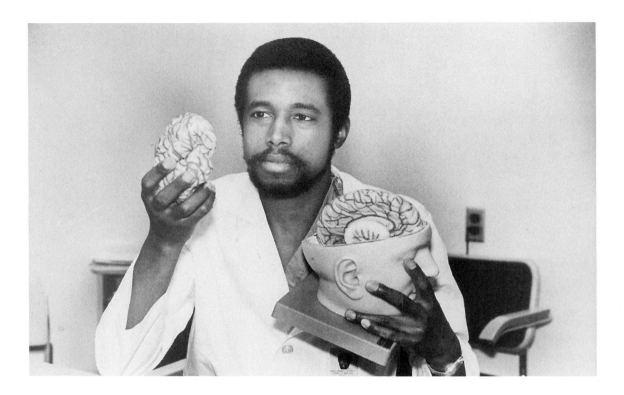

Ben Carson with a model of the human brain

Reputation spreads

Carson's skills became known throughout the medical community. He was especially adept at safely performing operations that were usually considered high-risk procedures. He gained renown for dealing with hemispherectomies (a complex operation in which a portion of the brain of a critically ill seizure victim, or other neurologically diseased patient, is removed to restore normal functioning) and for separating Siamese twins.

One of his most difficult cases occurred in 1985 when he operated on Christopher Pylant, a four-year-old from Atlanta, Georgia, with a malignant tumor of the brain stem (a malignant tumor, as opposed to a benign tumor, is one that spreads and causes physical harm). Other physicians had stated that the cancer could not be removed with surgery, but Carson told the boy's father he could save the boy. When he operated, Carson could not even see the brain stem; it appeared to have been destroyed by cancer. Carson removed what he safely could and then delivered the sad news to the parents. But over the next few weeks Pylant improved, and a brain scan indicated a brain stem still existed. Three weeks later Carson operated again and removed the remaining tumor. Pylant eventually made a complete recovery.

Another notable case involved four-year-old Maranda Francisco of Denver, Colorado, who suffered from multiple seizures—up to 120 a day. Her right side was paralyzed, and she had a rare brain disease that, if unchecked, would have left her with serious neurological damage. Carson removed the diseased left hemisphere of Francisco's brain during a ten-hour operation. Six months later she had regained nearly complete use of her right arm and leg and was free of seizures. The right side of her brain had taken over functions of the left.

The ultimate test

Carson's most famous medical operation occurred in 1987, when he led a surgical team of doctors, nurses, and technicians to separate a pair of West German Siamese twins who shared a blood vessel in the back of their heads. Carson devised a plan to separate the twins by completely shutting down their blood flow, severing their common blood vessel, and then restoring their individual vessel systems. While the entire procedure lasted twenty-two hours, Carson and another surgeon had only one hour to conduct the actual surgery and restoration. The operation went smoothly until Carson noticed the vessels that carried blood from the brain of each child were more tangled than had been expected. Twenty minutes after stopping the twins' circulation, Carson made the final cut. He then had forty minutes to reconstruct the severed blood vessels and close. Just a few minutes before the hour limit, the twins were separated, and the operating tables were wheeled apart. Carson told *Ebony,* "Not only was it exciting to be part of a history-making event, but the significant fact is that we put together an incredibly complex scene with a team of incredibly competent people who submerged their egos and pulled off what was perhaps the most complex surgical feat in the history of mankind."

Carson is a contributor to numerous journals, including the prestigious *Journal of the American Medical Association.* He has written two technical books in his field and is the co-author of *Gifted Hands: The Ben Carson Story*, a 1990 book that outlines his rise from troubled urban youth to world-famous surgeon. In 1992 he published *Think Big: Unleashing Your Potential for Excellence,* a book that encourages young people to set high goals and work hard to reach them.

Honors and awards

Carson has received numerous awards and honors for his work. Some of his honors include an American Black Achievement Award from *Ebony* in 1988, the Candle Award for Science and Technology from Morehouse University in 1989, and an *Essence* award in 1994. He has also been awarded honorary degrees from a number of colleges and universities.

Despite the honors bestowed on him, Carson has remained modest about his accomplishments. A devout Seventh Day Adventist, Carson places his achievements in a religious context. "God created the body. He knows more about it than anybody else and can heal virtually every problem. It's only a matter of whether we're willing to let Him work through us," he told *Ebony.* He also credits his mother for helping him with his success. In an article he wrote for *Ebony,* he credited his motivation to her philosophy of "no excuses for anything" and "if anybody can do something, you can do it better."

Carson and his wife, Candy, live in Columbia, Maryland, with their three children, Murray Nedlands, Benjamin Solomon, and Rhoeyce Harrington. He raises his children on the two books a week rule and speaks to other kids about staying away from drugs and violence. "It doesn't matter if you come from the inner city. People who fail in life are people who find lots of excuses," he told *People.* "It's never too late for a person to recognize that they have potential themselves."

Further Reading

Carson, Benjamin, with Cecil Murphey, *Gifted Hands: The Ben Carson Story,* Zondervan Books, 1990.

Carson, Benjamin, *Think Big: Unleashing Your Potential for Excellence,* Zondervan Books, 1992.

Kramer, Linda, "The Physician Who Healed Himself First," *People,* fall 1991, pp. 96-99.

Phillips, Christopher, "Ben Carson: Man of Miracles," *Reader's Digest,* April 1990, pp. 71-75.

"The Seventh Essence Awards," *Essence,* May 1994, p. 103.

"Surgical Superstar," *Ebony,* January 1988, pp. 52-58.

Kenneth B. Clark

Born July 24, 1914
Panama Canal Zone

Kenneth B. Clark conducted landmark research on the effect of segregation on black schoolchildren.

Kenneth Bancroft Clark is among the most prominent black social scientists of the twentieth century. (Social science is the study of human society and individual relationships within it, and includes the fields of sociology, psychology, anthropology, economics, political science, and history.) For many years a professor of psychology at City College of New York (now City College of the City University of New York), Clark achieved national recognition when his work was cited by the United States Supreme Court in its 1954 ruling that racially segregated (seperate) schools were unequal and therefore unconstitutional. That decision helped inspire the civil rights movement of the 1960s, and Clark went on to author a series of highly influential books about ghetto life, education, and the ways to end poverty.

Clark was born on July 24, 1914, in the Panama Canal Zone, the son of Miriam Clark and Arthur Bancroft Clark, a native of the West Indies who worked as a superintendent of cargo for the United Fruit Company. Despite the family's relatively comfortable situation in Panama, Miriam Clark, a Jamaican woman, insisted that the Clark children should be raised in the United States, where they would get better education and employment opportunities than in Panama. Kenneth and his sister, Beulah, accordingly moved with their mother to the Harlem district of New York City when Kenneth was four–and–a–half years old. Their father, however, refused to relocate to a country where his color would prevent him from holding a job similar to his position with the United Fruit Company. This did not change the mind of Miriam Clark, who found work in Harlem as a seamstress and proceeded to raise the children on her own.

Learns lessons of equality in school

Attending classes in New York City schools, young Clark was held to the same high standards as his fellow students, most of whom were white. As he told *New Yorker* magazine many years later, "When I went to the board in Mr. Ruprecht's algebra class, . . . I had to do those equations, and if I wasn't able to do them he wanted to find out why. He didn't expect any less of me because I was black." This idea is the basis of the educational philosophy Clark would maintain throughout his career: schools must be open to students of every race, and teachers must expect the same performance from each child. In such an environment, some students will naturally perform better than others, but not according to racial categories.

When he finished the ninth grade, Clark was faced with a critical turning point in his education. School counselors advised most black youths to attend vocational high school, where they could learn skills appropriate to the limited employment opportunities available to blacks at the time. When Clark's mother heard of this plan she went directly the counselor's office and told him that under no circumstances would her son go to trade school; she had not come all the way from Panama to raise a factory worker. Instead, Clark was sent to George Washington High School, where he excelled in all subjects and grew especially fond of economics. He had thoughts of becoming an economist until he was

≋IMPACT≋

The 1897 Supreme Court decision in the case of *Plessy v. Ferguson* allowed school districts to create separate schools for black students and white students. The court decision argued that "separate but equal" facilities would not be harmful to children. In the 1940s, Kenneth B. Clark studied the effects of segregated schools on black children, and in a 1950 report he charged that such a system did have a negative impact on a child's psychological outlook and self-esteem. Clark's findings were at the heart of the 1954 Supreme Court case, *Brown v. Board of Education,* which overturned the *Plessy* decision and ruled segregated schools unconstitutional. Clark did not believe that the court victory effectively solved the issue of segregated schools and went on to write about other factors that often keep black children from receiving educational opportunities equal to those of whites.

denied an award for excellence in economics by a teacher who apparently could not bring himself to so honor a black student. Clark remembers this as his first direct experience of discrimination.

Turns to psychology studies

Upon entering Howard University in 1931, Clark originally intended to become a medical doctor. In his second year at the all-black institution, however, he took a class in psychology taught by Francis Sumner that changed forever the course of his studies. Clark was excited by the idea of using a systematic approach like psychology to explain the complex workings of human behavior and interaction, particularly racist behavior. He determined that he would follow the example of Sumner in the field of psychology, and after receiving a master's degree in 1936, he joined the Howard faculty for a year of teaching.

At that point Clark came to another critical fork in his career. He could have remained to study and teach at Howard, but at the urging of his mentor, Sumner, and a number of other faculty members, Clark went on to Columbia University to obtain his doctorate and to teach at the integrated college. He became the first black doctoral candidate in psychology at Columbia and completed his degree in 1940.

Clark was married in 1938 to Mamie Phipps, a fellow psychology student at Howard who would co-author many of the articles that later made the couple famous. After graduation from Columbia, Clark taught briefly at the Hampton Institute in Virginia and then served for two years in the U.S. Government's Office of War Information. Clark joined the faculty of City College of New York in 1942, becoming an assistant professor seven years later. In 1960 he became a full professor—the first black academic to be so honored in the history of New York's city colleges.

Studies effects of segregated schools

As a black psychologist, Clark had always been deeply concerned with the nature of racism, and in the 1940s he and his wife, Mamie, began publishing the results of their research concerning the effect of segregated schooling on kindergarten students in Washington, D.C. Between 1939 and 1950, the Clarks wrote five articles on the subject and became nationally known for their work in the field. In 1950 Kenneth Clark wrote an article for the Midcentury White House Conference on Children and Youth, summarizing his own work and other psychological literature on segregation. This report came to the attention of the National Association for the Advancement of Colored People (NAACP) during its campaign to overturn legalized segregation. In its landmark 1954 decision declaring such segregation unconstitutional, the Supreme Court cited the Clark report as representative of "modern authority" on the subject.

Clark was intimately involved in the long legal struggle that culminated in *Brown v. Board of Education* (the name of the court's 1954 desegregation decision). He testified as an expert witness at three of the four cases leading up to the Supreme Court's review of *Brown,* and his report on the psychology of segregation was read carefully by the justices. Psychological findings were critical to the NAACP's case, in which it asked the court to overturn the 1896 decision in *Plessy* that upheld the concept of "separate but equal" schooling for the races.

Influences Supreme Court case

In *Plessy v. Ferguson,* the court had held that as long as separate schools were of equal quality, they did not inherently "deny . . . the equal protection of the laws" guaranteed by the Fourteenth Amendment to the Constitution. The NAACP challenged the Plessy decision by asserting that, in reality, "separate" meant "unequal" for blacks. In his testimony before one of the lower courts, Clark defined the harmful effects of segregated schooling as "a confusion in the child's own self esteem—basic feelings of inferiority, conflict, confusion in his self-image, resentment, hostility toward himself." Such effects would be felt, Clark and the NAACP argued, regardless of the relative merits of the schools involved; or, as the court eventually stated, "Separate educational facilities are inherently unequal."

Brown v. Board of Education was not only a milestone in the modern civil rights movement, it also made Kenneth Clark into something of an academic superstar. Clark went on to become the most influential black social scientist of his generation. He received honorary degrees from more than a dozen of the nation's finest colleges and universities. But despite the respect his work received from fellow academics, his goal of integrated, adequate schooling for blacks had not became a reality even four decades after the announcement of the monumental court decision.

Develops Harlem education plan

America's schools did not suddenly integrate themselves the day after *Brown v. Board of Education;* in most urban areas the growth of black ghettoes only reinforced the segregation of black and white schoolchildren. Clark understood that in order to improve the education of students of color, the African American community as a whole needed to lobby for funding and commitment from the federal government and private citizens. In the early 1960s, Clark was given the opportunity to reform the entire school system in Harlem. As part of the social plans introduced by the administrations of Presidents John F. Kennedy and Lyndon Johnson (under Kennedy the plans were part of his "New Frontier" policies—under Johnson they were part of the "Great Society" initiative), federal funds were provided in 1962 to create Harlem Youth Opportunities Unlimited (HARYOU), a group devoted to

studying the causes of juvenile delinquency in the Harlem area and suggesting remedies.

Clark was appointed chair of HARYOU, which over the next two years produced a 620-page report recommending, among other things, the "thorough reorganization of the schools" in Harlem. This would include increased integration, a massive program to improve reading skills among students, stricter review of teacher performance, and, most important, a high level of participation by the residents of Harlem in putting these changes into practice. HARYOU was the first example of what would later be known as a community-action program.

Writes about ghetto life

For political reasons, many of the HARYOU recommendations were never followed in New York. While this frustration made the experience with HARYOU a negative one for Clark, it did inspire him to write his best-known book, *Dark*

Kenneth B. Clark

Ghetto: Dilemmas of Social Power. In this work, Clark goes beyond his HARYOU research to write an overview of black ghetto life that has become required reading in sociology classes around the country.

In 1967 Clark formed and presided over a nonprofit corporation known as The Metropolitan Applied Research Center (MARC Corp.), composed of a group of social scientists and other professionals who hoped to identify and solve problems of the urban poor. MARC's most significant work was undertaken in 1970, when the school board of Washington, D.C., asked Clark and his associates to design a new educational program for the city's 150,000 schoolchildren, 90 percent of whom were black and the majority of whom were poor. The Washington, D.C., school system offered Clark the chance to test his theories of education on a large scale and under ideal conditions. Clark outlined a program similar to the HARYOU program for New York, calling for a massive and immediate upgrading of reading skills, teacher evaluation based on student performance, and community involvement in the schooling process.

Once again, though, real–world politics frustrated Clark's work. The Washington, D.C., teachers refused to make their pay and position dependent on student performance, and a new superintendent of schools refused to cooperate with the plan. The superintendent even challenged Clark's central thesis that children of the ghetto could and should be expected to perform at "normal" levels. Ghetto life, argued this administrator, was anything but normal, and it would be unfair to hold teachers and schools responsible for the performance of students handicapped by living under such conditions.

Clark's defeat at the hands of political reality, however, did not dampen his belief in integrated schooling. He also did not cave in to the demands of the black separatist movement in the late 1960s and early 1970s. He opposed the creation of any organization based on racial exclusivity, including such projects as a black dormitory at the University of Chicago and Antioch College's Afro American Institute. As a result, Clark was attacked as a "moderate" at a time of black radicalism, in some instances receiving personal threats for his total rejection of racial separatism.

Continues work on racial issues

After his retirement from City College in 1975, Clark and his wife and children founded a consulting firm called Clark, Phipps, Clark & Harris, Inc. The company helped large corporations design and implement minority hiring programs. The firm flourished, attracting prestigious clients such as AT&T, Chemical Bank, and Consolidated Edison. Clark remained active in the growing field of minority concerns in the workplace into the 1990s. In addition, he has continued to voice his outrage over the country's lack of educational progress in academic, social, and psychological terms. The means of successful change, Clark maintains, is by educating children in an atmosphere in which all people are treated with dignity and respect. Clark's career of research and activism has earned him a number of awards, including the Springarn Medal of the NAACP in 1961 and the Franklin Delano Roosevelt Four Freedoms Award in 1985.

Further Reading

Clark, Kenneth B., *Dark Ghetto: Dilemmas of Social Power,* Harper, 1965.

Clark, Kenneth B., "Unfinished Business: The Toll of Psychic Violence," *Newsweek,* January 11, 1993, p. 38.

Current Biography, H. W. Wilson, 1964, pp. 80-83.

Hentoff, Nat, "Profiles," *New Yorker,* August 23, 1982, pp. 37-40+.

Nicolaus Copernicus

Born February 19, 1473
Torun, Poland
Died May 24, 1543
Frombork, Poland

"We revolve about the Sun like any other planet."

Nicolaus Copernicus is considered the founder of modern astronomy for proving that the solar system is heliocentric, or organized around the Sun. By making scientific observations and mathematical calculations to support this idea, Copernicus also provided a model for the modern scientific method (formulating, testing, and proving a theory). In this way, Copernicus helped to overthrow the popular reliance on the unproven, and often incorrect, ideas of ancient Greek philosophers that had dominated scientific thought until his time.

Privately studies astronomy

Copernicus was born into a well-to-do family in Torun, Poland, on February 19, 1473. His father, a copper merchant, died when Copernicus was ten, and the boy was taken in by an uncle who was a prince and bishop. Because of his family circumstances, Copernicus was able to afford a good education. He entered the University of Cracow in 1491 and studied mathematics and painting. He graduated in 1494, by which time he had first become interested in astronomy.

His uncle arranged for Copernicus to serve as a canon (a member of the staff of a cathedral) at the cathedral at Frombork, even though this was a position usually held by priests. This job provided Copernicus with a generous income throughout his life and support for further studies. In 1496 he went to Italy for ten years in order to study medicine and religious law.

When he was not working on his official studies, Copernicus began investigating astronomy on his own, making his earliest astronomical observations in 1497. The year 1500 was probably the most influential time during Copernicus's stay in Italy. In that year he attended a conference in Rome dealing with calendar reform. Explanations of the movement of heavenly bodies at that time were based on the idea that the Sun and the other planets revolved around Earth, but this system could not be used to create an accurate calendar. This problem eventually set Copernicus on a quest to find a better method for calculating the length of the year. On November 6, 1500, Copernicus experienced another career-shaping moment when he witnessed a lunar eclipse (in which the Moon passes either wholly or partially into the shadow created by Earth's position in front of the Sun, that is, when the three bodies align thus: Moon—Earth—Sun). After completing his studies in 1503, Copernicus returned to Poland in either 1505 or 1506.

Shows Earth revolves around Sun

The problem of calculating planetary positions and an accurate calendar continued to hold Copernicus's interest back in Poland. The tables of planetary positions that were in use at the time were very complex and inaccurate. Predicting the positions of the planets over long periods of time was haphazard at best, and the seasons were out of step with the position of the Sun. Copernicus realized as early as 1507 that tables of planetary positions could be calculated much more easily, and accurately, if he made the assumption that the Sun, not Earth, was

Astronomer Nicolaus Copernicus saw that the system used to predict the position of the planets in the early 1500s simply did not work. That system said that Earth was the central point around which the Sun and all the other planets revolved, but this did not seem to be the case when Copernicus actually observed the movements of the heavenly bodies himself. He found that the idea of the planets revolving around the Sun actually fit his observations more closely. Although these ideas were considered dangerous by religious authorities of the time, Copernicus's ideas gained favor among scientists. His scientific work, presented in his book *De revolutionibus orbium coelestium* ("Revolution of the Heavenly Spheres") provided a basis for further exploration and explanation of the solar system by such astronomers as Galileo Galilei (1564-1642) and Johannes Kepler (1571-1630).

the center of the solar system, and that the planets, including Earth, orbited the Sun. In order to explain the rising and setting of the Sun, if the Sun did not travel around Earth, Copernicus suggested that Earth itself was spinning, which created the appearance of the Sun's movement in the sky.

Reviving an ancient idea

Copernicus was not the first person to introduce the concept that the Sun, not Earth, was the center of the solar system. The astronomer Aristarchus of Samos had come up with the idea in ancient Greece around 270 B.C., but his thought was overshadowed by the teachings of the Alexandrian astronomer Ptolemy, whose theory, proposed in the second century, had been dominant for 1,300 years and was the accepted view of the powerful Roman Catholic Church. Ptolemy claimed Earth was at the center of the universe, and all the planets (including the Sun and Moon) were attached to invisible spheres that rotated around it.

Uses science to support new system

Copernicus's truly unique contribution to astronomy was providing a mathematical system proving that the Sun-centered system was the case. In order to achieve this, he used his own observations, building a small observatory for this purpose in 1513. Copernicus was not an especially good astronomical observer. It is said he never saw the planet Mercury (which never gets very far from the Sun), and he made an incorrect assumption about planetary orbits—he decided they were perfectly circular. The true nature of planetary orbits were not understood until the early 1600s, when German astronomer **Johannes Kepler** (for more information, see pp. 126-132) discovered that planets travel in elliptical (oval-shaped) orbits.

Even so, the heliocentric model developed by Copernicus fit the observed data better than the ancient Greek concept. For example, the periodic "backward" motion in the sky of the planets Mars, Jupiter, and Saturn was more readily explained by the fact that those planets' orbits were outside Earth's. Thus, Earth "overtook" them as it circled the Sun. Planetary positions throughout the year could also be predicted much more accurately using Copernicus's model.

Ideas contradict Church teachings

Copernicus had completed a first draft of a paper explaining his new system by May 1514, but he only allowed a few close friends to see it. He called this work "Sketch of Hypotheses Made by Nicolaus Copernicus on the Heavenly Motions." Copernicus was very reluctant to make his ideas public. He realized his theory not only contradicted the Greek scientists, it also went against the teachings of the Catholic Church, which could impose harsh penalties on people it considered to be promoting heretical ideas (that is, those that go against accepted Church opinions). But in 1530 he finally allowed a summary of his ideas to circulate among scholars, who received it with great enthusiasm.

De Revolutionibus orbium coelestium

It was not until just shortly before his death in 1543, however, that Copernicus's entire book was published. German mathematician Georg Rheticus (1514-1574), who was a devoted follower of Copernicus's ideas, was finally able to convince Copernicus to give him permission to print it. Unfortunately, Rheticus was forced into exile after the Church condemned his ideas. The publication of Copernicus's book was turned over to a Lutheran minister named Andreas Osiander (1498-1552).

Jean-Bernard-Léon Foucault, French Physicist

Jean-Bernard-Léon Foucault (1819-1868) was an extremely successful experimental physicist. He, like Italian astronomer and physicist Galileo Galilei (1564-1642), believed experimentation and innovation were the best ways to accurately uncover the properties of the natural world. He was responsible for a number of discoveries and inventions, including the first use of silvered glass in reflecting telescopes, an improved measurement of the speed of light, the navigational tool known as the gyroscope, and a device known as Foucault's pendulum.

Working with French physicist Armand H. Fizeau (1819-1896), Foucault produced the first photographs of the Sun's surface in 1845. In order to produce a clear picture, Foucault had to design a device for their solar camera that could follow the Sun as it moved across the sky. This apparent movement, of course, is actually caused the movement of Earth as it rotates. In his device Foucault used a machine invented in the 1600s called a siderostat, or clock-drive, that uses a pendulum (an object hung from a fixed point that swings back and forth) to run a clock. The clock was then used to turn his camera. As he worked with the clock-drive, Foucault noticed that the pendulum kept swinging in the direction in which it started. This gave him an idea about how to demonstrate that Earth rotates: theorizing that the direction in which a pendulum swings remains absolutely constant, he proposed that, if Earth rotates, the line traced by the swing of the pendulum would appear to change. In fact, this is the case—the line appears to rotate in a clockwise direction, proving (given the absolute fixity of the pendulum's swing) that Earth rotates in a counter-clockwise direction.

After carrying out his demonstration successfully in private, Foucault constructed a massive pendulum, made of a large iron ball suspended from a wire more than 200 feet long. Staging a dramatic exhibition with the device in 1852, Foucault set the pendulum swinging before a large crowd in Paris. A spike attached to the bottom of the ball scratched a line in a plot of sand scattered on the floor. As time passed, the line shifted, proving that Earth was rotating under the pendulum. Three hundred years after Nicolaus Copernicus proposed that Earth rotates on its axis, Foucault had provided the observational evidence.

Osiander found he was in a difficult position; Lutheran leader Martin Luther (1483-1546) had come out firmly against Copernicus's new theory, and Osiander was obligated to follow his superior. "This Fool wants to turn the whole Art of Astronomy upside down," Luther had said. Copernicus had dedicated his book to Catholic leader Pope Paul III, perhaps to gain favor, but Osiander went one step further; he wrote a preface in which he stated the heliocentric theory was not being presented as actual fact, but just as an abstract concept to allow for better calculations of planetary positions. He did not sign his name to the preface, making it appear that Copernicus had written it and was debunking (or admitting the incorrectness of) his own theory. Copernicus, suffering from a stroke and close to death, could do nothing to defend himself. It is said he died only hours after seeing the first copy of the book, entitled *De revolutionibus orbium coelestium* ("Revolutions of the Heavenly Spheres"). Johannes Kepler discovered the truth about the preface in 1609 and cleared Copernicus from the blame of writing it.

Church bans book

The immediate reaction to the book was subdued. This was primarily due to Osiander's preface, which weakened Copernicus's theories. In addition, only a small number of books were printed, they were very expensive, and therefore not many people ever saw a copy of the work. The book did convince a number of people to accept Copernicus's ideas, but a reader had to be a mathematician to fully understand the theories. Still, *De revolutionibus* was placed on the Roman Catholic Church's list of prohibited books where it remained until 1835.

Although considered controversial for many years, Copernicus's work and writings soon proved to have a profound influence on science. Almost as significant as his proving the correctness of heliocentric solar system was Copernicus's questioning of the ancient Greek scientists. Ptolemy had bent the facts to fit his preconceived theory and his teachings had been accepted, without question, for centuries. Copernicus, on the other hand, did his best to develop his theory to match observed facts. It was the dawning of modern scientific methods. In honor of Copernicus's place in scientific history, a statue was raised near the house where he was born by French leader Napoleon Bonaparte (1769-1821) in 1807.

Further Reading

Asimov, Isaac, *Asimov's Biographical Encyclopedia of Science and Technology,* new revised edition, Doubleday, 1972, pp. 68-70.

Dictionary of Scientific Biography, Volume III, Scribner's, 1971, pp. 401-11.

The McGraw-Hill Encyclopedia of World Biography, McGraw-Hill, 1973, p. 129-31.

Patricia S. Cowings

Born December 15, 1948
New York City

atricia S. Cowings pioneered the use of biofeedback techniques to help astronauts cope with and avoid symptoms of motion sickness (biofeedback is a method of learning to gain some voluntary control over involuntary bodily functions, such as heartbeat or blood pressure). Her career-long focus on the relatively new field of biological feedback, also known as biofeedback, enabled her to devise innovative techniques for teaching people how to suppress this illness. As an African American female working in a scientific field, Cowings has had to deal with both gender and racial barriers, but she has overcome such obstacles to achieve a successful position at the National Aeronautics and Space Administration (NASA) Ames Research Center in California.

Patricia Suzanne Cowings was born in New York City on December 15, 1948. Her father, Albert S. Cowings, owned a neighborhood grocery store, and her mother, Sadie B. Cowings, earned a degree at the age of sixty-five, becoming an assistant teacher for the New York Board of Education. Cow-

Patricia Cowings has used biofeedback techniques to address the physical problems of astronauts living in zero gravity.

ings has three brothers: the oldest is a two-star general in the U.S. Army, another is a professional jazz vocalist, and the youngest is a professional disc jockey and musician.

Pursues interest in science

By the age of eleven, Cowings had become interested in science, particularly in astronomy (the study of objects and matter outside of Earth's atmosphere). After high school, she pursued her interest in science and attended the State University of New York at Stony Brook and studied psychology. She received her bachelor's degree with honors in 1970 and then enrolled in the graduate program in psychology at the University of California at Davis. In 1971 the university gave her its Distinguished Scholarship Award, and in 1973 she was awarded both her masters and doctoral degrees in psychology. That same year she received a National Research Council post-doctoral associateship, which enabled her to conduct research at NASA's Ames Research Center at Moffett Field, California, for two years.

Cowings's teaching career began at Stony Brook in 1968, where she was a research assistant in the department of psychology. She continued in the same position upon entering the University of California, Davis. From 1972 to 1975, she was a graduate research assistant in the university's department of psychology. In 1987 she returned to teaching, accepting the position of adjunct associate professor of psychology at the University of Nevada at Reno.

Begins career with NASA

Since 1977, however, she has held a full-time position as a researcher at the Ames Research Center. It was during her graduate school years that Cowings first made contact with the National Aeronautics and Space Administration, serving in its NASA Summer Student Program in both 1971 and 1972, and then working at Ames Research Center after graduate school from 1973 to 1975. After leaving Ames for two years to work as a research specialist at the San Jose State University Foundation, Cowings returned to NASA in 1977 as a research psychologist and principal investigator in Ames's Psychophysiological Research Laboratory. (Psychophysiology is the branch of psychology that focuses on combined mental and bodily processes).

Trains astronauts with biofeedback

Cowings then began in earnest her research on what was called the "zero-gravity sickness syndrome." Once NASA had decided to fly a space shuttle and keep its astronaut crews in space for increasingly longer periods, this syndrome—similar to the more common motion sickness—became a real concern. Cowings was asked to devise a program that might help astronauts minimize these symptoms without drugs. She then designed twelve half-hour sessions in which astronauts were taught biofeedback techniques to prevent this sickness.

Cowing's program used fifty volunteers who were taught how to monitor themselves and how to mentally raise their body temperature and to relax certain muscles at the onset of motion sickness. Sixty-five percent of those trained were able to suppress the symptoms completely, and eighty-five percent were at least able to improve their ability to withstand the effects of zero gravity. None of Cowings's control group of sixty volunteers (those who received no biofeedback training) could show any improvement over time. Cowings's work was finally put to use in space during a September 1992 Spacelab-J mission. During this eight-day flight of the space shuttle *Endeavour,* members of the crew wore a harness apparatus to monitor their ability to suppress the onset of motion sickness.

IMPACT

As space exploration has become more advanced, astronauts have been required to spend longer periods of time in the zero-gravity conditions of space. Living on a spacecraft without gravity, however, often causes a syndrome similar to motion sickness. Psychologist Patricia Cowings has conducted research in which she was able to reduce the symptoms of what is known as "zero-gravity sickness syndrome" by using biofeedback to teach astronauts to relax and control their bodies. Her work to help the human body adapt to this unique environment is crucial for the success of future space ventures, such as a permanent space station, that will involve having people in space for long periods of time.

Recognized for outstanding work

Cowings has also conducted research on exercises that will allow astronauts to maintain muscle strength while in zero gravity for extended periods of time. Cowings's research has been the subject of several Public Broadcasting System television programs. A member of the Aerospace Medical Association, the Society for Psychophysiological Research, the New York Academy of Sciences, and other professional organizations, she is also the recipient of several awards, including the NASA Individual Achievement Award (1993), the Black United Fund of Texas Award (1991), and the Innovative Research Award of the Biofeedback Society of California (1990). She is married to William B. Toscano, a colleague at Ames with whom she has collaborated on many scientific papers. The couple has one son, Christopher Michael Cowings Toscano.

Further Reading

Air Progress, December 1980, p. 30.

Savvy, January 1985, p. 16.

"Sickness in Motion," *SciQuest,* July/August 1980, p. 4.

Seymour Cray

Born September 28, 1925
Chippewa Falls, Wisconsin
Died October 5, 1996
Colorado Springs, Colorado

Seymour Cray, an electronics engineer, was one of the founding fathers of the computer industry. His pioneering work in computer design featured the semiconductor as a component to store and process information. (A semiconductor is a substance, such as silicon, that can either resist or easily pass the flow of electric current.) By densely packing hundreds of thousands of semiconductor chips, Cray reduced the distance between signals, enabling him to create very large and powerful "supercomputers."

Seeking to process the vast amounts of mathematical data needed to simulate physical phenomena such as weather patterns and nuclear weapon explosions, Cray built what many consider to have been the first supercomputer, the CDC 6600, which was made up of 350,000 transistors. To such fields as engineering, meteorology, and eventually biology and medicine, the supercomputer represented a technological revolution that greatly accelerated the speed of research. For many years Cray computers dominated the supercomputer industry. A

Seymour Cray is considered the father of the supercomputer.

devoted fan of *Star Trek*, a 1960s television show about space travel, Cray included aesthetically pleasing touches in his computers, such as transparent blue glass that revealed their inner workings.

Enthusiasm for science

Cray was born on September 28, 1925, in Chippewa Falls, Wisconsin, a small town in the heart of Wisconsin's dairy farm country. The eldest of two children, Cray revealed his talent for engineering while still a young boy. He tinkered with radios in the basement and built an automatic telegraph machine by the time he was ten years old. Cray's father, a city engineer, and his mother fully supported his scientific interests, providing him with a basement laboratory equipped with chemistry sets and radio gear. Cray's early aptitude for electronics was evident when he wired his laboratory to his bedroom and included an electric alarm that sounded whenever anyone tried to enter his room. While attending Chippewa Falls High School, Cray sometimes taught the physics class in his teacher's absence. During his senior year, he received the Bausch & Lomb Science Award for high achievement in science.

While serving in the U.S. Army during the final years of World War II (1939-45), Cray used his natural gifts in electronics as a radio operator and decipherer of enemy codes. After the war, he enrolled in the University of Wisconsin but later transferred to the University of Minnesota in Minneapolis. There he received his bachelor's degree in electrical engineering in 1950 and a master's degree in applied mathematics the next year.

Joins early computer firm

Cray began his corporate electronics career when he was hired to work for Engineering Research Associates (ERA). When Cray joined the company, it was among a small group of firms on the cutting edge of the commercial computer industry. One of his first assignments with ERA was to build computer pulse transformers for navy use. Cray credited his success on the project to a top-of-the-line circular slide rule that enabled him to make the multitude of calculations needed to build the transformers. In a speech before his colleagues at a 1988 supercomputer conference, Cray recalled feeling "quite smug" about his accomplishment until he encountered a more experienced engineer working at the firm who told Cray that he did not use complicated slide rules or many of the other standard engineering approaches in his work, preferring to rely on intuition. Intrigued, Cray put away his slide rule and decided that he would do likewise.

For his next computer project, Cray and his colleagues developed a binary programming system. (The binary system uses the numbers 1 and 0 to correspond to the on or off states of electric current.) With the addition of magnetic core memory, which allowed Cray and his coworkers to program 4,096 words, the age of the supercomputer dawned. With a thorough knowledge of circuits, logic, and computer software design, Cray designed the UNIVAC 1103, the first digital computer, which processes numbers and words, to become commercially available.

Creates computers with transistors

Despite his growing success, Cray became dissatisfied with the large corporate atmosphere of ERA, which had been renamed the Sperry Rand Corporation. A friend and colleague, William Norris, who also worked at Sperry Rand, decided to start his own company, Control Data Corporation (CDC), and recruited Cray to work for him. Lacking the financial resources of larger companies, Cray and Control Data set out to make affordable computers. To accomplish this, Cray built

IMPACT

When the United States agreed to sign a nuclear test ban treaty, the decision was at least partly due to the fact that a supercomputer had been developed that could simulate the effects of a new bomb—actually detonating the explosive was no longer necessary. This is only one arena in which the supercomputers designed by Seymour Cray affected the world. Supercomputers were the first machines capable of processing the immense amounts of calculations needed to address complex physical events; this allowed scientists to electronically determine things like the power of an atomic bomb, the path of a storm, or the body's reaction to a new drug. Actual experiments on such topics could be dangerous, time-consuming, costly, and even physically impossible. Using a supercomputer opened up many new possibilities for science, and research took a huge leap forward with the increased speed and scope of the computers pioneered by Cray.

computers out of transistors, devices that use a semiconducting material to amplify or switch electronic signals. He purchased the transistors at an electronics outlet store for 37 cents each. This allowed Cray to successfully replace the cumbersome and expensive tubes and radio "valves" that were then standard in the computer industry. The first computer to use transistors was Cray's CDC 1604, produced in 1960.

First supercomputer is born

Control Data began developing a line of computers that, like the CDC 1604, were immensely successful tools for scientific research. Cray developed the CDC 6600 in 1964, the most powerful computer of its day and the first to employ freon, a gas commonly used in air conditioners, to cool its 350,000 transistors. The CDC 6600 is considered by many to have been the first supercomputer. But Cray continued to design even faster machines. In 1969 the corporation introduced its next supercomputer, the CDC 7600. Capable of 15 million computations per second, the 7600 placed CDC at the top of the supercomputer industry—which did not please the IBM corporation, CDC's primary competitor.

Starts computer company

But as Control Data grew, so did its bureaucracy. Cray never enjoyed working in an atmosphere where business concerns interfered with his research. As Russell Mitchell recounted in *Business Week,* Norris once asked Cray to develop a five-year plan. What Norris received in return was a short note that said Cray's five-year plan was "to build the biggest computer in the world," and his one-year plan was "to achieve one-fifth of the above." Cray became even more frustrated after the company refused to market the CDC 8600 computer he had developed. In 1972, Cray decided to leave CDC and set up his own company, Cray Research Corporation. Norris and CDC graciously invested $500,000 to assist Cray in his fledgling business effort.

Designs more powerful supercomputers

Cray Research immediately set out to build the fastest supercomputer. In 1976 the CRAY 1 was introduced. Incorporating a revolutionary vector processing approach, which allowed the computer to solve various parts of a problem at once, the CRAY 1 was capable of performing 32 calculations at the same time, outpacing even the best CDC computer. When the National Center for Atmospheric Research agreed to buy the computer for $8.8 million, Cray Research finally had a solid financial footing to continue building faster and more affordable computers. For Cray, this meant manufacturing one product at a time, an unusual approach in the computer industry.

The first CRAY 2 was marketed in 1985 and featured a phenomenal 2-billion byte memory that could perform 1.2 billion computer operations per second, a tenfold performance increase over the CRAY 1. Capable of providing computerized models of physical phenomena described mathematically, the CRAY computers were essential in accelerating research. For example, in such areas as pharmaceutical development, a supercomputer could be used to create a model of a drug's molecules and its biological components. This would eliminate the trial and error involved in research and reduce the time necessary to solve complicated mathematical equations.

Experiments with new computer chip

In 1983, Cray turned his attention to developing the CRAY 3, in which Cray planned to use gallium arsenide (GaA) circuits. Although the successful CRAY 2 was based on silicon chips, Cray saw that the future of high-speed processing would require a breakthrough like GaA chips. Gallium arsenide computer chips marked a major advance in computer circuitry because they are able to conduct electrical impulses with less resistance than silicon. Adding even more speed to the computer, the GaA chip also effectively reduces both heat and energy loss. However, GaA chips are extremely difficult to work with because they are fragile and break easily. Many of Cray's fellow computer engineers, as well as the business staff of Cray Research, felt that Cray's plans were impractical. Not receiving support from Cray Research for his Cray 3 project, Cray formed Cray Computers Corporation in 1989 to continue working on his ideas.

While Cray's advances in computer technology enabled him to corner the market on the supercomputer industry for many years, the advent of parallel processing allowed others in the industry to make inroads into the same market. Utilizing hundreds of mini-computers to work on individual aspects of a problem, parallel processing is a less expensive approach to solving huge mathematical problems. Although Cray for many years denounced parallel processing as impractical, he eventually accepted this approach and made plans with other companies to incorporate it into his computer research and business. Cray began working on the CRAY 4, but high development costs and lack of sales, primarily due to cuts in government budgets, caused his company serious financial problems. Cray Computers Corporation eventually stopped work on the Cray 4 and declared bankruptcy in 1995. Cray quickly bounced back from this setback, forming another company, SRC Computers, in August 1996. He announced that this company was beginning plans for a CRAY 5 computer.

A dedicated researcher

Cray's first wife, Verene, was a minister's daughter. Married shortly after World War II, they had two daughters and two sons, who have characterized their father as a man intensely dedicated to his work; in fact, Cray demanded their absolute silence while traveling in the car so that he could think about his work on supercomputers. In 1975, Cray and Verene divorced. Five years later he wed Geri M. Harrand. Although he engaged in outdoor pursuits with his new wife, such as windsurfing and skiing, Cray remained devoted to his research. In September of 1996, Cray suffered severe injuries to his head in a car accident in Colorado Springs, Colorado, where he was living. He died a few weeks later, on October 5, 1996, at the age of 71. It was unclear at that time whether the work he had begun on the CRAY 5 would be continued by his associates at SRC Computers. But the work that had been accomplished by Cray in his lifetime had already placed him among the most important figures in the history of the computer. Because of his innovative work in creating some of the most powerful machines in the computer industry, he is remembered as the father of the supercomputer.

Further Reading

Anthes, Gary H., "Seymour Cray: Reclusive Genius," *Computerworld,* June 22, 1992, p. 38.

Elmer-Dewitt, Philip, "Computer Chip off the Old Block: Genius Seymour Cray and the Company He Founded Split Up," *Time,* May 29, 1989, p. 70.

Markoff, John, "Seymour Cray, Computer Industry Pioneer and Father of the Supercomputer, Dies at 71," *New York Times,* October 6, 1996, p. 19.

Mitchell, Russell, "The Genius," *Business Week,* April 30, 1990, pp. 80-88.

Slater, R., *Portraits in Silicon,* MIT Press, 1989, pp. 195-204.

Raymond A. Dart

Born February 4, 1893
Toowing, Australia
Died November 22, 1988
Johannesburg, South Africa

Raymond Dart discovered fossils of Australopithecus africanus, a species of two-legged erect primates that appears to be an evolutionary link between apes and humans.

A doctor and surgeon by training, Australian scientist Raymond A. Dart was drawn into the field of anthropology, the study of the origin and physical and cultural characteristics of human beings, early in his career. Shortly after taking a teaching post at a medical school in South Africa, Dart discovered the first fossils of *Australopithecus africanus*. Dart claimed that this creature was an early ancestor of humans, representing the "missing link" in the evolution of humans from apes that the English naturalist **Charles Darwin** (1809-1882; for more information, see Volume 1, pp. 203-210) had proposed in the 1870s. While his findings were initially resisted by the scientific community, Dart was later proved correct, and his discoveries served as the basis of the development of modern paleoanthropology, the study of human fossils.

Raymond Arthur Dart was born in Toowong, Australia, on February 4, 1893. He was the fifth of nine children of Samuel Dart, a general store operator, and Eliza Anne Brimblecombe Dart. Dart's parents were devout Baptists and pioneers in the settlement of Queensland, Australia. They raised Dart in the Brisbane suburb of Toowong, later moving the family to a bush farm in Blenheim, where the future scientist spent his youth milking cows and hiking to school. In 1911, Dart won a scholarship to Brisbane's newly founded University of Queensland, where he earned both a bachelor's degree and a master's degree in biology. Another scholarship sent him in 1914 to St. Andrew's College at the University of Sydney. There, before the completion of his second year of medical studies, he was appointed a tutor in biology and named a member of the college staff.

First interest in fossils

The year 1914 also saw the outbreak of World War I (1914-18) in Europe as well as the meeting of the British Association (a prestigious scientific organization) in Sydney. Dart attended the gathering, which brought in noted scientists such as Australian-born anatomist and anthropologist Grafton Elliot Smith (1871-1937) and English geologist W. J. Sollas (1849-1936). Dart became intrigued by the announcement of the discovery of Australia's first human fossil find, the Talgai Skull from Queensland, unearthed by Antarctic geologic explorer T. Edgeworth David. The description of the fossil was presented by James T. Wilson, head of the University of Sydney's department of anatomy. Soon after the conference, Dart became an assistant to Wilson on research in neurology, or the study of the nervous system.

Dart's intentions to conduct more in-depth neurological research were hampered by his own schoolwork and administrative roles as instructor in anatomy and acting vice principal of St. Andrew's College. After receiving his bachelor's degree in medicine and a master's degree in surgery in August 1917, he enlisted in the Australian Army Medical Corps, finishing his service in France as a captain. Upon his release from the military in 1919, he was immediately appointed to the post of senior demonstrator, or instructor, in anatomy at University College in London, England, by Grafton Elliot Smith. In 1920, at Smith's recommendation, the Rockefeller Foundation

IMPACT

Raymond A. Dart altered scientific thought about the origin of human beings when he declared that the fossils he had named *Australopithecus africanus* belonged to an early form of man that lived three million years ago. While the English naturalist Charles Darwin (1809-1882) had predicted that humans evolved from apes in Africa, the belief favored by scientists of the early twentieth century was that human beings arose in Asia. Dart's fossils, uncovered in South Africa, were the first physical record of a pre-human species. His work stimulated research in paleoanthropology (the search for and study of fossilized remains of early human ancestors), and the focal point of research in this field became Africa. There, evidence of other types of pre-humans have been uncovered, such as the famous "Lucy" skeleton, which is a three-and-a-half million year old specimen (the oldest pre-human ever unearthed) found in Ethiopia by American anthropologist **Donald Johanson** (1943– ; for more information, see volume 2, pp. 515-523).

awarded Dart one of its first two foreign fellowships, allowing him the opportunity to teach at Washington University in St. Louis, Missouri, and to study at the Woods Hole marine research station in Massachusetts.

Moves to South Africa

By 1922, Dart had rejoined the faculty of University College as a lecturer in histology, the study of microscopic plant and animal tissues, and embryology, the study of the development of animals before birth. At the insistence of Smith, however, Dart applied for the position of chair of anatomy at the newly established School of Medicine at the University of Witwatersrand in Johannesburg, South Africa. Dart had never heard of the place, and was initially reluctant to go there. "The very idea revolted me; I turned it down flat instantly," he recalled in the *Journal of Human Evolution* in 1973.

After some reflection, Dart changed his mind and arrived in South Africa in January 1923. Dart found the School of Medicine in dire need of equipment, facilities, and a collection of bones for a proper anatomy museum. To acquire some bone specimens for the museum, Dart encouraged his students to search for fossil bones during holidays. In the summer of 1924, a fossilized baboon skull was brought to Dart's attention by Josephine Salmons, one of his student assistants. She had secured the skull from E. G. Izod of Rand Mines Limited. The fossil had been detected while Izod's company was mining a sheet of limestone at Taungs (now Taung) in the Bechuanaland Protectorate, where other fossil baboon skulls had been discovered as early as 1920. Curious about the skull, Dart asked his colleague, geology professor R. B. Young, to look for similar specimens since Young was going to investigate the lime deposit at Taungs. By November 28, 1924, Dart had in his hands a fossil skull that would change the course of paleoanthropology.

Acquires important fossil

Young sent back two crates full of bones, one of which held a face and skull still embedded in the rock in which it was discovered. The collection also included a cast, or mold, of the inside of a cranium found by one of the quarry workers. After a quick examination of this cast, Dart realized that the fossils could be an important find. In his earlier neurological studies with Smith, Dart had learned that convolutions, or irregular ridges, toward the back of the brain of primates (the order of mammals that includes humans, monkeys, apes, and similar animals) cause two fissures that are farther apart in humans than in apes. Smith had attributed this difference between apes and humans to the expansion of the cerebrum (the uppermost tissue that covers the rest of the brain) that had occurred during human evolution. Yet, the cast Dart held in his hand had fissures that were farther apart than those of any non-human primate he had ever seen.

Dart freed the face and skull from the fossil's rock casing shortly before Christmas of 1924. The face was nearly complete, and the features of the skull revealed a creature that was more like a human than an ape. The shape of the jaw and alignment of the teeth resembled those of humans, as did the set of emerging molars that Dart likened to those of a six-year-old child or a young ape. Because of the near completeness of the specimen, Dart was able to measure the position of the foramen magnum—the opening at the base of the skull through which the spinal cord enters the cranial cavity.

Proposes existence of "man-ape"

In his first account of the specimen, published in the journal *Nature* on February 7, 1925, Dart noted that the foramen magnum's position suggested that the creature would have stood more erect than any modern anthropoid, or ape-like animal. "The specimen is of importance because it exhibits an extinct race of apes intermediate between living anthropoids and man," Dart declared in his report. He believed he had found the "missing link" and that his discovery might support Charles Darwin's earlier idea that man's origins were linked to Africa. He named the creature *Australopithecus africanus,* the "southern ape of Africa."

Findings create controversy

Dart's views were immediately met with scorn by the general public and strong disagreement by many of his own colleagues, including Smith and Scottish anatomist and anthropologist Arthur Keith. Keith immediately categorized the find within the fossil family that evolved into modern gorillas and chimpanzees. Dart's opponents argued that he did not have enough evidence about the fossil's structure or age, and they were appalled that the discovery was made in Africa. During that era, Asia was believed to be the cradle of humankind.

Yet Dart had defenders—most notably Scottish anthropologist Robert Broom, whose defense of Dart has been compared to English biologist Thomas Henry Huxley's staunch support of Charles Darwin's evolutionary theory. Broom's successive series of Taung-like fossil discoveries in Sterkfontein in 1936 and Kromdraii in 1938 (both sites in South Africa) would turn the tide of evidence in favor of Dart's South African man-ape.

Conducts other expeditions

Despite the controversy that surrounded him, Dart was elected president of the Anthropological Section of the South African Association for the Advancement of Science in 1925. He became dean of Witwatersrand's School of Medicine in 1926, and was appointed vice president of the Anthropology Section of the British Association in 1929. The following year,

Robert Broom, Scottish Paleontologist

Robert Broom (1866-1951) was a Scottish medical doctor and paleontologist (a scientist who studies fossils) who is best known for his work investigating the origins of mammals. Broom believed that mammals were descended from reptiles, not amphibians, as other scientists believed in the late 1800s and early 1900s. He studied fossils of early reptiles, particularly reptile skulls, and found similarities with mammals that pointed to an evolutionary connection between the two groups of animals. Broom conducted his early research in Australia, where he also practiced medicine. But while visiting London in 1896, Broom went to an exhibit of reptile fossils from South Africa that had many more mammal-like characteristics than other reptiles he had seen. Sensing that these fossils could be important to his theory of mammal evolution, he set off for South Africa.

Broom's most important work in South Africa was classifying an enormous number of fossils at a site called the Karroo deposits. He payed close attention to the different animal specimens he found at each level of sediment; he knew that each level he uncovered represented a different time period that would allow him to observe changes in fossils structures through time. When describing the things he found, Broom would often sketch the specimen, using his imagination to fill in missing parts of an animal and give an idea of what it looked like when it was alive. Eventually Broom's work at Karroo allowed him to show that the development of mammals in Africa was similar to the same process in North America.

In his later years, Broom also worked with human fossils and theories of human evolution. When Raymond Dart reported his discovery of *Australopithecus africanus* in 1925, Broom decided to examine the fossil himself. Many well-known scientists doubted Dart's claim that *Australopithecus africanus* was an early ancestor of human beings—they thought it was just an early gorilla, or some other non-human primate. But Broom found that the fossil skull did indeed have human-like characteristics that would place it between apes and humans in evolutionary development. Broom decided to conduct a hunt for more examples of early human fossils, uncovering specimens in deposits at Sterkfontein, Kromdraai, and Swartkrans in South Africa in the 1930s and 1940s, continuing his field work well into his eighties. Broom's investigations and opinion helped to convince scientists that Dart had made an important scientific find and inspired others to continue scientific inquiry into human evolution.

with a growing belief in the African origins of human beings, he set out on a series of archeological and anthropological expeditions. His joint venture with the Italian African Scientific Expedition of 1930 gave him his first glimpse of the gorilla in its natural habitat, which led to his sponsorship of the University of Witwatersrand's Gorilla Research Unit in the late 1950s.

The year 1945 brought another turning point in Dart's scientific career. Again, baboon fossils had been found in South Africa, this time at Makapansgat in the northern Transvaal. Just as the baboon specimens had foreshadowed the appearance of *Australopithecus africanus* at Taung and Sterkfontein, so they did at Makapansgat. The excavation of the site during April of 1947 turned up some three dozen *Australopithecus* fossils, a number of fossilized baboon skulls, and thousands of animal bone fragments. Fractures were found in many of the baboon skulls at Makapansgat, Sterkfontein, and Taungs, as well as in six australopithecine skulls. This observation led Dart to the conclusion that *Australopithecus africanus* had inflicted the deadly blows that had caused the fractures using bone weapons such as the upper arm bones of antelope, which were found in large numbers around the Makapansgat site. He further concluded that their culture was able to manufacture tools and weapons from bones, teeth, and horns, and thus named it the osteodontokeratic culture. While this theory was ultimately rejected by the scientific community, Dart's observations helped create a new field of science called taphonomy, concerning the environmental circumstances that act upon bones after death.

Divorced from his first wife, Dora Tyree, in 1934, Dart married again on November 28, 1936. His second wife, Marjorie Gordon Frew, was chief librarian of the Witwatersrand Medical Library. They had two children, Diana Elizabeth and Galen Alexander. Dart retired from the chair of anatomy at Witwatersrand in 1958. From 1966 to 1986, he spent half of each year in Johannesburg and the other half in Philadelphia, Pennsylvania, where he had been appointed United Steelworkers of America Professor of Anthropology in the Avery Postgraduate Institute of the Institutes for the Achievement of Human Potential.

Just before his eightieth birthday, Dart remarked upon his achievements in the *Journal of Human Evolution.* "To open closed doors, to find lost things, or to shed light where gloom enshrouded understanding, these are but types of the privileges common to all intelligent individuals." Dart died in Johannesburg, South Africa, on November 22, 1988.

Further Reading

Broom, Robert, *Finding the Missing Link,* Watts, 1951.

Dart, Raymond A., with Dennis Craig, *Adventures with the Missing Link,* Harper, 1959.

Dart, Raymond A., "*Australopithecus africanus:* The Man-Ape of South Africa," *Nature,* February 7, 1925, pp. 195-99.

Dart, Raymond A., "Recollections of a Reluctant Anthropologist," *Journal of Human Evolution,* 1973, pp. 417-27.

Johanson, Donald, and James Shreeve, *Lucy's Child: The Discovery of a Human Ancestor,* Avon Books, 1989, pp. 53-58.

Alice Evans

Born January 29, 1881
Neath, Pennsylvania
Died September 5, 1975
Alexandria, Virginia

Alice Evans discovered that a bacterium in cow milk causes disease in humans, leading her to campaign for the pasteurization of milk.

Bacteriologist Alice Evans was a pioneer both as a scientist and as a woman. (A bacteriologist is a scientist who studies the single-cell microorganisms known as bacteria.) She discovered that brucellae (pronounced bru-'se-lee, this is the plural form of brucella) bacteria from cows and their milk cause undulant fever in humans. Evans knew that undulant fever—a disease marked by recurring fever, weakness, and pain and swelling in the joints—could be prevented if milk was pasteurized, a process that uses heat to destroy dangerous bacteria. She called upon the dairy industry and the U.S. government to pasteurize all milk, and her efforts were eventually successful. She was the first woman president of the Society of American Bacteriologists (now the American Society of Microbiology). Although she experienced prejudice early in her career because she was a woman, Evans overcame many obstacles and lived to see the importance of her discoveries confirmed by others. She had a major impact on microbiology in the United States and the world and received honors for her numerous achievements in the field.

Discovers love of science

Alice Catherine Evans was born on January 29, 1881, in the mainly Welsh town of Neath, Pennsylvania, the second of the two children of William Howell and Anne Evans. William Howell, whose father was from Wales, was a surveyor, teacher, farmer, and Civil War veteran. Anne Evans, also Welsh, emigrated from Wales at the age of fourteen. Alice Evans received her primary education at the local district school. She went on to study at the Susquehanna Institute in Towanda, Pennsylvania. She wished to go to college but, unable to afford tuition, she took a post as a grade school teacher. After teaching for four years she enrolled in a tuition-free, two-year course in nature study at the Cornell University College of Agriculture. The course was designed to help teachers in rural areas inspire an appreciation of nature in their students. But Evans was so excited about this glimpse into the world of science that she set upon a new course in life.

Evans continued her studies at Cornell University and eventually received a bachelor of science degree in agriculture. She then decided to pursue an advanced degree in bacteriology and was recommended by her professor at Cornell for a scholarship at the University of Wisconsin. She received the scholarship—becoming the first woman ever to win it—and under the supervision of University of Wisconsin professor E. G. Hastings she studied bacteriology with a focus on chemistry. In 1910 she received a master of science degree in bacteriology from Wisconsin.

Investigates cow milk

Although encouraged to pursue a doctoral degree, Evans accepted a research position with the University of Wisconsin Agriculture Department's Dairy Division and began researching cheese-making methods in 1911. In 1913 she moved with

Since 1905, it has been known that the disease brucellosis, caused by the brucella bacteria, could be passed from infected goats to humans who drank goat milk. But for many years after that discovery, no investigation was made into whether a similar connection existed between cow milk (an important source of milk in America) and humans. In the early twentieth century, people believed that many cow diseases could not be transmitted to humans, and the raw (untreated) milk of cows suffering from infections continued to be sold. In the 1920s, Alice Evans proved that those diseases could be passed to humans. To prevent cases of brucellosis, she argued that all milk should be pasteurized before being sold in order to remove any dangerous bacteria. Through her scientific findings as well as her campaign for a safe milk supply, Evans was responsible for the now-common practice of the pasteurization of milk that has greatly reduced the number of brucellosis infections in humans.

the division to Washington, D.C., where she served as bacteriological technician on a team that was attempting to identify sources of contamination in raw cow milk. There was suspicion that some diseases were related to drinking cow milk, and at that time, scientists believed that the disease-causing agents were introduced to milk after the milk was taken from the cow.

Finds link between cow and human disease

Evans, however, began to suspect that milk could be contaminated by bacteria carried inside cows. She started her own research on the subject, and by 1917 she had found that the bacterium responsible for undulant fever in humans was similar in important respects to the bacterium associated with spontaneous abortion—the death of an unborn animal caused by a problem in the body—in cows. Evans exposed guinea pigs to the two types of bacteria and found that they produced similar effects on the animals. By finding the same kind of bacteria in humans and cows, Evans challenged the belief held by many of her colleagues that bovine, or cow-related, diseases could not be transmitted to humans. That year she presented her discovery to the Society of American Bacteriologists; her ideas were received with a skepticism that seems to have been due more to her gender and level of education than to the quality of her research.

In 1918 Evans was asked to join the staff of the U.S. Public Health Service by director George McCoy. There she was absorbed in the study of meningitis, a disease in which the thin tissues surrounding the brain and spinal column become inflamed. Although she was unable to continue her milk studies during this time, support for Evans's findings was trickling in from all over the world. By the early 1920s it was recognized that undulant fever and Malta fever were both caused by the brucella bacterium. It had been proven in the late 1800s that brucellae bacteria could be transmitted from goats to humans through the drinking of goat milk. This information seemed to support Evans's theory that the same thing could happen with cow milk.

Documents cases of brucellosis

But there was still resistance to the idea that humans could contract brucellosis (any disease caused by the brucella bacterium) by drinking the milk of infected cows. Proving the connection was difficult because the symptoms of brucellosis were similar to diseases such as influenza, typhoid fever, tuberculosis, malaria, and rheumatism; for this reason, brucellosis was not often correctly diagnosed. To try to gain more accurate numbers of the rate of brucellosis, Evans began documenting cases of the disease among humans in the United States and South Africa. But it was not until 1930, after brucellosis had claimed the lives of a number of farmers' children in the United States, that public health officials began to recognize the need for pasteurization of cow milk.

In 1922, Evans herself, like many others who researched the brucella bacterium, became ill with brucellosis. Her condition was chronic, plaguing her on and off for almost 23 years and perhaps providing her with new insight into the disease. As the problem of chronic illness became widespread, Evans began surveying different parts of the United States to determine the number of infected cows whose raw milk had been sold and the number of people with chronic cases of brucellosis resulting from the milk.

Argues for pasteurization

In 1925 Evans was asked to serve on the National Research Council's Committee on Infectious Abortion. In this

David Bruce, Scottish Microbiologist

David Bruce (1855-1931), an Australian-born Scottish microbiologist (a scientist who studies microscopic forms of life), is known for, among other things, his work in identifying the causes of brucellosis. Bruce collaborated with his wife, Mary Elizabeth Steele Bruce, in his scientific work throughout his life. The Bruces served in Great Britain's Army Medical Service and in 1884 were assigned to the island of Malta, located south of Italy in the Mediterranean sea. There Bruce investigated Malta fever, an often fatal disease striking British soldiers. The disease caused chills, sweats, and weakness. Using a microscope, Bruce found the cause of the disease to be what he called a "micrococcus" growing in the spleen of patients. Danish scientist Bernhard L. F. Bang (1848-1932) later isolated the bacteria that Bruce had discovered. In 1905 Bruce found that soldiers were contracting Malta fever by drinking the milk of goats infected with the same bacteria. Goat milk was thus eliminated from the soldiers' diet and the disease vanished. The bacterium was eventually named brucella, and the disease it caused brucellosis, in honor of the Scottish scientist. However, the fight against the disease would not be over for more than twenty years, when Alice Evans in the United States discovered that brucellosis was often transmitted by the milk of cows as well as goats. The occurrence of the disease began to decline after a successful drive to pasteurize all milk products.

capacity Evans argued for the pasteurization of milk, a practice that later became an industry standard. In recognition of her achievements, Evans was elected the first woman president of the American Society of Bacteriologists in 1928. She was further recognized as a leader in her field when in 1930 she was chosen, along with Robert E. Buchanan of Iowa State University, as an American delegate to the First International Congress of Bacteriology in Paris. She attended the second Congress in London in 1936 and was again able to travel widely in Europe. She returned to the United States and eventually was promoted to senior bacteriologist at the Public Health Service, by then called the National Institute of Health. By 1939 she had changed the focus of her research to the subject of immunity to streptococcal infections. (Streptococcus are bacteria that cause various diseases in humans, such as strep throat.) She retired from her post in 1945. Evans, who never married, died at the age of 94 on September 5, 1975, in Alexandria, Virginia, following a stroke.

Further Reading

"Alice Evans, 94, Bacteriologist, Dies," *Washington Post,* September 8, 1975, p. B4.

Kass-Simon, G., and P. Farnes, *Women of Science,* Indiana University Press, 1990, p. 278.

MacKaye, Milton, "Undulant Fever," *Ladies Home Journal,* December, 1944, pp. 23, 69-70.

O'Hern, Elizabeth M., "Alice Evans, Pioneer Microbiologist," *American Society for Microbiology News,* September, 1973.

O'Hern, Elizabeth M., *Profiles of Pioneer Women Scientists,* Acropolis, 1985, pp. 127-38.

Siegel, J. P., and R. T. Finley, *Women in the Scientific Search,* Scarecrow, 1985, pp. 67-70.

Henry Ford

Born July 30, 1863
Dearborn, Michigan
Died April 7, 1947
Detroit, Michigan

Henry Ford, an innovator of the moving assembly line, produced the first automobile that was affordable to the average worker.

Henry Ford—mechanic, inventor, industrialist, and social activist—launched the era of the automobile, and in doing so provided the tools necessary for the mass production of consumer goods. The founder of the Ford Motor Company, Ford is associated with the creation of the assembly line, an industrial innovation that allowed cars—and later a variety of manufactured goods—to be produced quickly and efficiently. In realizing his goal of making inexpensive, high-quality automobiles available to the ordinary person, Ford played a large role in bringing about the modern consumer age.

Mechanical interests develop on family farm

Henry Ford was born in Springwells, Michigan (now part of Dearborn), on July 30, 1863, the first child of William and Mary Litogot Ford. The Fords were prosperous farmers who had around ninety-one acres of land under cultivation. Though Ford's father expected his eldest son to follow in his footsteps, young Henry was never interested in the demanding life that a frontier farmer led in the mid-1800s. Instead, he decided to leave the farm and make his living as a mechanic. At the age of sixteen, with only seven years of formal education, Ford left his parents' farm to seek his fortune in nearby Detroit.

Ford had shown a mechanical inclination at an early age. He had tinkered with the farm machinery he used and he had invented a number of labor-saving devices to ease his farm chores. With these mechanical abilities, he quickly found a position in Detroit as an apprentice at the James Flowers and Brothers Machine Shop, a small company that was busily manufacturing valves and fire hydrants for the rapidly-growing city. While working for Flowers and Brothers, Ford earned a meager salary of two dollars and fifty cents a week—a dollar a week less than his rent in a Detroit boarding house. To supplement his income he took a night job repairing clocks and watches—no small sacrifice considering his day job required twelve hours of labor a day, six days a week.

Ford, however, was forward-looking and determined to become a wealthy man. He saw his position with Flowers and Brothers as only the first step in a career. Nine months later, he left the machine shop in order to work for the Detroit Dry Dock Company. His new wage was fifty cents a week less, but he felt the experience he would get working on steam engines at the dry dock company would be more valuable to him in the long term. By the time he was twenty, Ford was a traveling "engine expert" for the Westinghouse company. His job took him all across southern Michigan repairing Westinghouse traction engines, which were self-propelled threshing machines (machines used in harvesting to separate grain from the rest of the plant). It was during these travels that he gained his first exposure to a new machine, the internal combustion engine. The internal combustion engine was an important development because it allowed fuel to be burned within a cylinder housing a piston, thus directly capturing a much greater amount of the potential energy of the fuel than had been possible before; it also allowed for a smaller, lighter engine. The steam engine, the widely-used predecessor of the internal combustion engine, by comparison burned fuel to heat water;

The concept and practice of mass production had been in place in the United States for more than one hundred years before Henry Ford adapted assembly line techniques for the creation of his successful Model T automobile. Beginning in the late 1700s, people such as Eli Whitney (1765-1825; inventor of the cotton gin), George Eastman (1854-1932; producer of photographic film), and Cyrus McCormick (1809-1884; developer of mechanical reapers, machines used to harvest grain) had experimented with ideas such as interchangeable parts and assembly lines to speed production and insure that the quality of products was consistent. Henry Ford further refined the concept of the moving assembly line. He found ways to produce cars faster and for less money, passing the savings along to consumers and the profits along to workers. By placing the automobile within the reach of the average person, Ford revolutionized not only industry but the lifestyle of people in the United States and in much of the world.

the resulting steam was then transferred to the engine to push the piston. The steam engine lost a great deal of the potential energy of the fuel in these various steps and was therefore not very efficient.

Begins work on a "horseless carriage"

Ford had taken up residence in Dearborn in 1882 when he took his job as a traveling engineer with Westinghouse. In 1888, he married Clara Bryant, quit his traveling job, and settled down on a farm in Dearborn. Ford did not find farming any more attractive as a young husband in his twenties than he had as a teenager. He spent most of his time over the next three years tinkering with machinery. It was during this period that Ford built his first internal combustion engine, a two-cylinder device he used to power a bicycle.

In 1891, convinced that electricity was the key to building an effective mechanical vehicle, Ford took a position as a night engineer with the Detroit Illuminating company, which was owned by American inventor Thomas Alva Edison (1847-1931). Two years later, Ford had risen to chief engineer and was earning an impressive salary of $100 per month. With this new wage Ford was able to support both his family—his only child, Edsel, was born in 1893—and his experiments with the "horseless carriage."

Working mainly at night (and using most of his family's income in the process) Ford began developing his first horseless carriage soon after he was hired at Detroit Illuminating. He tested his new engine on

Christmas Eve, 1893, in the family kitchen. He clamped his invention to the kitchen sink, provided a spark with household electrical current, and fed gasoline to the engine's cylinders by dribbling it in from a tea cup. It took Ford two and a half years to refine this crude engine and to design and build the vehicle that it would power. But finally, in June 1896, the Ford Quadricycle was ready to be tested on the cobblestone roads of old Detroit. Although it was not the first gasoline-powered car—the Duryea brothers had built one in Springfield, Massachusetts, three years previously and Gottlieb Daimler had demonstrated his horseless carriage at least six years before—the Quadricycle caused something of a sensation in Detroit. In addition, it displayed many of the properties that were to become hallmarks of Ford automobiles: it was light, inexpensive, easy to repair, and reliable.

The Ford racers

On August 5, 1899, with the backing of William Murphy, a wealthy Detroit businessman, Ford founded the Detroit Automobile Company. Although Ford's first business venture would soon end in economic failure, the company gave him the chance to concentrate all of his energies on designing and building automobiles. During this period his understanding of the automobile and the automobile manufacturing process grew immeasurably. Soon after the Detroit Automobile Company failed, Ford developed a four-cylinder, twenty-six-horsepower racing engine and mounted it on the chassis, or frame, of his company's last prototype (a prototype is the original model of a product). The crucial test of the new car came on October 10, 1901, in a ten-mile race just outside of Detroit. Ford matched his vehicle against what was then the world's fastest automobile, a car designed and driven by Alexander Winton. In an exciting race, Ford's first as a driver, he caught and passed the much more experienced Winton in the eighth lap on the one-mile oval and went on to win by a quarter mile.

The publicity from this important victory allowed Ford to raise more money for his second and third automobile-making

GENTLEMEM
OUR
COUNTRY

Ford in his first car

ventures, the Henry Ford Company (later renamed Cadillac) and the Ford Motor Company (formed in 1903). Although the new companies were founded to build automobiles for the public, Ford instead became obsessed with building race cars, which he felt provided excellent free publicity as well as a practical laboratory for refining his ideas. He built two racers, the Arrow and the 999, that were to set several world records. One of his most memorable publicity stunts, however, involved plowing a four-mile course on the frozen surface of Lake St. Clair northeast of Detroit. Slipping and sliding on the cinder-covered ice, Ford set a new world's record, covering one mile in 36 seconds (an average speed of 100 miles per hour) on January 9, 1904, with the new Ford Motor Company's Model B. The resulting publicity helped the company to sell 1,700 cars in 1904, for a total of more than one million dollars. After two failed attempts, Henry Ford had launched a hugely successful car company.

A car for the common man

Prior to 1908, the horseless carriage was typically considered a rich person's toy. Most automobiles then being manufactured were built for wealthy individuals, who would be able to hire someone to both drive and, when necessary, repair the vehicle. Ford's vision was different. He saw the automobile as the tool that would end the dreary isolation of the American farmer and that would allow the inhabitants of the teeming urban slums to move to the outskirts of the great cities where there was plenty of room for new housing developments but no transportation to the factories. To do this, Ford knew the automobile must be priced within the range of the common man, it would have to be reliable, and it would require interchangeable and inexpensive replacement parts.

In 1906, the Ford Motor Company came out with the Model N, a $600 vehicle, and on October 1, 1908, the Model T. The Model T was exactly the car Ford had dreamed about, a light-weight, inexpensive, reliable automobile, priced to be available to the average working consumer. In its first year, Ford sold 8000 Model Ts. Over the course of the next three years Model T sales increased dramatically with 18,000 sold in 1909, 34,000 in 1910, and 78,000 in 1911. In 1916, the year of its greatest production, 730,000 of the automobiles were sold. By 1922, Ford was the richest man in America. And, unlike most of his wealthy contemporaries, Ford was greatly appreciated by many Americans.

Ford and mass production

Ford is often credited with inventing the moving assembly line, a system for carrying an item that is being manufactured past a series of stationary (staying in one place) workers who each assemble a particular portion of the finished product. Ford made the first industrial application of the idea, and the result revolutionized manufacturing, making the modern consumer society possible. (Without the moving assembly line, televisions, medical products, home computers, and many other goods we take for granted would be too expensive for most people.) It should be noted, however, that the moving assembly line was probably the invention of dozens of Ford production supervisors; Ford undoubtedly contributed to its development and certainly approved of the idea and rewarded the persons responsible for perfecting it.

Using the moving assembly line, Ford was able to realize his vision of the Model T as a mass-produced consumer item designed for the common man. The Ford Motor Company built fifteen million Model Ts between 1908 and 1927, an impossible feat in the days prior to the advent of interchangeable parts and the moving assembly line. The addition of a conveyor belt that carried preassembled parts to the point in the factory where they were to be bolted onto the Model T chassis allowed the process of automobile mass production to reach its full height.

Ford as a social activist

Ford's deeply-held belief in his duty (as a wealthy man) to work for the common good led him to share the benefits of mass production with both the people who bought his automobiles and with the workers who made them. After the second year of production, Ford either dropped the price or enhanced the features of the Model T every year, carrying out his stated goal of increasing the Model T's value annually. The price of the Model T, initially $850 in 1908, dropped to as low as $260 in 1924, while the quality of the car itself had been much improved.

In January 1914, Ford decided to share the success of the Model T with his workers. He doubled the pay of the average worker in the Ford plants from $2.50 to $5.00 a day and cut the work day from nine hours to eight. While reviled by Ford's fellow industrialists, this move was wildly popular with his

Gottlieb Daimler, Automobile Inventor

Although Henry Ford made the automobile an affordable consumer product, the invention of the automobile is credited to a number of people from as early as the 1600s. The first model that had many of the basic characteristics of the modern automobile was probably built by the German engineer Gottlieb Daimler (1834-1900) in 1887.

Daimler and his collaborator, Wilhelm Maybach, set up a factory in 1882 to develop a light, high-speed, internal combustion engine that could be used to power a vehicle. While other inventors worked primarily with coal-gas powered engines, Daimler and Maybach built a small gasoline engine that was far superior because it used a carburetor (device that vaporizes the fuel with air to form an explosive mixture that produces the engine's energy). In an attempt to find a commercial use for his engine, Daimler fitted it to a boat in 1882. Three years later, Daimler and Maybach fitted their engine to a wooden bicycle—creating the first motorcycle—and drove it on the streets of Mannheim, Baden, Germany. In 1887, they adapted their gasoline engine to power a four-wheeled vehicle, creating one of the first true automobiles. The unique features of this vehicle included a belt-drive mechanism to turn the wheels, a "tiller" for steering, and a four-speed gearbox. In 1890 the Daimler Motor Company was formed. A car powered by a Daimler engine won the first international car race, the 1894 Paris-to-Rouen race in France. The competition focused attention on the Daimler Motor Company and promoted the concept of automobile use in general.

workers. Ford saw his action not only the right thing to do, but also as a good economic decision. In one move he drastically reduced the turnover of his workers, raised employee morale, and created a new class of industrial workers who could afford to buy Ford automobiles. Ford regarded low wages as "the cutting of buying power and the curtailment of the home market." And by increasing his workers' salaries, he forced his fellow industrialists to pay their workers more, putting the Model T Ford within their economic reach as well.

Ford was also far ahead of his time in employing the physically challenged. He felt, given a chance to work, the blind and the deaf would work much harder than other workers. In addition, he believed in hiring former criminals, thereby providing them with an alternative to a life of crime.

Ford's image

As the Model T gained popularity, Ford gained respect from his fellow Americans. He also developed a high opinion of himself. This development caused him to attempt some seemingly impossible tasks and to take some very questionable positions.

The peace ship

In 1915 Ford financed and sailed on the "Peace" ship, his ill-fated attempt to end World War I (1914-18) in Europe before the United States was drawn into the conflict. According to Ford, war was nonproductive and something that should not be indulged in no matter how badly a nation's "honor" had been sullied. But at that time war was widely viewed as a "manly contest of arms," and Ford was ridiculed for his views. Once his ship arrived in Europe, Ford found that the German government did not want to talk to his peace group and that other European leaders questioned his mission. After two weeks, the ship returned home.

The "international Jewish conspiracy"

After the war, in 1919, Ford took up a crusade against what he imagined was an international conspiracy of Jews to rule society. (Throughout history, Jews have been made scapegoats—the ones arbitrarily and unjustly blamed—for many of society's ills by people who did not understand their religious or social beliefs.) Ford bought a newspaper, the *Dearborn Independent,* and used it to publish his bitter anti-Semitic (anti-Jewish) diatribes (a diatribe is an abusive, mean-spirited piece of writing or speech); Ford, and a significant number of others in the United States and Europe at this time, believed that Jews were in a giant conspiracy to gain control of world economies. He published pamphlets describing what he thought was the excessive influence of Jews in America. He attacked a man named Aaron Shapiro, whom he despised not only because he was Jewish but because he attempted to help farmers by organizing a farm union; Ford hated the idea of a unionized (organized) labor force almost as much as he hated Jews. Shapiro sued Ford, who consequently claimed innocence on the grounds that his writings had not hurt anyone.

When challenged to prove the existence of a conspiracy, Ford pointed to an editor of the *Jewish Tribune,* Herman Bernstein, whom Ford said had first told him about the Jewish conspiracy. Bernstein denied the charge, and accused Ford of inciting pogroms (organized massacres) against Jews in Europe. Ford offered to apologize if Bernstein found any evidence in Europe that Jews had been hurt because of his accusations. Bernstein personally traveled to Europe and uncovered a great deal of evidence. Ford apologized and went out of the newspaper business, but much damage had been done. Through questionable political activities as well as his anti-Semitic actions, Ford's reputation had been sullied in the eyes of many Americans.

Resists changes to company

Ford's final years were ones of decline. By 1920 he had bought out the other shareholders in the Ford Motor Company and was solely in charge. He ignored the advice of his business experts, chased away many of his best executives, and by 1927, the last year of the production of the Model T, his company had fallen behind General Motors. In 1933 he defied President Roosevelt by refusing to take part in the National Recovery Act (legislation that attempted to institute cooperation between industries—under the guidance of the government—in order to ease the economic problems of the Great Depression of the 1930s). Roosevelt's National Labor Relations Act was also designed to get America out of economic depression by giving certain benefits to the working person. Ford strongly opposed this act and refused to join other car makers in adopting its proposals.

Fights unions in factories

Because of Ford's disagreement with the government act, he fought to keep the United Auto Workers (UAW) union from gaining a foothold in Ford plants. Violent strikes erupted in 1937 and 1941, as workers attempted to overcome Ford's strong anti-union position. In 1941, Ford received a court order to allow his employees to enroll in the UAW and to rehire twenty-two union organizers whom he had fired for their actions. Forced to allow a union vote, Ford found that his popularity with his employees had dwindled. More than 70 percent of the Ford workers voted to join the UAW.

Ford suffered a stroke in 1938. His only son, Edsel, died of cancer in 1943, another terrible blow. Ford himself died on April 7, 1947, leaving a legacy that includes the concept of mass production and the moving assembly line, his car company—the second largest in the world, with more than a hundred billion dollars in yearly sales—and the Ford Foundation, a charitable fund that he dedicated to the purpose of "advancing human welfare."

Further Reading

Bennett, Harry, and Paul Marcus, *Ford: We Never Called Him Henry,* TOR, 1951.

Collier, Peter, and David Horowitz, *The Fords: An American Epic,* Simon and Schuster, 1987.

Dahlinger, John Coté, and Francis Spatz Leighton, *The Secret Life of Henry Ford,* Bobbs-Merrill, 1978.

Ford, Henry, with Samuel Crowther, *My Life and Work,* Doubleday, 1922.

Nevins, Allan, and F. E. Hill, *Ford: The Times, the Man, the Company,* 3 volumes, Scribners, 1954.

Rae, John B., editor, *Great Lives Observed: Henry Ford,* Prentice-Hall, 1969.

Dian Fossey

Born 1932
San Francisco, California
Died December 27, 1985
Karisoke Research Centre, Rwanda

Dian Fossey conducted ground-breaking research on the endangered mountain gorillas of central Africa and actively fought to protect them from human interference and exploitation.

Dian Fossey is remembered by her fellow scientists as the world's foremost authority on mountain gorillas. But to the millions who came to know Fossey through her articles and book, she will be remembered as a martyr (person who suffers or makes great sacrifices to further a cause). Throughout the nearly 20 years she spent studying mountain gorillas in central Africa, the American primatologist (scientist who studies the order of mammals that includes monkeys and apes) stubbornly fought the poachers (people who kill or take wild animals illegally) who threatened to wipe out the endangered primates. She was brutally murdered at her research center in 1985 by what many believe was a vengeful poacher.

Early love of animals

Fossey was born in 1932, the only child of George Fossey, an insurance agent, and Kitty (Kidd) Fossey, a fashion model. Fossey's parents divorced when she was six years old.

A year later, Fossey's mother married a wealthy building contractor named Richard Price, a strict disciplinarian who showed little affection for his stepdaughter. Although Fossey loved animals, the only kind she was allowed to have as a pet was a goldfish. When it died, she cried for a week.

Fossey began her college education at the University of California at Davis in the pre-veterinary medicine program. There she excelled in writing and botany, but failed her chemistry and physics courses. After two years she transferred to San Jose State University, where she earned a bachelor of arts degree in occupational therapy in 1954 (branch of medicine that promotes physical recovery by means of activity). While in college Fossey became a prize-winning equestrian (horseback rider). In 1955 her love of horses drew her away from California to Kentucky, where she directed the occupational therapy department at the Kosair Crippled Children's Hospital in Louisville.

Inspired by book on gorillas

Fossey first became interested in African gorillas when she read *The Mountain Gorilla: Ecology and Behavior* (1963) by primatologist George Schaller. She was intrigued by the book's description of the largest and rarest of the three subspecies of gorilla, *Gorilla gorilla beringei*. These giant apes make their home in the mountainous forests of Rwanda, Zaire, and Uganda. The males grow up to six feet tall and weigh 400 pounds or more, with arms that span up to eight feet; the smaller females weigh about 200 pounds. Inspired by the book, Fossey decided to travel to Africa. Against her family's advice she took out a bank loan for $8,000 to finance a seven-week safari.

While in Africa, Fossey met **Louis Leakey** (1903-1972; for more information, see volume 2, pp. 575-587), the celebrated paleoanthropologist (scientist who studies human fossils), who had encouraged British primatologist **Jane Goodall** (1934– ; for more information, see volume 2, pp. 405-444) in her research of chimpanzees in Tanzania. Leakey was

The mountain gorillas of central Africa, hunted by poachers and harassed by cattle grazers, number only in the hundreds and are faced with the possibility of extinction. The fact that the mountain gorillas have managed to survive to the present day at all is largely credited to the work of Dian Fossey. Fossey brought the cause of the threatened mountain gorilla before the public eye, raising awareness about them through articles and her book, *Gorillas in the Mist.* Her writings describe the way she was accepted by the gorillas, who were often tender and human-like in their interactions. When some of her gorilla subjects in Rwanda were killed, Fossey went a step further in her efforts to preserve the animals and personally began a campaign against the poachers. Her struggle against the poachers (people who hunt animals illegally, usually in order to sell them), many of whom turned to such work because of the widespread poverty in Rwanda, was widely suspected to have been a key factor in her murder in 1985.

impressed by Fossey's plans to visit the mountain gorillas. Those plans, however, were nearly destroyed when Fossey shattered her ankle during a fossil dig with Leakey. But just two weeks later, Fossey hobbled on a walking stick up a mountain in the Congo (now Zaire) to her first encounter with the great apes. The sight of six gorillas set the course for her future. Fossey would later recall in her book, *Gorillas in the Mist,* that "I left Kabara (a gorilla site) with reluctance but with never a doubt that I would, somehow, return to learn more about the gorillas of the misted mountains."

Begins research in Africa

Her opportunity came three years later, when Leakey was visiting Louisville on a lecture tour and Fossey convinced him to hire her to study the mountain gorillas. With funding from the L. S. B. Leakey and Wilkie Brothers foundations, as well as the National Geographic Society, Fossey began her career in Africa. She first made a visit to Goodall in Tanzania to learn the best methods for studying primates and collecting data. She then set up camp early in 1967 at the Kabara meadow in the Parc National des Virungas in Zaire, where Schaller had conducted his pioneering research a few years earlier. The site was ideal for Fossey's purposes. Because Zaire's park system protected them from human intrusion, the gorillas showed little fear of Fossey's presence. Unfortunately, six months after Fossey arrived, civil war in Zaire forced her to abandon the site.

Fossey established a permanent research site on September 24, 1967, on the slopes of the Virunga Mountains in the tiny country of Rwanda. She called the site Karisoke Research Centre, taking the name from the neighboring mountains of Karisimbi and Visoke. Although Karisoke was just five miles from the first site, Fossey found a marked difference in Rwanda's gorillas. They had been harassed so often by poachers and cattle grazers that they initially rejected all her attempts to make contact.

Poachers threaten gorilla population

Theoretically, the great apes were protected from such intrusion within the park. But the government of the impoverished (poor), densely populated country failed to enforce the park rules. Native Batusi herdsmen used the park to trap antelope and buffalo, sometimes inadvertently snaring a gorilla. Most trapped gorillas escaped, but not without seriously mutilated limbs that sometimes led to gangrene (rotting of tissue) and death. Poachers could earn up to $200,000 for one gorilla by selling the skeleton to a university and the hands to tourists. From the start, Fossey's mission was to protect the endangered gorillas from extinction (being killed off completely)—she accomplished this both by researching and writing about them, and by destroying traps and warning poachers.

Wins gorillas' trust

Fossey focused her studies on some 51 gorillas in four family groups. Each group was dominated by a sexually mature silverback, named for the characteristic gray hair on its back. Younger bachelor males served as guards for the silverback's harem (group of females associated with one male) and their young offspring. When Fossey began observing the gorillas—which usually avoid other creatures—she followed the advice of earlier scientists by concealing herself and watching from a distance. But she soon realized that the only way she would be able to observe their behavior as closely as she wanted was by "habituating" the gorillas to her presence (getting them used to her). She did so by mimicking their sounds and behavior. She learned to imitate their belches that signal contentment, their barks of curiosity, and a dozen other sounds. To convince them she was their kind, Fossey pretended to munch on the foliage that made up their diet. Her tactics worked. One day early in 1970, Fossey made history when a gorilla she called Peanuts reached out and touched her hand. Fossey called it her most rewarding moment with the gorillas.

She endeared Peanuts and the other gorillas to the public by writing articles about them for *National Geographic* magazine. She drew attention to the way gorillas, much like humans, nurture their young and engage in play. Her early articles also dispelled the myth that gorillas are vicious. In her 1971 *National Geographic* article she described the giant beasts as ranking among "the gentlest animals, and the shiest." In later articles, Fossey acknowledged a dark side to the gorillas. Six of 38 infants born during a 13-year-period were victims of infanticide (the killing of an infant). She speculated that the practice was a silverback's means of perpetuating his own lineage (ensuring he would have direct descendents) by killing another male's offspring so he could mate with the victim's mother.

Poachings inspire conservation efforts

Three years into her study, Fossey realized she would need a doctoral degree to continue receiving financial support for Karisoke. She temporarily left Africa to enroll at Cambridge University in England, where she earned her Ph.D. in zoology in 1974. Then in 1977 she suffered a tragedy that would permanently change her mission at Karisoke. Digit, a young male gorilla she had grown to love, was slaughtered by poachers. When Digit's death was reported on television, interest in gorilla conservation surged. Fossey took advantage of that interest and established the Digit Fund, a nonprofit organization to raise money for anti-poaching patrols and equipment.

But the money was not enough to save the gorillas. Within six months a silverback and his mate were shot to death

Biruté Galdikas, Orangutan Researcher

Like Jane Goodall and Dian Fossey, Biruté Galdikas began her career as a primatologist after studying with British paleoanthropologist Louis Leakey. Leakey was interested in having someone study the lives of orangutans. In 1969, he met Galdikas, an anthropology graduate student at the University of California in Los Angeles (UCLA), and chose her for the job.

Establishing her research in the Tanjung Puting reserve in Indonesia, Galdikas found that orangutans posed some unique problems for scientific research. They are much less social than chimpanzees or gorillas, and they rarely appear on the ground where they can be observed, preferring to stay high in the trees. In addition, the apes were not at all welcoming, often throwing branches at Galdikas or defecating on her to signal their displeasure. Galdikas's patience and careful observations, however, eventually paid off. After 12 years of work, she was finally able to get an orangutan comfortable in her presence.

Galdikas's research has provided numerous insights into the mysterious life of the orangutan. Her discoveries about orangutan behavior—including the facts that adolescents travel together and that adults tend to keep an individual mate for long periods of time—overturned previous assumptions about the apes. Galdikas has become increasingly concerned with the plight of primates in the wild. She continues to work at her research center in the Tanjung Puting Reserve, largely through the support of the conservation group Earthwatch.

Fossey with a group of gorillas in Africa

while defending their three-year-old son who had been shot in the shoulder; the juvenile later died from his wounds. The deaths prompted Fossey to step up her fight against poachers by terrorizing them and raiding their villages.

Forced to leave Africa in 1980 because of a serious calcium deficiency, Fossey spent three years as a visiting associate professor at Cornell University in Ithaca, New York. During that time she completed her book about her life and work in Africa, *Gorillas in the Mist*, which was published in 1983. Fossey returned to Karisoke that year. Lacking outside funding, she operated the site with her own money, focusing her work more on animal conservation than scientific studies. Two years later, on December 27, 1985, she was found murdered in her bedroom, her skull split by a large weapon. She was 54 years old. The crime remains a mystery that has prompted much speculation. Many believe an angry poacher was responsible.

A legacy of animal activism

Fossey's final resting place is at Karisoke, surrounded by the remains of Digit and more than a dozen other gorillas she had buried. Fossey's legacy lives on in the Virunga Mountains, where her followers have taken up her battle to protect the endangered mountain gorillas. The Dian Fossey Gorilla Fund, formerly the Digit Fund, finances scientific research at Karisoke and employs camp staff, trackers, and anti-poaching patrols. The motion picture *Gorillas in the Mist,* which tells the story of Fossey's life, pioneering work, and violent death, was released in 1988, further spreading knowledge of Fossey's work and the plight of the mountain gorilla. The Rwanda government, which for years had ignored Fossey's pleas to protect the mountain gorillas, recognized her scientific achievement in 1990 with the Ordre National des Grandes Lacs, the highest award ever given a foreigner.

Further Reading

Brower, Montgomery, "The Strange Death of Dian Fossey," *People,* February 17, 1986, pp. 46-54.

Fossey, Dian, *Gorillas in the Mist,* Houghton Mifflin, 1983.

Fossey, Dian, "The Imperiled Mountain Gorilla," *National Geographic,* April 1981, pp. 501-22.

Fossey, Dian, "Making Friends with Mountain Gorillas," *National Geographic,* January 1970, pp. 48-67.

Fossey, Dian, "More Years with Mountain Gorillas," *National Geographic,* October 1971, pp. 574-85.

Hayes, Harold T. P., *The Dark Romance of Dian Fossey,* Simon and Schuster, 1990.

Montgomery, Sy, *Walking with the Great Apes: Jane Goodall, Dian Fossey, Biruté Galdikas,* Houghton Mifflin Company, 1991.

Morell, Virginia, "Called 'Trimates,' Three Bold Women Shaped Their Field," *Science,* April 16, 1993, pp. 420-25.

Mowat, Farley, *Woman in the Mists: The Story of Dian Fossey and the Mountain Gorillas of Africa,* Warner Books, 1987.

Galileo Galilei

Born February 15, 1564
Pisa, Italy
Died January 8, 1642
Arcetri, Italy

Galileo Galilei's astronomical observations with a telescope provided proof that Earth is not the center of the universe.

alileo Galilei is credited with establishing the modern experimental method. Before Galileo, knowledge of the physical world advanced by scientists and thinkers was for the most part a matter of hypothesis (untested ideas) and guesses. In contrast, Galileo introduced the practice of proving or disproving a scientific theory by conducting tests and observing the results. His desire to increase the precision of his observations led him to develop a number of inventions and make numerous discoveries, particularly in the fields of physics and astronomy.

Discovers principles of the pendulum

The son of Vincenzo Galilei (c.1520-1591), an eminent composer and music theorist, Galileo (who is commonly known by his first name) was born in Pisa, Italy, on February 15, 1564. He received his early education at a monastery near Florence, and in 1581 he entered the University of Pisa to study medicine. While a student he observed a hanging lamp that was swinging back and forth and noted that the amount of time it took the lamp to complete a single swing remained constant, even as the arc, or curve, of the swing steadily decreased. He later experimented with other suspended objects and discovered that they behaved in the same way, suggesting to him the principle of the pendulum—a suspended body that once set swinging can be used to regulate the movements of a machine, such as a clock. From this discovery he was able to invent an instrument that measured time, which doctors found to be useful for measuring a patient's pulse rate. Dutch mathematician and astronomer Christiaan Huygens (1629-1695) later adapted the principle of a swinging pendulum to build a reliable pendulum clock in 1656.

Establishes scientific reputation

While at the University of Pisa, Galileo listened in on a geometry lesson and was so fascinated with it that he decided to abandon his medical studies and devote himself to mathematics. However, he was unable to complete a degree at the university due to lack of funds. He returned to Florence in 1585, having studied the works of Greek mathematician Euclid (who lived in the third century B.C.) and Greek mathematician Archimedes (c.287-212 B.C.). He expanded on Archimedes's work in hydrostatics (a branch of physics dealing with the amount of pressure in fluids) by creating a hydrostatic balance, a device designed to measure the density, or mass, of objects by weighing them in water. The following year, he published an essay describing his new invention, which earned him a reputation throughout Italy as a talented scientist.

Challenges ideas of Aristotle

In 1592 Galileo was appointed professor of mathematics at Padua University in Pisa, where he began conducting experiments with falling objects. The ancient Greek philosopher Aristotle (384-322 B.C.), whose ideas were still considered to

Mathematician and astronomer Galileo Galilei took a bold stand in the early 1600s when he declared that he had evidence that Polish astronomer Nicolaus Copernicus had been right when he said that Earth was not the center of the universe, as the second-century Alexandrian astronomer Ptolemy had claimed. His statement convinced many people to accept the Copernican theory, even though it directly contradicted the teachings of the Catholic Church of the time, which supported Ptolemy's geocentric (or Earth-centered) theory of the solar system; the Church prosecuted Galileo for teaching a different view. Galileo also disproved many of the teachings of the Greek philosopher Aristotle (384-322 B.C.), proving, for example, that objects of different weight fall at the same speed, that the speed of a falling object increases at a steady rate, and that the universe is not "perfect" and unchanging. Galileo's studies of motion and falling objects eventually led to English mathematician Isaac Newton's formulation of the laws of motion.

be scientific law, had stated that a heavier object should fall faster than a lighter one. It is said that Galileo tested Aristotle's assertion by climbing the leaning tower of Pisa, dropping objects of various weights, and proving once and for all that all objects, no matter what their weight, fall at the same rate. There is no real evidence to prove that Galileo did perform such a demonstration, though a similar experiment had been conducted by Flemish mathematician Simon Stevin (1548-1620) a few years earlier. Whether Galileo conducted this famous experiment or not, his end result was the same—he had successfully disproved the long-standing physics of Aristotle.

Develops early thermometer

In 1593 Galileo invented one of the first measuring devices to be used in science: the thermometer. His thermometer employed a bulb of air that expanded or contracted as temperature changed and in so doing caused the level of a column of water to rise or fall. Though this device was inaccurate because it did not account for changes in air pressure, it was later followed by more accurate instruments that did allow for new breakthroughs in scientific observation.

Studies speed of falling objects

From 1602 to 1609 Galileo studied the motion of pendulums and other objects as they moved along arcs and inclines. Using inclined planes that he built, he concluded that falling objects accelerate at a constant rate. This law of uniform acceleration later helped English mathematician and physicist Isaac Newton (1642-1727) derive the law of gravity.

Attention turns to astronomy

Galileo did not make his first contribution to astronomy until 1604, when a supernova, or a massive explosion of a star, suddenly appeared in the night sky. Galileo reasoned that this object was farther away than the planets and pointed out that this violent event in the sky meant that the "perfect and unchanging heavens" that Aristotle had claimed surrounded Earth were not unchanging after all.

Telescope revolutionizes astronomy

It was a few years after this event that he first heard about the invention of the telescope in 1608 by Hans Lippershey (c.1570-1619), a Danish spectacle maker. Galileo is often mistakenly given credit for inventing the telescope, partly because of his major improvements to Lippershey's device and partly because he claimed at one point to have done so. When Galileo learned of the invention in mid-1609, he quickly built one himself and made several improvements. His altered telescope could magnify objects at nine power (nine times the power of vision with the naked eye), three times the magnification of Lippershey's model. Galileo's telescope proved to be very valuable for the business of sailing ships, and Galileo was rewarded for his work with a lifetime appointment to the University of Venice.

Publishes *The Starry Messenger*

He continued to work on the telescope, and by the end of the year he had built one that could magnify at 30 power. He had the idea to turn his telescope up to observe the stars and planets. The discoveries he made with this instrument revolutionized astronomy. Through the telescope, Galileo saw jagged edges on the Moon, which he realized were the tops of moun-

Galileo and his telescope

tains. He assumed that the Moon's large dark areas were bodies of water, which he called *maria,* the Latin name for seas
(though we now know there is no water on the Moon). When
he observed the Milky Way (the galaxy of which the Sun and
Earth are part and which appears as a luminous band of light
in the night sky), Galileo was amazed to discover that the
cloudy body was actually made up of individual stars. He pub-

lished these and other early discoveries in March 1610 in a book titled *Sidereus nuncius* ("The Starry Messenger"). The book increased Galileo's fame, and his discoveries—though questioned by some—were praised by many scientists, including the German astronomer **Johannes Kepler** (1571-1630; for more information, see pp. 126-132).

New information about the solar system

Galileo did not stop with this first round of discoveries. Also in 1610 he observed that the planet Venus had light and dark phases (regularly recurring states) like the Moon, and for the same reasons: Venus did not make its own light, but was illuminated by the Sun. Looking at the Sun itself, he saw dark spots on its disc. The position of the spots changed from day to day, allowing Galileo to determine the rate at which the Sun rotated on its axis.

When he looked at Saturn, it looked like an oval. His telescope was not strong enough to make out the planet's famous rings; he concluded that the odd shape was due to some satellites that were very close to the planet. In observing Jupiter he was able to clearly see that the planet had four moons; he later called them "satellites," a term suggested by Kepler. Galileo named the moons of Jupiter Sidera Medicea ("Medicean stars") in honor of Cosimo de Medici (1519-1574), the Grand Duke of Tuscany, whom Galileo served as "first philosopher and mathematician" after leaving the University of Pisa in 1610. By observing the moons over a few weeks, he was able to see the satellites being eclipsed, or blocked from view, by Jupiter. This brought Galileo to the conclusion that the four moons rotated around Jupiter, and he even calculated the length of time it took each moon to circle the planet. While this idea is now an accepted fact of science, in Galileo's time this was observation revolutionary.

The two views of the universe

Since the second century, the most widely accepted view of the universe was based on the theory of the Alexandrian

Simon Stevin, Flemish Mathematician and Engineer

Simon Stevin (1548-1620) is best known as a contributor to two branches of physics: statics (the science of forces producing equilibrium, or a balanced state) and hydrostatics (the science of the force produced by liquids). His most important book in the field of statics was *De Beghinselen der weeghconst,* published in 1586. In this work, Stevin described his most famous discovery, the law of inclined planes, which states that a smaller weight on a steep slope can balance a heavier weight on a gentler slope. His other well-known publication, *De Beghinselen des waterwichts,* was the first work since ancient times to study the principle of displacement (the idea that the weight of an object can be calculated by how much water it moves—displaces—when immersed) of Greek mathematician Archimedes (c.287-212 B.C.). He added many new ideas of his own, including one that is the fundamental principle of hydraulics (using the movement of water to accomplish a mechanical task): the pressure exerted by a liquid depends only on its height, not the shape of its container. This meant that a small amount of fluid could produce a large amount of pressure if it were held in a long, narrow tube.

In another branch of science, Stevin was upstaged by another scientist of his time: Galileo Galilei. Although credit has historically been given to the Italian, it was Stevin who first proved wrong the idea of ancient Greek philosopher Aristotle that heavier bodies fall faster than light ones. He dropped two lead balls, one ten times heavier than the other, from a height of 30 feet and found that they hit the ground at the same time. Stevin published his findings years before Galileo, but never received the same amount of fame.

Stevin was also influential in supporting the use of a decimal system of mathematics. In two works published in 1585, he described the usefulness of decimal fractions in everyday life. Until that time, decimals had only been used in the scholarly field of trigonometry, and even then they were used only occasionally. Although awkward by modern standards, Stevin's system of writing fractions was a vast improvement over sixteenth-century methods, and decimal fractions were soon in wide use. Stevin also proposed a decimal system for weights, measures, and currency, ideas that were not adopted for hundreds of years.

astronomer Ptolemy, who said that Earth was the center of the universe, and the Sun and all the planets and other heavenly bodies rotated around it. This was the established teaching of the powerful Roman Catholic Church as well. But in the early 1500s, the Polish astronomer **Nicolaus Copernicus** (1473-1543; for more information, see pp. 48-54) had suggested that Earth, along with the other planets, circled the Sun. Copernicus had begun compiling evidence for his ideas based on the positions of the planets throughout the year, but his proof was mostly mathematical—he did not have the physical evidence that a telescope could provide. Copernicus's ideas had been banned by the Catholic Church.

Supports Copernican theory

In 1613 Galileo published a book called *Letters on Sunspots,* in which for the first time he presented evidence for and openly defended the model of the solar system earlier proposed by Copernicus. Presenting his findings on Venus, the Sun, and Jupiter, Galileo showed that not all moving bodies in the universe revolved around the Earth. While there was some support even among Church authorities for Galileo's proof of the Copernican theory, the Roman Catholic leadership ultimately determined that it would not change the long-held astronomical teachings of the Church. Thus, in 1616 an order was issued by the Church declaring the Copernican system "false and erroneous," and Galileo was instructed not to support this system.

Following this run-in with the Catholic church, Galileo turned his attention to the less controversial issue of determining a ship's longitude (east-west) position while at sea, which required a reliable clock. (Using an accurate time-keeping system, a person on board a ship could compare the changes in position of a certain heavenly body at the same time every day and calculate how far east or west the ship had traveled.) Galileo thought it possible to measure time by observing eclipses of Jupiter's moons. Unfortunately, this idea was not practical because eclipses could not be predicted with enough accuracy and observing celestial bodies from a rocking ship was nearly impossible.

Book angers Church leaders

Galileo wanted to have the Church's position against the Copernican theory reversed, and in 1624 he traveled to Rome to make his appeal to the newly elected pope, Urban VIII. The pope would not change the Church's ruling, but Galileo was given permission to write about the Copernican system, with the restriction that it would not be given preference over the church-supported Ptolemaic model of the universe.

With this sign of approval from Urban, Galileo wrote his *Dialogue Concerning the Two Chief World Systems—Ptolemaic and Copernican,* published in 1632. Despite his agreement not to favor the Copernican view, the objections to it in the *Dialogue* are made to sound unconvincing and even ridiculous. Galileo was soon called to Rome to stand before the Inquisition, a court of the Catholic Church that was designed to uncover and punish people who held beliefs that went against the teachings of the Church. Galileo was accused of violating the original ruling of 1616 forbidding him to promote the Copernican theory. Put on trial for heresy (going against Church belief), he was found guilty and ordered to admit that his ideas were wrong. By this time, Galileo was almost seventy years old, and not wishing a harsh sentence, he did as he was told. According to legend, however, after making the required statement that the Copernican ideas were incorrect, Galileo said quietly, "And yet it moves," referring to the Copernican teaching that Earth rotates on its axis.

Final work published

While the judgment against Galileo included a term of imprisonment, the pope lightened this sentence to house arrest at Galileo's home near Florence. He devoted himself to work in physics, including a study of projectile motion (the movement of a body thrust forward by an external force, for example, a cannonball shot out of a cannon). Although officially forbidden to publish any further works, a book on his work in physics, titled *Two New Sciences,* was printed in France in 1638.

By the time of his last book's publication, Galileo had become completely blind, perhaps due in part to his many observations of the Sun through a telescope. He died at Arcetri, Italy, just outside of Florence, on January 8, 1642. Even after the scientist's death, the Church refused to allow his work to be recognized. It was not until almost 100 years later that the Church finally gave permission for a monument acknowledging Galileo's accomplishments to be placed at his grave.

Further Readings

Asimov, Isaac, *Asimov's Biographical Encyclopedia of Science and Technology,* Doubleday, 1972, pp. 91-96.

Dictionary of Scientific Biography, Volume V, Scribner's, 1972, pp. 237-49.

The McGraw-Hill Encyclopedia of World Biography, Volume 4, McGraw-Hill, 1973, pp. 289-92.

Alice Hamilton

Born February 27, 1869
New York, New York

Died September 22, 1970
Hadlyme, Connecticut

Alice Hamilton conducted pioneering research into workplace safety and was instrumental in setting industrial safety standards.

Alice Hamilton was a pioneer in correcting the medical problems caused by industrialization, awakening the United States in the early twentieth century to the dangers of industrial poisons and hazardous working conditions. Through her efforts, toxic substances were identified in the mining, rubber, paint, and rayon industries, among others, and safeguards were put in place to protect workers from such dangers. A medical doctor and researcher, she was the first woman to serve on the faculty at Harvard University.

Hamilton was born on February 27, 1869, in New York City, the second of the five children of Montgomery and Gertrude (Pond) Hamilton. When she was only six weeks old, her family moved to Fort Wayne, Indiana, where she and her three sisters grew up. The children enjoyed a sheltered, comfortable existence in the "Old House" that belonged to her father's family. Their only brother was born there when Hamilton was 17. Her grandfather, Allen Hamilton, had settled in Fort Wayne when it was still a military post, and her grandmother had become a leader in the city's charitable and religious life. In opposition to her husband's rather conservative family, Gertrude Hamilton encouraged her daughters' aspirations, education, and independence, teaching Hamilton that personal liberty was to be valued most in life. The four girls were educated at home where their parents taught them history, literature, and languages, and a governess introduced them to mathematics. Then, at 17, in accordance with family tradition, Hamilton was sent to Miss Porter's School in Farmington, Connecticut, for two years.

Chooses medical career

By the time she returned to Fort Wayne, her father's business was in serious trouble. Like her sisters, Hamilton needed to find a career in order to support herself financially. Despite the objections of her family, she decided on the only profession open to women in the late nineteenth century that would allow her to make money while performing useful, independent work. She decided to study medicine. She made this choice not because she had an overwhelming interest in science, but because she believed that "as a doctor I could go anywhere I pleased—to far-off lands or to city slums—and could be quite sure that I could be of use anywhere." She took courses in physics, chemistry, and anatomy at the Fort Wayne College of Medicine before enrolling in the University of Michigan's medical department, where she received her M.D. in 1893. Hamilton then interned (served a period of training under the supervision of experienced doctors) at the Northwestern Hospital for Women and Children in Minneapolis, Minnesota, and the New England Hospital for Women and Children in Boston, Massachusetts.

Convinced that she did not want to establish a private practice, she decided to devote her career to bacteriology (the study of the single-cell microorganisms known as bacteria) and pathology (the study of the cause and behavior of disease). In 1895, she and her older sister Edith (who was to become well known as a writer, educator, and Greek scholar) went to Germany. There Hamilton studied bacteriology and pathology

Before the early 1900s, industrial workplaces were often filled with toxic substances and unsafe conditions that made life in the factories dangerous, even deadly, for the people who worked there. Alice Hamilton became the first U.S. expert in industrial hygiene, the study of the safety of the substances and practices used in industry. Her pioneering studies established that workers who were exposed to materials such as lead, arsenic, mercury, and radium suffered serious health problems, and she lobbied business leaders to protect their employees from such substances. The information she gathered was instrumental in passing laws to protect workers in Illinois and Pennsylvania, setting standards for the entire country.

at the universities of Leipzig and Munich. She spent another year studying pathological anatomy at the Johns Hopkins Medical School in Baltimore, Maryland.

Moves to Hull House

In 1897, Hamilton was appointed professor of pathology at the Woman's Medical School of Northwestern University in Chicago, Illinois, and became a resident of social reformer Jane Addams's Hull House, a settlement house (community center) designed to bring reform workers into urban neighborhoods to live and work among the poor and disadvantaged. At first, Hamilton felt isolated and overwhelmed in her new environment of poverty, trade unions, and social activism. But she soon enjoyed the support and friendship of Addams and other residents of Hull House, and through the settlement she met many well-known reformers and intellectuals of the day. During her years at Hull House, Hamilton's contributions to the work of the settlement included teaching medical-education classes and operating a baby clinic.

Hull House was a center of public health reform efforts during Hamilton's association with it. But she began to be discouraged when she realized that her efforts would never match the tremendous needs of the poor there. In addition to her teaching and work at Hull House, Hamilton carried out laboratory research at the University of Chicago, but at times her scientific work seemed "remote and useless," while the pressures of settlement work left her exhausted and overwhelmed.

When the Woman's Medical School closed in 1902, Hamilton joined the new Memorial Institute for Infectious Diseases as assistant to the eminent pathologist Dr. Ludwig Hektoen, who was the Institute's director. Hektoen encouraged his assistant to publish scientific papers and become active in Chicago's medical and reform communities. Hamilton had now found a more rewarding type of work in which she could combine her interests in scientific research and social reform. Her studies of a typhoid fever epidemic (rapidly spreading disease caused by bacteris in food or water, marked by high fever and intestinal bleeding) that struck Chicago in 1902 earned her considerable recognition. During this time, she brought attention to the role of flies in spreading typhoid and was instrumental in reorganizing Chicago's health department.

Studies occupational diseases

Through her work at Hull House, Hamilton had become aware that many workers became invalids (disabled) because of the poisonous substances they encountered in the factories, foundries, and steel mills. "Living in a working-class quarter," she wrote, "coming in contact with laborers and their wives, I could not fail to hear tales of the dangers that workingmen faced, of cases of carbon-monoxide gassing in the great steel mills, of painters disabled by lead palsy, of pneumonia and rheumatism among the men in the stockyards." Reading Sir Thomas Oliver's book *Dangerous Trades* further focused her attention on the problems of workers suffering from industrial diseases. Her readings on the subject revealed that while industrial medicine was an established medical discipline in Britain, Germany, Austria, Holland, Scandinavia, Italy, and Spain—with some European nations establishing factory inspection systems—in the United States, diseases of the workplace were totally ignored and no occupational safety laws existed to protect workers. Hamilton noted, "The American Medical Association had never had a meeting devoted to this subject, and except for a few surgeons attached to large companies operating steel mills, or railways, or coal mines, there were no medical men in Illinois who specialized in the field of industrial medicine."

In 1908, Governor Charles S. Deneen appointed Hamilton to the Illinois Commission on Occupational Diseases; she later became managing director of the commission. A pioneer who combined field studies of industrial poisons with modern laboratory techniques, Hamilton began studying lead—one of the most common industrial poisons—and identified lead-using industrial processes while proving that hundreds of workers were victims of lead poisoning. As a result of the survey, Illinois passed a workmen's compensation law requiring safety measures in factories and medical examinations of workers.

In 1910, Hamilton attended the International Congress on Occupational Accidents and Diseases in Brussels, Belgium, where she presented a paper on occupational diseases in the United States. As a result of her paper's impact, in 1911 she became a special investigator for the U.S. Bureau of Labor. Her work conducting industrial surveys for the federal government took her to Washington, D.C., and to many other parts of the country, but she remained a resident of Hull House until 1919. Until the death of Jane Addams in 1935, Hamilton spent several months each year at the settlement house. She held her unpaid federal post from 1911 to 1921. As compensation for her work, the government purchased her reports when they were ready for publication.

Becomes industrial medicine authority

By 1916, Hamilton was internationally known as America's leading authority on industrial poisoning and industrial medicine. Having established the dangers of lead dust, she went on to investigate the hazards of arsenic, mercury, organic solvents, radium, and many other toxic materials—especially in the rubber industry and ammunition plants. Hamilton served as an advocate (spokesperson) for abused workers, a public health crusader, and a skilled negotiator who was often able to persuade factory owners to improve safety conditions.

After World War I (1914-18), interest in industrial hygiene increased, but, because the field was new and still not widely supported as a science, it was of limited interest to men. Hamilton attributed some of her success and opportunities to this situation. Indeed, she noted with amusement that she became Harvard's first woman professor in 1919 because she was "the only candidate available." Although she became assistant professor of industrial medicine at the Harvard Medical School, Hamilton insisted on a half-time appointment that allowed her to spend six months of the year doing field work. Harvard attached three stipulations to her appointment because of her sex: she was not to enter the all-male Harvard Faculty Club, march in the graduation procession, or claim her quota of football tickets.

Publishes work on industrial poisons

The 1925 publication of Hamilton's *Industrial Poisons in the United States,* the first text on the subject, provided detailed proof of the dangers of industrial poisons and established her as one of the field's two major authorities in the world (along with Sir Thomas Legge in England). In addition to advancing the cause of worker protection through her teaching, writing, and research, Hamilton spoke out in public and testified persuasively for protective legislation, child labor laws, pacifism (opposition to war), birth control, and other social reforms.

Increasingly interested in international affairs, from 1924 to 1930 Hamilton served as a member of the Health Committee of the League of Nations (a world organization formed after World War I to promote peace and cooperation); she was the only woman member of the committee. At the invitation of its Department of Health, she visited the Soviet Union in 1924 and noted achievements made in industrial hygiene but was disappointed by the country's abuse of power and suppression of free speech. Following a visit to Nazi Germany in 1933, she published a series of articles warning of Nazi anti-intellectualism, repression, and persecution of the Jews. After German Nazi leader Adolf Hitler (1889-1945) ordered the invasion of Western Europe in 1940, she abandoned her pacifist stance and urged support for the war effort against Germany.

Continues industrial studies

Hamilton retired from Harvard in 1935 as assistant professor emeritus of industrial medicine. She and her sister Margaret became year-round residents of the home they had purchased in Hadlyme, Connecticut. At the request of Frances Perkins, the U.S. secretary of labor, Hamilton became a consultant in the Division of Labor Standards. In this role she conducted intensive investigations of the rayon industry from 1937 to 1938; her demonstration of the toxicity of the rayon processes led to Pennsylvania's first compensation law for occupational diseases. She also completed an analysis of silicosis (a disease of the lungs caused by breathing in fine particles of dust) and other occupational diseases of miners in 1940.

Well past the standard age of retirement, Hamilton continued to write, lecture, serve as a consultant, and participate in reform movements. She also published an autobiography, *Exploring the Dangerous Trades,* in 1943. In 1959, the authors of the *Textbook of Toxicology* described Hamilton as a "frail, courageous, and tenacious physician" who was one of the great leaders of the struggle for "the rights of the individual to hygienic working conditions." In her 80s, she continued to enjoy her hobbies of gardening and painting. Hamilton was 101 when she died of a stroke at her home in 1970.

Further Reading

DuBois, Kenneth P., and E. M. K. Geiling, *Textbook of Toxicology,* Oxford University Press, 1984.

Hamilton, Alice, *Exploring the Dangerous Trades: The Autobiography of Alice Hamilton, M.D.,* Little, Brown, 1943.

McPherson, Stephanie Sammartino, *The Workers' Detective: A Story about Dr. Alice Hamilton,* Carolrhoda Books, 1992.

Noble, Iris, *Contemporary Women Scientists of America,* Messner, 1988, pp. 13-14.

Notable American Women: The Modern Period, Harvard University Press, 1980, pp. 303-306.

Sicherman, Barbara, *Alice Hamilton, a Life in Letters,* Harvard University Press, 1984.

Frédéric Joliot-Curie

Born March 19, 1900
Paris, France
Died 1958
France

Irène Joliot-Curie

Born September 12, 1897
Paris, France
Died March 17, 1956
France

Irène Joliot-Curie and Frédéric Joliot-Curie were French nuclear physicists who discovered artificial radioactivity. For their discovery they received the 1935 Nobel Prize in chemistry. Their efforts made nuclear fission and the subsequent development of both nuclear energy and the atomic bomb feasible. The couple met while working at the Radium Institute at the University of Paris. Irène Joliot-Curie was the daughter of **Marie and Pierre Curie** (for more information, see volume 1, pp. 181–191), the Nobel Prize winners who discovered the element radium and founded the Radium Institute. Irène and Frédéric became lifelong research collaborators and they usually published their findings under the combined form of their last names, Joliot-Curie.

Irène and Frédéric Joliot-Curie were awarded a Nobel Prize for their discovery of artificial radiation.

Frédéric influenced by liberal family

Jean-Frédéric Joliot was born on March 19, 1900, in Paris, France, to Henri Joliot and Emilie Roederer. According

117

to family tradition, all the Joliot men were named Jean in honor of Jean Hus (1372?-1415), a Czech religious leader and champion of spiritual freedom who was burned at the stake by the Catholic Church. Henri Joliot came from a long line of liberal thinkers and had been part of the French Communard movement, a rebel government created at the end of the Franco-Prussian War in the 1870s. He became a dry goods merchant and the family was settled into a middle-class life, yet Henri remained passionate about his political concerns. He also had a great love of the outdoors and of music, combining the two by composing a number of calls for the hunting horn. His son Frédéric would become an avid outdoorsman as well despite his busy scientific career. Frédéric's mother Emilie was also from a liberal family, and Frédéric was exposed to progressive social ideas at a young age. The social and political leanings of his parents had a profound influence on young Frédéric and he was an atheist (person who does not believe in the existence of God) and political leftist his entire life.

Frédéric was educated at the Lycée Lakanal in a suburb of Paris, then at the École Primaire Supérieure Lavoisier in Paris. In 1920 he was admitted to the École Supérieure de Physique et de Chimie Industrielle of Paris, a preparatory school that turned out most of France's industrial engineers at the time. The director of the school, a brilliant physicist named Paul Langevin, recognized Frédéric's interest and aptitude for scientific research and became Frédéric's lifelong mentor. After graduating at the head of his class, Frédéric worked in industry for a short time. Following Langevin's advice, however, he took a position as research assistant at the Radium Institute in Paris.

Irène receives extraordinary education

Irène Curie was born on September 12, 1897, in Paris to the Nobel-winning scientists Marie and Pierre Curie. She had a rather extraordinary childhood, growing up in the company of brilliant scientists. Her mother, the former Marie Sklodowska, and her father, Pierre Curie, had been married in 1895 and had become dedicated physicists, experimenting with radioactivity in their laboratory. Marie Curie was on the threshold of discovering the element radium when little Irène, or "my little Queen" as her mother called her, was only a few months old. As Irène grew into an intelligent yet shy child, she was very possessive of her mother, who was often busy with her experiments. If, after a long day at the laboratory, the little Queen greeted her exhausted mother with demands for fruit, Marie Curie would turn right around and walk to the market to get her daughter fruit. After her father's accidental death in 1908, Irène became more influenced by her paternal grandfather, Eugène Curie. It was her grandfather who taught young Irène botany and natural history as they spent summers in the country. The elder Curie was also somewhat of a political radical and atheist, and it was he who helped shape Irène's leftist political views and her rejection of organized religion.

Irène's education was quite remarkable. Marie Curie made sure she and her younger sister, Eve Denise (born in 1904), did their physical as well as mental exercises each day. The girls had a governess for a time, but because Madame Curie was not satisfied with the available schools, she organized a teaching cooperative in which children of the professors from Paris's famed Sorbonne University came to the laboratory for their lessons. Madame Curie taught physics, and some of her famous colleagues taught math, chemistry, language, and sculpture. Soon Irène became the star pupil as she excelled in physics and chemistry. After only two years, however, when Irène was 14, the cooperative ended and Irène enrolled in a private school, the Collège Sevigné, and soon earned her degree. Irène then enrolled at the Sorbonne to study for a diploma in nursing.

IMPACT

Nuclear physicists Irène Joliot-Curie and Frédéric Joliot-Curie continued the research into radioactivity that had first begun with Irène's famous parents, Marie and Pierre Curie (1867-1934 and 1859-1906, respectively), the discoverers of radium and the concept of radioactivity. The Curies had discovered elements—like radium and polonium—that were naturally radioactive; the Joliot-Curies developed a method to artificially create radioactive isotopes of elements (an isotope is one of two or more atoms of a chemical element that have the same structure but different physical properties). Artificial radiation has since been used in a number of scientific experiments that have led to greater knowledge of biochemistry (the study of chemical processes of living organisms), mineralogy (the study of minerals), and other fields. The Joliot-Curies also paved the way for the discovery of nuclear fission, the reaction that creates the energy in nuclear power and atomic bombs.

Irène Joliot-Curie

During World War I (1914-18), Madame Curie went to the battlefront, where she used new X-ray equipment to treat soldiers. Irène soon learned to use the same equipment, working first with her mother and later on her own. Irène, who was shy and rather antisocial by nature, grew to be calm and determined in the face of danger. At age 21, she became her mother's assistant at the Radium Institute. There she became quite good at using the Wilson cloud chamber, a device that makes otherwise invisible atomic particles visible by the trails of water droplets left in their wake.

In the early 1920s, Irène Curie began to make her mark in the laboratory. Working with Fernand Holweck, chief of staff at the Institute, she performed several experiments on radium, resulting in her first scientific paper in 1921. By 1925 she had completed her doctoral thesis on the emission of alpha rays from polonium, an element that her parents had discovered. Many colleagues in the lab, including her future husband, thought her to be much like her father in her almost instinctive ability to use laboratory instruments.

Work together leads to marriage

Frédéric was several years younger than Irène and untrained in the use of the equipment at the Institute. When she was called upon to teach him about radioactivity, Irène started out in a rather uninterested manner, but soon the two began taking long walks in the country. They married in 1926 and decided to use the combined name Joliot-Curie to honor her notable scientific heritage. After their marriage, Irène and Frédéric began doing their research together, signing all their scientific papers jointly even after Irène was named chief of the laboratory in 1932.

In 1930, Frédéric completed his doctoral thesis, which was titled "A Study of the Electrochemistry of Radioactive

Elements." Irène and Frédéric's shared interest in radioactivity drew them into the field of nuclear physics, particularly after they read of the experiments of the German scientists Walther Bothe and Hans Becker in that same year.

New discoveries in nuclear physics

Nuclear physics was a fairly new field of study at that time. Only at the turn of the century had scientists discovered that atoms contain a central core, or nucleus, made up of positively charged particles called protons. Outside the nucleus are negatively charged particles called electrons. Irène's parents had done their work on radioactivity, a phenomenon that occurs when the unstable nuclei of certain elements disintegrate and release particles or emit energy. Some emissions are called alpha particles, which are relatively large particles resembling the nucleus of a helium atom and thus contain two positive charges. In their Nobel Prize-winning work, the elder Curies had discovered that some elements, the radioactive elements, emit particles on a regular, predictable basis. Bothe and Becker had discovered that very strong radiation was also emitted from some of the lighter elements when they were bombarded with alpha rays (streams of alpha particles).

Creation of artificial radioactivity

Irène Joliot-Curie had in her laboratory one of the largest supplies of radioactive materials in the world, primarily the element polonium. The polonium released alpha particles that Irène and Frédéric used to bombard different elements. In 1933 they used alpha particles to bombard aluminum nuclei. What they produced was radioactive phosphorus. Here's how: Aluminum usually has 13 protons in its nuclei; when bombarded with alpha particles, each of which contains two positive charges, aluminum nuclei "absorb" the two new positive charges—forming a nucleus with 15 protons—and thus form a new element, phosphorus. The phosphorus produced in this way, however, is different from naturally-occurring phosphorus because it is radioactive; it is known as a radioactive isotope of phosphorus.

The two researchers used their alpha bombardment technique on other elements, finding that when a nucleus of a particular element combined with an alpha particle, it would transform that element into another, radioactive element with a higher number of protons in its nucleus. What Irène and Frédéric Joliot-Curie had done was to create artificial radioactivity. They announced this breakthrough to the Academy of Sciences in January of 1934.

The Joliot-Curies' discovery was of great significance not only for its pure science, but for its many applications. Since the 1930s many more radioactive isotopes have been produced and used in medical diagnoses as well as in countless experiments. The success of the technique encouraged other scientists to experiment with releasing the power of the nucleus.

Awarded Nobel Prize

It was a bittersweet time for Irène Joliot-Curie. An overjoyed but ailing Marie Curie knew that her daughter was headed for great recognition, but died in July of 1934 from leukemia (disease of the blood) caused by many years of radiation exposure. Several months later the Joliot-Curies were informed of their Nobel Prize. Although they were nuclear physicists, the pair received an award in chemistry because of their discovery's impact in that area.

After winning the Nobel Prize, Irène and Frédéric were the recipients of many honorary degrees and named officers of the Legion of Honor (French order recognizing Civil or military merit). But all these awards made little impact on Irène, who preferred spending her free time reading poetry or swimming, sailing, skiing, or hiking. Frédéric was also known for his love of the outdoors. It was said that instead of keeping pictures of his family in his wallet, he carried a picture of a giant pike he had once caught on a fishing trip. He was a very sociable man, telling not only fish stories, but entertaining both colleagues and family with his wit and charm. As their children, Hélène and Pierre, grew, Irène became more interested in social movements and politics. An atheist and politi-

Georg von Hevesy, Swedish Radiochemist

Georg von Hevesy (1885-1966) developed radioactive tracer analysis, a method widely used to determine the movement of elements in chemistry and medicine. For this accomplishment—which had far-reaching consequences in physiology (a branch of biology that deals with the functions and chemical processes of cells, tissues, and organs), biochemistry, and mineralogy—he was awarded the 1943 Nobel Prize in chemistry. He was also the co-discoverer of the element hafnium. Hevesy began his lifelong research with radioactive tracers while working at the University of Manchester in England with the research team of English physicist **Ernest Rutherford** (1871-1937; for more information, see volume 3, pp. 805-813) beginning in 1911. There he was given the assignment of separating "radium-D," a decay product of the element radium, from a large pile of radioactive lead. Over many months, he tried every chemical separation he knew, but he was not successful. It is now known that radium-D is the radioactive isotope lead-210; it is, in other words, a form of lead that has the same number of protons and electrons (and therefore the same chemistry) as any other kind of lead, but with a different number of neutrons in its nucleus. Separation of isotopes can be done only by difficult physical methods, and chemical separation is impossible.

Having failed to separate the radium-D, Hevesy attempted to make something good out of a bad situation by using radium-D to trace the course of lead in chemical processes. By mixing a small amount of radium-D with regular lead, he could discover the amount of lead used up in a chemical reaction by measuring the amount of radioactivity in the end product. In the 1920s, Hevesy began to apply his work with radioactive lead tracers to biology, studying the amount of lead taken in by bean seedlings.

When Irène and Frédéric Joliot-Curie announced in 1934 that they had succeeded in producing artificial radioactive isotopes by alpha particle bombardment, Hevesy immediately saw great uses of this knowledge in his research. He used the same method to create radioactive phosphorus-32 from sulfur-32. This isotope was a major advance in the study of physiology. Phosphorus is an element central to all animal physiology, and the new isotope allowed researchers to follow the way the element was taken in, circulated, exchanged, and excreted from the body. A number of discoveries resulted from the use of this tracer, including information about the creation and distribution of deoxyribonucleic acid (DNA) and ribonucleic acid (RNA), the "genetic codes" that govern all aspects of development in living organisms.

cal leftist, she also took up the cause of woman's suffrage (the right to vote). She served as undersecretary of state in French leader Léon Blum's Popular Front government in 1936 and then was elected professor at the Sorbonne in 1937.

Research leads to nuclear fission

Continuing their work in physics during the late 1930s, Irène and Frédéric Joliot-Curie experimented with bombarding uranium nuclei with neutrons. They showed that uranium could be broken down into other radioactive elements. This groundbreaking experiment paved the way for another physicist, Otto Hahn, to prove that uranium bombarded with neutrons can be made to split into two atoms of comparable mass. This phenomenon, called fission, results in the release of large amounts of energy and is the foundation for the practical applications of nuclear energy—the generation of nuclear power and the atom bomb.

During the early part of World War II (1939-45), Frédéric and Irène both became part of the French Resistance, the movement that fought against the German Nazi forces (and the French forces that collaborated with them) that had taken over France. Frédéric became especially involved in political activities, becoming a member of the Communist Party in 1942 after a friend of his was killed by the Nazis. After being arrested twice for his activities, Frédéric went into hiding, and Irène and their children fled France for Switzerland.

Radical politics cause suspicion

After the war Irène returned to France and was appointed director of the Radium Institute. Frédéric was instrumental in convincing the post-war government of Charles de Gaulle to establish an Atomic Energy Commission in France, modeled after the similar agency in the United States. After being appointed its Commissioner, Frédéric oversaw the installation of a major nuclear research center. But with the onset of the Cold War, a period of tensions between the Soviet Union and

Western countries, his membership in the Communist Party and his radical activism made the French government suspicious of him. Fearing that his Communist politics would make him loyal to the Soviet Union instead of France, the government removed him from the position of high commissioner of Atomic Energy in 1950.

Radiation exposure causes death

While her health was slowly deteriorating, Irène continued to put in long days in the laboratory and to lecture and present papers on radioactivity. She and Frédéric spoke out on the use of nuclear energy for the cause of peace. Irène was a member of the World Peace Council and made several trips to the Soviet Union. Also a victim of Cold War suspicion because of her politics, Irène was rejected by the American Chemical Society when she applied for membership in 1954. Her final contribution to physics came as she helped plan a large particle accelerator (machine that bombards atomic nuclei with high-speed atomic particles) and laboratory at Orsay, south of Paris, in 1955. Her health worsened and on March 17, 1956, Irène Joliot-Curie died—as her mother had before her—of leukemia resulting from a lifetime of exposure to radiation.

Frédéric succeeded her as head of the Radium Institute and continued her efforts to build a new physics laboratory south of Paris. At the age of 58, with his liver badly damaged by exposure to radiation, Frédéric Joliot-Curie died following an operation to treat internal bleeding.

Further Readings

Opfell, Olga S., *The Lady Laureates: Women Who Have Won the Nobel Prize,* Scarecrow, 1978.

Pflaum, Rosalynd, *Grand Obsession: Madame Curie and Her World,* Doubleday, 1989.

Johannes Kepler

Born December 17, 1571
Weil, Germany
Died November 15, 1630
Regensburg, Germany

Johannes Kepler developed three laws of planetary motion that revolutionized astronomy and led to Sir Isaac Newton's discovery of the laws of gravity.

Johannes Kepler was born to a poor family in Weil, near Würtemburg, Germany, on December 17, 1571. His father served as a soldier in the duke's army and later owned a tavern where Johannes was employed from ages nine to twelve. His mother, Catherine, who was noted for her fiery temperament, also worked at the tavern and cared for her home and family.

When Kepler was only four years old, he suffered a severe attack of smallpox. The illness did permanent damage to his eyesight and left him very weak. For the rest of his life he was unable to go out at night because of his frail constitution. With outdoor activities severely limited, Kepler turned to reading and writing. He was fascinated by numbers and continually asked questions—especially about the way the universe worked.

Studies astronomy

At the age of seventeen Kepler enrolled at the University of Tübingen, where he studied astronomy (the study of objects in outer space) and religion and graduated second in his class. In college he was exposed to the ideas of **Nicolaus Copernicus** (1473-1543; for more information, see pp. 48-54), the first astronomer to assert that the Sun was the center of our solar system. The Catholic Church at that time held that Earth was the center of the universe, so Copernicus's position was strongly opposed. But Kepler believed in Copernicus's model and defended it in debates at his university. He earned a master's degree in 1591, and for the next two years worked within the Lutheran Church. Like his mother, however, Kepler had a fiery disposition, and he clashed with Lutheran authorities over the strictness of the church. In 1594, when the opportunity arose for him to teach astronomy at the University of Gratz, he left the church and became a professor.

Life of a sixteenth-century astronomer

During the sixteenth century, astronomy was closely tied to astrology. At that time, like today, astrology represented a not-quite scientific body of knowledge that asserted that the positions of the stars and planets dictate human destiny and control everything from weather patterns to political events. Therefore, the job of an astronomer in Kepler's time was not only to make accurate calendars but to forecast weather, prepare horoscopes, and make political predictions. Kepler's first years at Gratz were spent pursuing these activities, but he also spent long nights poring over books, making calculations, and guessing as to the nature of the universe.

First book and theory

Kepler sought to find a connection between the number of planets (then it was believed there were only six: Mercury, Venus, Earth, Mars, Jupiter, and Saturn), their times of revolution, and their distance from the Sun. In his 1596 publication *Mysterium Cosmographicum,* he put forth a mathematical hypothesis (theory) to explain such a connection. Although the hypothesis is now known to be flawed, at the time it was widely acclaimed and helped establish Kepler as a first-rate astronomer and intellectual.

Although Johannes Kepler struggled during most of his life and saw much of his work banned, he ultimately succeeded in revolutionizing astronomy. Kepler used many of the observations gathered by the Danish astronomer Tycho Brahe (pronounced 'Tee-ko 'Brahee), and together their work formed the basis of modern astronomy. Kepler's three laws of planetary motion proved that planets orbit a stationary star—in other words, Earth travels around the Sun, not vice versa as was widely believed—and provided the foundation for Sir Isaac Newton's laws of gravity.

After years of hard work and calculation, Kepler was thrilled at his first discovery and wrote: "The intense pleasure I have received from this discovery can never be told in words. I regretted no more the time wasted; I tired of no labour; I shunned no toil of reckoning, of days and nights spent in calculation, until I could see whether my hypothesis would agree with the orbits of Copernicus, or whether my joy was to vanish in air." The book captured the attention of two famed astronomers, Tycho Brahe (1546–1601) and **Galileo Galilei** (1564–1642; for more information, see pp. 100-109), who would later become very involved in Kepler's life and lead him to his greatest achievements.

Brahe and brilliance

Though Kepler had always been a brilliant thinker, he lacked the data to calculate, develop, and prove his theories. After his first book came out, he began corresponding with Danish astronomer Tycho Brahe, who had spent more than twenty years compiling celestial observations.

Kepler sent Brahe a copy of his book and the two began corresponding by letter. Although Brahe had an idea about the organization of the solar system that was very different from that of Copernicus and Kepler, he greatly respected Kepler's work. For several years, the two had friendly and frank exchanges in which Brahe continually tried to convert Kepler to his "Tychonic System"—which placed Earth at the center of the solar system, with the Sun and other planets revolving around it. Kepler politely but forcefully argued otherwise.

When Kepler was forced to leave his teaching position at Gratz in 1599, he called on Brahe, who was then Imperial Mathematician of the Holy Roman Empire. Brahe was by this time old and weak, and Kepler realized that no one had yet tapped his vast store of knowledge. He offered to examine Brahe's compilation of observations and use them to perfect theories of planetary motion. Brahe eagerly accepted Kepler's proposal, saying: "Come not as a stranger, but as a very welcome friend; come and share in my observations with such instruments as I have with me, and as a dearly beloved associate."

Kepler's first two laws of planetary motion

The timing could not have been better for the meeting of two such brilliant minds. Brahe was near death, and Kepler was able to access his lifetime's accumulation of knowledge before he passed away. Brahe put Kepler to work calculating the movements of Mars. Kepler also worked with Brahe on the *Rudolphine Tables* (which described planetary movements) and pledged, as the older astronomer's health worsened, that he would complete them. After Brahe's passing in 1601, Kepler was named Imperial Mathematician and continued to work at Brahe's observatory at Benatky Castle.

For six years Kepler struggled to explain the way the planets move. After trying hundreds of hypotheses, Kepler finally came up with a brilliant guess that was verified by Brahe's data. The vision of planets moving in ellipses (ovals) apparently came to Kepler in a dream; when he awoke, he spent the rest of the night and the next day testing his theory. At last he had discovered the first two laws of planetary motion: a planet orbits the Sun in an ellipse, and it moves faster when nearer the Sun and slower when farther away.

Setbacks and hardship

While Kepler searched for the answers to more questions about the planets, he suffered many hardships in his personal life. By 1611 both his wife and his young son had died. He was left alone to care for his two remaining small children.

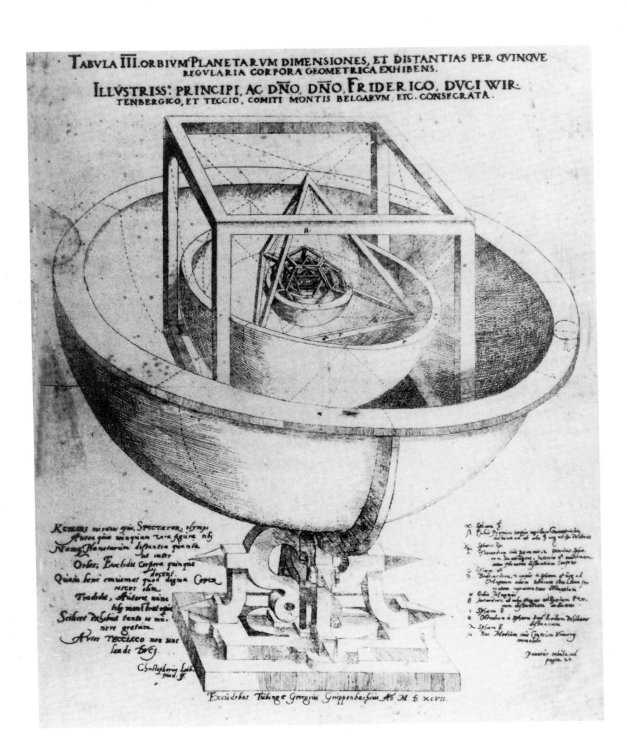

Kepler's life was further complicated by Emperor Rudolf II's death in 1612. The emperor had been his patron, and after he died, Kepler's salary was cut off. In order to provide for his children, Kepler was forced to leave Benatky and set aside work on Brahe's research.

Third law

Kepler once again became a professor of astronomy, this time at the university in Linz. To make extra money, he published an almanac that predicted future political events and weather patterns. In 1618, after sixteen years of investigation, Kepler finally hit upon his third law. Kepler's third law of planetary motion states that the square of the time of each planet's revolution is proportional to the cube of its mean (average) distance from the Sun. In other words, using this mathematical formula, you could calculate a planet's distance from the Sun if you knew how long it takes the planet to complete one orbit.

At age forty-seven Kepler had fulfilled his lifelong dream and lived to see it published. However, because his third law was based on the Copernican idea of a Sun-centered solar system, his book was banned by the Church. The church decree adversely affected his career; he was never able to secure a publisher for his work again.

Tables published

For an entire decade Kepler was unable to publish his own work, so he once again took up the *Rudolphine Tables,* which Brahe had begun. They were published in 1627, but Kepler had to pay for the printing himself. He had promised Brahe at his death he would see them published and though he was very poor, he fulfilled his great friend's last request.

Unfortunately, Kepler's last years were ones of hardship and struggle. He was owed a considerable amount of money from the Holy Roman Empire and in 1630 he traveled to Prague to petition the government for his past-due wages.

Giovanni Domenico Cassini, Astronomer

French astronomer Giovanni Domenico Cassini (1625-1712) was the director of the Paris Observatory from 1669 to 1710. Between 1671 and 1684, Cassini discovered four moons of Saturn in addition to Titan, which had been detected by Dutch astronomer Christiaan Huygens (1629-1695) in 1656. Cassini was also the first to notice a dark gap that split the famous ring around Saturn. It has since been called "Cassini's Division." He also correctly predicted that the rings were made of objects too small to be seen separately.

Cassini is best known for his calculations concerning the size of the solar system. He first established the distance between Earth and Mars by comparing the difference in the position of Mars in the sky as it was simultaneously observed from two different places on Earth. For these figures he used measurements made by himself in Paris and those made by his colleague Jean Richer (1630-1696) in French Guiana in South America. This value of the distance from Earth to Mars allowed Cassini to calculate the astronomical unit (AU) or the distance from Earth to the Sun. His figure of eighty-seven million miles is considered by modern astronomers to be about 7 percent too low. Tycho Brahe believed the distance to be five million miles, while Johannes Kepler estimated it at fifteen million miles. In comparison, it is clear that Cassini's astronomical unit gave the world its first accurate assessment of the vast size of the solar system.

However, on the trip he became very ill, and in November of 1630, at age fifty-nine, he died. He was buried at St. Peter's Church in Ratisbon, Germany.

Further Reading

Lodge, Oliver, *Pioneers of Science,* St. Martin's, 1913.

Ronan, Colin, *The Astronomers,* Hill & Wang, 1964.

Rosen, Edward, ed., *Kepler's Conversation with Galileo's Sidereal Messenger,* Johnson Reprint Corporation, 1965.

Har Gobind Khorana

Born c. January 9, 1922
Raipur, India

Har Gobind Khorana is considered a major contributor to the science of genetics (a branch of biology that deals with the heredity and variation of organisms). In addition to developing a relatively inexpensive method of synthesizing acetyl coenzyme A (pronounced 'uh-see-t'l ko-'en-zim), a complex molecule used in biochemical research, he succeeded in cracking the genetic code of yeast by synthesizing parts of a nucleic acid molecule—an achievement for which he shared the Nobel Prize for physiology or medicine in 1968. Khorana went on to do other significant work, including the synthesis of the first completely artificial gene.

Har Gobind Khorana helped identify the way chemical compounds are organized in the genetic code of deoxyribonucleic acid (DNA).

Education in India

Khorana was born around January 9, 1922, in the small village of Raipur, India. He was the youngest of five children of Ganpat Rai Khorana, a tax collector for the British colonial government, and Krishna (Devi) Khorana. His family, although poor, was one of the few literate families in his village. He received his early education under a tree in outdoor classes conducted by the village teacher, and he went on to attend high school in Multan, Punjab (India). Khorana later studied chemistry on a government scholarship at Punjab University in Lahore, graduating with honors in 1943 and receiving a master of science degree with honors in 1945.

After obtaining his M.S., Khorana went to the University of Liverpool in England on a Government of India Fellowship to study organic chemistry, which is the science of carbon compounds, particularly those found in living things. There he earned a Ph.D. in 1948 for his research on the structure of the bacterial pigment (a substance that gives color) violacein. From England, Khorana went to Zurich, Switzerland, to study certain alkaloids (organic bases). After a brief visit to India in 1949, he returned to England. From 1950 to 1952, Khorana worked at Cambridge University under English chemist Sir Alexander Todd (1907–), who later received the 1957 Nobel Prize for his work with nucleic acids (large molecules in the nucleus of the cell). While working with Todd, Khorana, too, became interested in the biochemistry (the study of chemical compounds and processes in living things) of nucleic acids.

Achieves international recognition

In 1952, Khorana took a position as director of the British Columbia Research Council's Organic Chemistry Section, located at the University of British Columbia in Vancouver, Canada. There he made his first contribution to the field of biochemistry when he and a colleague, John G. Moffat, announced in 1959 that they had developed a process for synthesizing, or artificially creating, acetyl coenzyme A, an essential molecule in the processing of proteins, fats, and carbohydrates within the human body. A complex structure, this coenzyme had previously been available only by an extremely expensive method of isolating the compound from yeast. But Moffat and Khorana were able to use a kind of scientific "recipe" to create the coenzyme from a mixture of chemical elements and compounds, instead of extracting it ready-made from yeast. Their new process was much cheaper and made the coenzyme more widely available for research. This work made Khorana an internationally-known figure in the scientific community.

Begins genetic research

In 1960, Khorana moved to the University of Wisconsin in Madison to accept a position as co-director of the Institute for Enzyme Research. He became a professor of biochemistry in 1962, and in 1964 was named to the Conrad A. Elvelijem Professorship of the life sciences. Khorana then began focusing his research on genetics—specifically, on the biochemistry of nucleic acids, the biosynthesis (the creation of a chemical compound in the body) of enzymes, and on deciphering the genetic code.

At the time Khorana began his research in genetics, scientists already knew much about genes and how they determine heredity, the set of traits that are biologically passed on from parents to children. Researchers had discovered that genes are located on chromosomes in the cell nucleus, and that genes are made of deoxyribonucleic acid (DNA), a nucleic acid that controls the biochemical processes of the cell and governs an organism's inherited traits. DNA has a double-helix shape that resembles a spiral staircase with regularly spaced steps, each step consisting of a pair of chemical compounds called nucleotides. The four different types of nucleotides are arranged on the staircase in a pattern of heredity-carrying code "words."

To decipher this code, scientists needed to learn how those words were translated into a second "alphabet" consisting of 20

IMPACT

With other researchers, Har Gobind Khorana helped to create a more complete picture of the way chemical compounds are organized in DNA, deoxyribonucleic acid (pronounced dee-'ahk-see-ri-bo-noo-klee-ik), allowing scientists to better understand the way physical traits are passed on from one generation to the next. He also advanced the field of genetics by finding a way to synthesize, or artificially create, part of a nucleic acid molecule. Not stopping there, Khorana eventually synthesized an even more complex structure—a gene, the structure that controls heredity. Khorana's discoveries have provided researchers with tools for identifying the genes responsible for specific traits, opening the door for new possibilities in the medical diagnosis and treatment of genetic disorders.

Khorana with a model of the double helix structure of DNA

types of amino acids, the building blocks of protein. Part of this translation had been accomplished prior to Khorana's work. The DNA in the nucleus of a cell causes another nucleic acid called messenger ribonucleic acid (mRNA) to be produced; the messenger RNA then attaches itself to ribosomes, where the cell's proteins are produced. Another type of RNA, called transfer RNA, transports loose amino acids to the ribosomes, where messenger RNA uses them to construct proteins.

Scientists knew that the code word on each transfer RNA molecule indicated the kind of amino acid it would deliver and and where it would deliver it—to a complimentary messenger RNA that acted as a matching puzzle piece where the amino acid would fit. They had also figured out that there were 64 possible combinations of nucleotides, each with its own signal. What they did not know was which nucleotide word called for which amino acid.

Increases Knowledge of DNA

In 1961, Dr. Marshall Warren Nirenberg (1927-), a biochemist at the National Institutes of Health, successfully decoded most of the messages in the nucleotides. Khorana carried Nirenberg's work even further, adding more important details. In 1964 he synthesized parts of the nucleic acid molecule; he later was able to duplicate each of the 64 possible genetic words in the DNA staircase. He mapped out the exact order of the nucleotides, and showed that the code is always transmitted by three-letter words known as triplets, or codons. He also learned that certain nucleotides order the cell to start or stop making proteins.

Shares Nobel Prize

Khorana's research was based in part on work done separately by both Nirenberg and biochemist Robert W. Holley (1922-1993) of Cornell University, who identified all the parts of a complete nucleic acid molecule in 1966. For their contributions to deciphering the genetic code, these three scientists

Robert W. Holley, American Biochemist

Robert W. Holley (1922-1993) is best known for isolating transfer ribonucleic acid (tRNA) and explaining its structure. Essentially, tRNA "translates" the genetic instructions within cells by first "reading" genes, the fundamental units of heredity, and then creating proteins—the building blocks of the body—from amino acids. In the 1950s, Holley started investigating how the order of nucleotides (pronounced 'noo-klee-uh-tids), the "steps" in the "spiral staircase" shape of deoxyribonucleic acid (DNA), control the order of amino acids in proteins. It had been known that DNA did not directly create protein, but instead copied itself into strands of RNA. It was not known, however, how these long strands of RNA, called messenger RNA or mRNA, functioned in the creation of proteins. Holley believed that the much smaller tRNA molecules played a key role in this process.

Holley and his colleagues at Cornell University eventually succeeded in isolating a pure sample of tRNA. Holley then studied the molecular organization of the substance to get clues about how it worked. He knew that three consecutive bases, called a triplet or codon, make up the genetic code or instruction for the production of a protein. Other scientists had found that each triplet matches a particular amino acid. Holley found that tRNA produces triplets that allow it to match up, or bond, with mRNA. Once attached, amino acids from the two structures are combined into a new protein, following the chemical pattern—the instructions from the DNA—found in the mRNA. For his explanation of this process, Holley was one of three scientists to share the 1968 Nobel Prize for physiology or medicine.

were awarded the 1968 Nobel Prize for physiology or medicine. At the presentation ceremony, the three were commended for having "written the most exciting chapter in modern biology."

Creates first artificial gene

Two years later, Khorana made another contribution to the field of genetics when he and his colleagues succeeded in synthesizing the first artificial gene of yeast. Khorana announced his achievement in a characteristically modest way, by informing a small gathering of biochemists at the University of Wisconsin in June of 1970. He also announced that he and most of his research team would move to the Massachusetts Institute of Technology in the fall of that year. As he explained to a friend, "You stay intellectually alive longer if you change your environment every so often." Khorana joined MIT's faculty as the Alfred P. Sloan Professor of Biology and Chemistry.

Khorana's accomplishments in the laboratory also include the artificial synthesis of another gene found in Escherichia coli, an intestinal bacteria known commonly as E. coli. Outside the laboratory, his professional activities include membership in several scientific societies, including the National Academy of Sciences and the American Academy of Arts and Sciences. He also served on the editorial board of the *Journal of the American Chemical Society* for many years, and published more than 200 articles on technical subjects in that journal and other professional publications.

Khorana married Esther Elizabeth Sibler in 1952. The couple has two daughters, Julia Elizabeth and Emily Anne, and one son, Dave Roy. Khorana became an American citizen in 1966. Extremely committed to his work, he seldom takes time off, and once went 12 years without taking a vacation. He takes daily long walks, carrying with him an index card to record any ideas that might come to him. He also enjoys going on hikes and listening to music.

Further Reading

"Biographies of Three Nobel Laureates," *New York Times,* October 17, 1968, p. 41.

"The Code-breakers," *Time,* October 25, 1968, pp. 84-85.

Current Biography Yearbook, H. W. Wilson, 1970, pp. 222-24.

Nobel Prize Winners, H. W. Wilson, 1987, pp. 546-48.

Flemmie Pansy Kittrell

Born December 25, 1904
Henderson, North Carolina
Died October 3, 1980
Washington, D.C.

Flemmie Pansy Kittrell was an internationally known nutritionist (someone who studies the ways in which living organisms take in and make use of food) who drew much-needed attention to the importance of the home environment in the development of children and in family welfare. During her more than forty years as an educator, she traveled a great deal, helping to improve home-life conditions in many poor nations. She was a founder of Howard University's school of human ecology (the study of how people are affected by their physical and social environment) and the recipient of several major awards. The first African American woman to earn a Ph.D. in nutrition, she believed that women could play an important role in the world and pushed for higher education for women everywhere.

Family stresses learning

Kittrell was born in Henderson, North Carolina, on Christmas Day, 1904. She was the youngest daughter of Alice

Flemmie Pansy Kittrell was a well-known nutritionist who made important contributions to improving the upbringing of children.

141

Mills Kittrell and James Lee Kittrell, both of whom were descended from African American and Cherokee families. Learning was very important to Kittrell's parents, and her father often read stories and poetry to her and her eight brothers and sisters. Her parents knew the importance of encouragement and the children frequently received praise for their efforts and achievements.

After graduating from high school in North Carolina, Kittrell attended Hampton Institute in Virginia, receiving her bachelor of science degree in 1928. With the encouragement of her professors she enrolled at Cornell University, though there were not many black women during that era who became graduate students. In 1930 Kittrell received her master of arts degree from Cornell and in 1938 she was awarded her Ph.D. in nutrition with honors.

Broadens study of home economics

Kittrell had been offered her first job teaching home economics, the study of the practices involved in homemaking, in 1928 at Bennett College in Greensboro, North Carolina. After finishing her Ph.D. she returned to Bennett. She later became dean of women and the head of the home economics department at Hampton Institute in 1940, where she remained until 1944. In that year Kittrell accepted the personal offer of Howard University president Mordecai Johnson to head the home economics department at Howard University in Washington, D.C. At Howard, Kittrell developed a course of study that broadened the common perception of home economics so that it included such fields as child development research.

Studies nutrition around the world

In 1947 Kittrell began a lifelong program of international activism, carrying out a nutritional survey of the West African nation of Liberia sponsored by the United States government. Her findings concerning "hidden hunger," a type of malnutrition that occurred in 90 percent of the African nation's population, led to important changes in Liberian agricultural and fishing industries. Kittrell then received a 1950 Fulbright award that allowed her to work with Baroda University in India, where she developed an educational plan for nutritional research. In 1953, Kittrell went back to India as a teacher of home economics classes and nutritional seminars. Then, in 1957, Kittrell headed a team that traveled to Japan and Hawaii to research home economics-related activities in these cultures. Between 1957 and 1961, Kittrell was the leader of three more tours to Africa.

Founds school of human ecology

During this period Kittrell continued to hold her post at Howard University. In 1963, after struggling for fifteen years to obtain a building for a school of human ecology, a new facility for this purpose was finally dedicated. This innovative building attracted national attention as it provided a working example for the nation's Head Start program, a pre-kindergarten program to help poor children that was just getting off the ground. Kittrell retired from Howard University in 1972 and was named Emeritus Professor of Nutrition.

⊨IMPACT⊨

Nutritionist Flemmie Pansy Kittrell was a pioneer in applying scientific practices to the study of the home environment, particularly as it affects the development of children. Because of her research into the factors that affect child development, Kittrell was one of the experts in the field who helped design and put into practice the Head Start program. This government-funded program was created to provide poor children with proper nutrition and a stimulating learning environment so they could have the best chance possible of succeeding in school. Kittrell realized that proper nutrition and a supportive family life were critical to the physical and mental growth of children, and she spent much of her career traveling around the world educating people about how to improve in these areas.

Honored for accomplishments

Kittrell's achievements were recognized with a number of awards and honors. In 1961 she received the Scroll of Honor from the National Council of Negro Women in recognition of her special services. Also, a scholarship fund was founded in honor of Kittrell's career by the American Home Economics Association. Kittrell continued to work despite her retirement from teaching in 1972. From 1974 to 1976 she was a Cornell Visiting Senior Fellow, and she served as a Moton Center Senior Research Fellow in 1977 and a Fulbright lecturer in India in 1978. Kittrell died unexpectedly of cardiac arrest on October 3, 1980, in Washington, D.C. During her life she had credited much of her success not only to her education, but also to the strength, love, and family unity she enjoyed in her parents' home, where learning was a very important aspect of family life.

Further Reading

Sammons, Vivian O., *Blacks in Science and Medicine,* Hemisphere Publishing, 1990, pp. 143-44.

Smith, Jesse Carney, editor, *Notable Black American Women,* Gale, 1992, pp. 636-38.

Lewis H. Latimer

Born September 4, 1848
Chelsea, Massachusetts
Died December 11, 1928
Flushing, New York

Despite his lack of any formal education, Lewis H. Latimer, the son of an escaped slave, became a member of the research team of American inventor **Thomas Alva Edison** (1847-1931; for more information, see volume 1, pp. 244-254) and made several outstanding contributions to the development and commercialization of the electric light. Latimer was a self-taught draftsman who began as an office boy and rose to become chief draftsman for the General Electric company.

Lewis Howard Latimer was born in Chelsea, Massachusetts, on September 4, 1848. His father, George A. Latimer, a former slave in Virginia who had escaped to Boston to gain his freedom, deserted the family when Lewis was ten years old, forcing the boy to leave school and take a job to help support his mother, Rebecca (Smith) Latimer, and her other four children.

Lewis H. Latimer made important contributions to the early electric light industry.

Inventor Lewis H. Latimer was a key figure in the early years of the electrical lighting industry. While working for the United States Electric Lighting Company in the early 1880s, he invented a way of improving upon Thomas Edison's recent invention of the electric incandescent lamp. Latimer's new lamp lasted longer and was less expensive to produce and helped his company become a major competitor with Edison's electric light company. But when Latimer joined Edison's research team in 1884, he helped give Edison the lead again. Latimer not only continued to develop important improvements in electrical lighting, he served as a witness in court battles that eventually confirmed that Edison was the inventor of the carbon filament—a key part of the incandescent lamp.

Becomes a self-taught draftsman

In 1864, Latimer turned sixteen and fought in the Civil War (1860-64), enlisting in the Union Navy and serving on the gunboat U.S.S. Massasoit. Eventually, he became a lieutenant in the 4th Battalion of the Massachusetts Volunteer Militia. After receiving an honorable discharge in 1865, Latimer returned to Boston and accepted a job as an office boy in the patent firm of Crosby and Gould. It was there that Latimer first became interested in the craft of mechanical drawing, or drafting, and he soon began to teach himself the art.

An application for a patent (a government grant giving an inventor the right to be the only person to make or sell an invention for a set length of time) required that very detailed and accurate drawings of an invention be submitted, and Latimer was so fascinated by this craft that he saved his money to buy second-hand drafting tools and learned how to use them by reading library textbooks. Studying every night after work, Latimer eventually felt he was ready to ask his employers for permission to make the drawings for an invention; once they saw how skilled he was, they promoted him to the position of junior draftsman.

After ten years, Latimer was promoted to chief draftsman for Crosby and Gould. In this position he was responsible for perfecting the final drawings that decided the success or failure of patent applications. One of the firm's clients was American inventor Alexander Graham Bell (1847-1922), and it fell to Latimer to execute the drawings for Bell's historic invention, the telephone; in 1876, Bell received his patent.

Creates better carbon filament

Three years later, Latimer left Crosby and Gould to join the United States Electric Lighting Company. This new firm was the creation of American inventor and entrepreneur Hiram S. Maxim (1840-1916) and was one of the first to enter the new and rapidly expanding field of electric lighting. Thomas Edison had just invented the first electric incandescent (glowing) lamp, and Maxim was determined to improve upon Edison's invention and take the lead. With Latimer's help he did just that. By 1882, Latimer had invented an improved carbon filament (a thread-like object in a lamp that glows when electricity passes through it) that lasted longer at high temperatures than Edison's; in addition, he devised a cheaper method of making the filaments. The new light was called the "Maxim lamp" and was used in railroad stations throughout the United States, Canada, and other countries.

Begins long career at General Electric

Latimer left Maxim's company in 1882 and joined the Olmstead Electric Light and Power Company of New York where he could continue his experimentation on improved filaments. Staying there for only two years, Latimer then joined one of Edison's companies, the Excelsior Electric Company, in 1884. There Latimer worked as a draftsman and engineer and was able to continue his pioneering electrical research. After joining Edison, Latimer never switched companies again; when Excelsior later became part of the larger Edison General Electric Company—which became known simply as GE—Latimer became one of its key members.

Testifies in patent battle

The electric light industry by the end of the 1880s was full of confusion and arguments. The federal courts were asked to settle many lawsuits involving patent rights for incandescent lighting. One of the most significant legal contests involved Edison and the combined rival forces of the Westinghouse and Thompson-Houston companies. The legal issue centered on Edison's 1880 invention of the carbon filament lamp and his right to be the only person allowed to manufacture and sell it. The United States Electric Lighting Company, a smaller company within Westinghouse and Latimer's old employer, challenged Edison's claim to be the sole inventor of the carbon filament. The United States Electric Lighting Company planned to prove that it had played a role in inventing the carbon filament because a number of patents had been awarded to people in the company, including Latimer, for work on carbon filaments. Latimer was thus in a unique position. Edison needed to show that Latimer's own early designs did not qualify as patentable inventions. So he promoted Latimer to the company's legal department, where he began a career as an expert witness. His testimony aided Edison in eventually overcoming all the challenges of the other companies. Latimer would continue as an expert witness in many of the related trials that followed. He remained with General Electric until 1912, when his expertise as a witness was no longer needed.

Remains active in later years

A man of many talents, Latimer did not simply retire when he left General Electric at age 64. He worked as an independent electrical and mechanical engineer for another sixteen years and taught mechanical drawing to immigrants at the Henry Street Settlement in New York City. Latimer also loved to write, and in 1925 his friends and family published his *Poems of Love and Life*. Writing was nothing new to Latimer, however; in 1890 he had written a groundbreaking book on electric lighting, *Incandescent Electric Lighting: A Practical Description of the Edison System*. Latimer's curiosity led him to study art and music as well, but his major interest remained invention. He had demonstrated his abilities as an inventor as early as 1874, when he received a patent for an improved railroad car water closet (toilet) while working for Crosby and Gould. Later Latimer also obtained patents for such varied devices as an apparatus for cooling and disinfecting, a rack for hats, coats, and umbrellas that locked, and a new device for supporting books.

When Latimer died in Flushing, New York, on December 11, 1928, he left behind his wife, Mary Wilson (Lewis) Latimer, whom he had married on December 10, 1873, and two children, Louise Rebecca and Emma Jeanette. He had been a member of a wide range of organizations such as the New York Electrical Society, the Grand Army of the Republic, and the Negro Society for Historical Research. Most significantly, Latimer was the only African American member of the famous team of inventors called the "Edison Pioneers." On May 10, 1968, the Lewis H. Latimer public school in New York City was named in his honor, dedicated to the memory of a man who, while not as well-known as some of his fellow inventors, was a key figure in the history of electric lighting.

Further Reading

Contemporary Black Biography, Volume 4, Gale, 1993, pp. 148-50.

Dictionary of American Negro Biography, Norton, 1982, pp. 385-86.

Hayden, Robert C., *Eight Black American Inventors,* Addison-Wesley, 1972, pp. 78-92.

Klein, Aaron E., *The Hidden Contributors: Black Scientists and Inventors in America,* Doubleday, 1971, pp. 97-108.

Rita Levi-Montalcini

Born April 22, 1909
Turin, Italy

Nobel Prize-winner Rita Levi-Montalcini was the co-discoverer of the substance that causes nerve growth.

Rita Levi-Montalcini is recognized for her groundbreaking research on nerve cell growth. Her early experiments were conducted in private in a small laboratory in her home because, as an Italian Jew during the time of Benito Mussolini (1883-1945) and the fascist control of Italy, she was not allowed to hold a professional position. After World War II (1939-45), however, Levi-Montalcini returned to university laboratories to pursue her work. During the 1950s she discovered a protein in the human nervous system that she named the nerve growth factor (NGF). She later worked with biochemist Stanley Cohen (1922-) at Washington University in St. Louis, Missouri, where the two scientists succeeded in isolating, or obtaining a sample of, that substance. Their work has proven useful in the study of several disorders, including Alzheimer's disease, cancer, and birth defects. Levi-Montalcini's and Cohen's work was recognized in 1986 when they were jointly awarded the Nobel Prize for physiology or medicine. Levi-Montalcini became the fourth woman to receive the Nobel in that field.

Decides on medical career

Levi-Montalcini, the third of four children of Adamo Levi and Adele Montalcini, was born on April 22, 1909, into an upper-middle-class Jewish family in Turin, Italy. She had a traditional upbringing, and her father decided that she would be educated at an all-girls' high school that prepared young women for marriage. When she was eighteen, she graduated from high school, where she had been recognized as an extremely intelligent student. But because of the limited education that her family had chosen for her, she was unable to enter a university. Levi-Montalcini was uncertain what she wanted to do with her life, but she did know that she didn't want to get married and have children. It wasn't until three years later, when her beloved governess was stricken with cancer, that she decided to become a doctor.

After convincing her father to let her enter medical school, Levi-Montalcini passed the entrance exams with high marks. She enrolled in the Turin School of Medicine in 1930, where she studied under Dr. Giuseppe Levi, a well-known histologist (a scientist who studies microscopic plant and animal tissues) and embryologist (a person who studies the development of the body before birth). With Levi, Levi-Montalcini began research on the nervous system (the bodily system that includes the brain, spinal cord, and nerves). She graduated from medical school in 1936 and became Levi's research assistant.

In the late 1930s Italy was governed by fascists. Fascism is a political system that promotes the supposed needs of the nation—and often of a particular race—at the expense of individual human rights; a fascist government is led by a dictator, is characterized by centralized control of all aspects of society, and is highly repressive of all forms of opposition. "Racial laws" were established in fascist Italy and Jews were not allowed to work as professionals. Levi-Montalcini was forced to resign from her academic and clinical posts in 1938. The following year, she accepted a position at the Neurological Institute in Brussels, Belgium. When that country was invaded by Nazi Germany in 1939 at the beginning of World War II, she decided to return to her homeland.

Neurobiologist Rita Levi-Montalcini played a leading role in discovering nerve growth factor, or NGF, a protein that stimulates the growth of nerve cells. This knowledge of how nerve cells are created has led other researchers to investigate how NGF can be used to fight diseases that destroy nerve cells, such as Alzheimer's disease and cancer. Levi-Montalcini's work was considered so important to medical science that she was named a co-winner of the Nobel Prize for physiology or medicine in 1986.

Conducts research in hiding

Upon returning to Italy, Levi-Montalcini went to live in Turin with her family. Restrictions imposed upon Jews had increased during her absence, and Levi-Montalcini was forced to set up a private laboratory in her bedroom in order to continue her work. Again working with Levi, who had also been banned from his academic post, Levi-Montalcini began researching the nervous system of chicken embryos (developing unborn animals). In an autobiographical article published in *Women Scientists: The Road to Liberation,* Levi-Montalcini recalled: "Looking back to that period I wonder how I could have found so much interest in, and devoted myself with such enthusiasm to, the study of a small neuroembryological problem, when all the values I cherished were being crushed, and the triumphant advance of the Germans all over Europe seemed to herald the end of Western civilization. The answer may be found in the well-known refusal of human beings to accept reality at its face value, whether this be the fate of the individual, of a country, or of the human race." Her research at the time, in fact, laid the groundwork for her discovery of NGF.

By 1942 the bombing of Turin by the Allied forces (the countries fighting Nazi Germany and fascist Italy) forced Levi-Montalcini and her family to move to the countryside. There she continued to experiment on chicken embryos in order to study how nerve cells are differentiated, or how they are formed and assigned a particular function in the developing body. Respected German-born neuroembryologist (a person who studies the nervous system in embryos) Viktor Hamburger (1900-) had conducted studies on the same topic, and he believed that nerve cells found their appropriate places in the body by following signals sent out by specific organs. Levi-Montalcini had a different hypothesis (an untested idea):

she thought that a specific nutrient (a substance that provides nourishment) was essential for nerve growth.

When Nazi troops invaded northern Italy in 1943, Levi-Montalcini was again forced to move, this time to Florence, where she remained for the duration of the war under a false name. After Florence was freed from Nazi control in 1944, Levi-Montalcini worked as a doctor in a refugee camp. When northern Italy was liberated the following year, she went back to her post as research assistant to Levi in Turin. Hamburger, who was interested in a paper Levi-Montalcini had published on her wartime experiments, contacted her in 1946, inviting her to fill a visiting research position at Washington University in St. Louis. This temporary position ultimately lasted more than three decades.

Identifies nerve growth factor

Levi-Montalcini's early work at Washington University involved further experimentation on the growth processes of chicken embryos. In this research, she made observations that proved her theory about the existence of a factor that provided the essential nutrients for nerve cell differentiation. In 1950 she began studying mouse tumors that had been grafted (surgically connected) to chicken embryos; a scientist named Elmer Bueker had earlier demonstrated that this procedure would create the growth of nerve cells. After repeating Bueker's experiment, Levi-Montalcini reached a different conclusion. Instead of agreeing that the nerve cells grew in the chicken embryo as a response to the presence of the tumor, she realized that the nerve cells grew out of the tumor itself. In order to do this the tumor had to release a substance that caused the growth.

Collaborates with Cohen

Traveling to Rio de Janeiro, Brazil, in 1952, Levi-Montalcini further tested her hypothesis using cultures (living material grown in a laboratory from a cell sample) of tissue cells. Her tissue culture experiments were highly successful in

Stanley Cohen, American Biochemist

Biochemist Stanley Cohen (1922-) was a pioneer in the study of growth factors—the nutrients that determine how cells are differentiated, or take on specialized roles in the body. He is best known for isolating, or obtaining a sample of, nerve growth factor (NGF), the first known growth factor. He later discovered epidermal growth factor (EGF), the growth factor that creates skin cells.

In the early 1950s, neurobiologist Rita Levi-Montalcini had evidence proving the existence of nerve growth factor. She turned to Cohen, a colleague of hers at Washington University in St. Louis, Missouri, to help her isolate NGF. By 1956 Cohen succeeded in extracting NGF from a mouse tumor, and later found it in snake venom and the salivary glands of male mice. By the late 1950s he was able to purify NGF, allowing Levi-Montalcini to study its effects on the nervous system of rats. For this work, the two scientists were honored with the 1986 Nobel Prize in physiology or medicine.

Stanley Cohen receiving Nobel Prize in medicine.

Cohen left Washington University in 1959 to join a research group in Nashville, Tennessee, where he continued his work with growth factors. He found that baby mice injected with unpurified NGF opened their eyes several days earlier than untreated mice. Cohen searched for the mystery substance in the unpurified NGF that caused this to happen. By 1962, he had extracted and purified the unknown substance, a protein that promoted the growth of skin cells and the cornea (the outer covering of the eye). He named the substance epidermal growth factor (EGF). This protein has become an important part of treating severe burns; EGF can help burned skin to heal more quickly and can help skin grafts (pieces of healthy skin) bond to damaged tissue.

proving the presence of a nerve-growth substance in the tumor. She still, however, had not isolated a sample of this substance, which she called "the nerve-growth promoting agent" and later labeled nerve growth factor. Upon returning to Washington University, Levi-Montalcini worked with American biochemist Stanley Cohen between 1953 and 1959. During that time, they extracted NGF from snake venom and the salivary glands of male mice. Through these experiments, Cohen was able to determine the chemical structure of NGF, as well as produce NGF antibodies, or substances that can stop NGF from working in the body.

Levi-Montalcini continued her research into NGF. When she returned to Italy in 1961, she established a laboratory at the Higher Institute of Health in Rome to perform joint NGF research with colleagues at Washington University. By 1969 Levi-Montalcini had established and become director of the Institute of Cell Biology of the Italian National Research Council in Rome. Working six months out of the year at the Institute of Cell Biology and the other six months at Washington University, Levi-Montalcini maintained labs in Rome and St. Louis until 1977, at which time she became a full-time resident of Italy.

During this time she received numerous awards for her work. One special moment of recognition occurred in 1968 when she became the tenth woman to be elected to the National Academy of Sciences. Despite her success, Levi-Montalcini's laboratory was the only one conducting NGF research for many years. Later researchers, however, realized the important role that nerve fiber growth could play in treating degenerative diseases (diseases in which organs or tissues deteriorate and stop functioning properly) and have continued the work that Levi-Montalcini began in the late 1930s.

Receives Nobel Prize

Levi-Montalcini remains active in the scientific community. She has held the title of professor emeritus at Washington University since 1977 and has contributed a great deal to scientific studies and programs in her native country of Italy. After winning the Nobel Prize in 1986, she was appointed president of the Italian Multiple Sclerosis Association and also became the first woman member of the Pontifical Academy of Sciences in Rome. In 1987 she was awarded the National Medal of Science, the highest honor among American scientists.

Keeping up-to-date with the latest scientific trends, Levi-Montalcini continues to conduct research at the Institute of Cell Biology in Rome, focusing on the importance of NGF in the immune and endocrine systems (endocrine refers to the bodily structures that produce hormones, which are substances that stimulate cell activity). Additionally, with her twin sister, who is an artist, Levi-Montalcini has established educational youth programs that provide counseling and grants for teenagers interested in the arts or sciences. Levi-Montalcini's work has profoundly increased the understanding of human biochemistry and has markedly influenced the work of three generations of scientists.

Further Reading

Holloway, Marguerite, "Finding the Good in the Bad," *Scientific American,* January 1993, pp. 32, 36.

Levi-Montalcini, Rita, *In Praise of Imperfection: My Life and Work,* Basic Books, 1988.

Levi-Montalcini, Rita, "Reflections on a Scientific Adventure," *Women Scientists: The Road to Liberation,* edited by Derek Richter, Macmillan, 1982, pp. 99-117.

Levine, Joe, "Lives of Spirit and Dedication," *Time,* October 27, 1986, pp. 66-68.

Marx, Jean L., "The 1986 Nobel Prize for Physiology or Medicine," *Science,* October 31, 1986, pp. 543-44.

Randall, Frederika, "The Heart and Mind of a Genius," *Vogue,* March 1987, pp. 480, 536.

Schmeck, Harold M., Jr., "Two Pioneers in Growth of Cells Win Nobel Prize," *New York Times,* October 14, 1986, pp. A1, C3.

Suro, Roberto, "Unraveler of Mysteries," *New York Times,* October 14, 1986, p. C3.

Carolus Linnaeus

Born May 23, 1707
Södra Råshult, Småland, Sweden
Died January 10, 1778
Uppsala, Sweden

Carolus Linnaeus spent his entire life studying and classifying living things. His childhood fascination with plants grew into a scientific career in which he became the most respected botanist (scientist who studies plants) in Europe. He strongly believed in creating and maintaining a system of classifying plants and animals that would be used by the entire scientific world. By devising a system that categorized living things according to similarities in physical characteristics, Linnaeus created a logical structure that has remained in place for more than 200 years. This represented a major turning point in botany and zoology (the study of animals) in which the 2,000-year-old ideas of Aristotle were abandoned in favor of a system that better fit the expanding scientific knowledge of the time.

Carolus Linnaeus created the modern system used to classify living things.

The "little botanist"

Linnaeus was born in Södra Råshult, Sweden, on May 23, 1707. He was the oldest of the five children of Nils Linnaeus, a

157

By classifying plants and animals in specific categories, scientists have a way of sharing information about the huge number of species of living things in the world. Before the time of botanist Carl Linnaeus, there was no agreed upon way of categorizing and naming newly discovered plants and animals. Linnaeus created an outline of all the types of living things, separating types of plants and animals primarily based on the way in which they reproduce. He also declared that all living things should be given a scientific name created with the Latin terms for their genus and species. This provided a logical system of classification that soon became the accepted method of scientists worldwide. Today, new species are still labeled and named according to the system devised by Linnaeus in the 1700s.

clergyman who had a great love of flowers. Linnaeus grew up in the Swedish town of Stenbrohult, where his father kept a small botanical garden on the grounds of his parsonage (official residence of a clergyman). The young Linnaeus had his own little garden there, which he tended with such care and enthusiasm that he earned the nickname "little botanist." Linnaeus's early love of the natural world also was inspired by books that he read. His father gave him a copy of *Historia Animalium* by the ancient Greek philosopher Aristotle (384-322 B.C.), and the book became one of Linnaeus's favorites.

In 1716, Linnaeus entered a Latin school in the nearby city of Växjö, where natural history became his favorite subject. Overall he was only an average student, but his delight in learning about plants distinguished him from others. Although he entered the University of Lund in 1727 to study medicine, he maintained his contact with plants on the many botanical excursions he took in the area around the university. One year later he moved to the University of Uppsala, which was considered a better school for medicine. Upon arriving there, Linnaeus was disappointed to find that Uppsala's medical program did not have much more to offer than the University of Lund. But Uppsala did have something that made up for the shortcoming: a botanical garden containing rare foreign plants.

Investigates reproduction in plants

At Uppsala, Linnaeus pursued his botanical research with even more energy. He was particularly fascinated with the new concept of plant sexuality—the idea that plants have "male" and "female" parts that must work together to fertilize the plant and produce new seeds. He saw the possibility of using the sexual characteristics and structures of plants as a basis for a way to organize all types of plants into separate categories. Linnaeus presented his first thoughts about a sexual system of classification in a 1730 paper that he showed to his professor of medicine. The teacher was impressed with Linnaeus's abilities and gave him the position of lecturer in botany at the university.

Conducts botanical expeditions

During his student years at Uppsala, Linnaeus continued to go on botanical expeditions. In 1732 he made a five-month trip to the Arctic region of Lappland, gathering information about the little-known plants and people of the mountainous area. Two years later, he traveled to Dalarna in central Sweden to make a survey of the natural resources there for the Swedish government. It was during this trip that Linnaeus met Sara Moraea, to whom he became engaged.

Publishes major work

In order to complete his medical degree, Linnaeus moved to Holland in 1735. He stayed there for about three years; during that time he was awarded an M.D. and published a number of important works that earned him a reputation as the leading botanist in Europe. In 1735 he published *Systema Naturae,* a small but important book in which he first presented the basic outline of his new system for classifying and naming plants, animals, and minerals. This was the first published work in which Linnaeus presented his system for grouping types of plants. He intended *Systema Naturae* to be a complete and authoritative work containing all known information relating to natural history; to keep up with new information, Linnaeus published new versions of the book periodically. By the tenth edition, published in 1758 and 1759, the book—which by then included plant and animal species—had grown to a two-volume work of over 1,000 pages.

In 1739 Linnaeus returned to Sweden and began practicing medicine. That same year he married Sara Moraea, with whom he would have six children. Two years later he became the chair of botany, dietetics, and materia medica (a branch of science that deals with the uses, sources, and nature of drugs) at the University of Uppsala. For the rest of his life, Linnaeus remained in this position, while his fame as a top botanist spread throughout the world because of his work in replacing Aristotle's system of classification with a more scientific and useful method.

The need for a new system

Aristotle had devised the first classification system more than 2,000 years earlier when he established the basic principles of dividing and subdividing types of plants and animals into different categories. At that time, only about a thousand species were known. Therefore, he grouped them into very simple categories. Animals were divided into only two groups—creatures with backbones and without backbones. Plants were divided into different categories that dealt mostly with size and appearance. By the sixteenth century, however, the system was proving to be less and less adequate as the body of knowledge of plants and animals grew. As Europeans explored and traveled to other places around the world, they brought back numerous new plants; between 1550 and 1770 the number of plants known by Europeans quadrupled. Aristotle's system was not a convenient way of categorizing all the new specimens, so modified systems were developed. But scientists could not agree on which new system to use—they all seemed complex and difficult.

New method becomes scientific standard

Linnaeus's new system provided a well-organized way of classifying known plants and animals, while at the same time providing a method of naming and grouping new specimens. In creating his system, Linnaeus's primary consideration was the number of observable characteristics of the organism,

Georges Cuvier, French Naturalist

Although Georges Cuvier (1769-1832) was trained as an anatomist (a scientist who studies the structure of living organisms), his contribution to the science of biology and the organization of plants and animals was so substantial that he is known today as the founder of comparative anatomy and paleontology (the study of early life forms through the examination of fossils). Throughout his academic career, Cuvier conducted zoological research (research relating to animals); in 1805 he published his first work, *Lessons in Comparative Anatomy.* After he discovered the fossil of the flying dinosaur called the pterodactyl (pronounced ter-uh-'dak-t'l)—which he named—he assembled a vast collection of animal fossils for research and study.

Cuvier's thorough examination of animal specimens and fossils convinced him that the system for classifying animals developed by Carolus Linnaeus did not acknowledge the high level of development of some animals. Linnaeus's system was based mainly on the outward appearance of animals; Cuvier modified Linnaeus's system so that animals were instead classified by their internal structures. He also changed the basic categories of animals, creating four major groups, called phyla, within the animal kingdom (phyla, pronounced 'fi-luh, is the plural form of phylum). These included *mollusca* (such as snails and cuttlefish), *radiata* (with starfish and jellyfish), *articulata* (with worms and insects), and *vertebrata* (which included all the higher animals). Cuvier presented his ideas and fossil evidence in his book *The Animal Kingdom, Distributed According to Its Organization,* published in 1817.

specifically its physical structure and details of reproduction. Based on his observations, Linneaus created a multi-level system of nomenclature (naming) in which living organisms were grouped according to their similarities or number of physical traits they had in common. The ranking of the system, going from general to specific, is kingdom, phylum (or division), class, order, family, genus, and species. The more specific the level, the more traits shared by the organisms placed in that level. Humans and gorillas share many physical characteristics. For this reason, they are placed in the same kingdom (Animalia), phylum (Chordata), class (Mammalia), and order (Primates). However, their similarities stop here, and their specific physical differences place them in different families (Hominidae for humans, Pongidae for gorillas). This hierarchical system (one consisting of levels of increasing importance) provided scientists with a way of understanding the relationships among different organisms or groups of organisms.

Linneaus also developed a two-part naming system (called binomial nomenclature) in which each living organism was given a two-part Latin name to distinguish it from all other organisms. The first name (italicized and capitalized) is the genus of the organism, while the second name (italicized but not capitalized) is its species. For example, all oak trees belong to the genus *Quercus*. The scientific name of a white oak is *Quercus alba* (*alba* is Latin for **white**), while a red oak is *Quercus rubra* (*rubra* means **red**). Since each species has only one name under this naming system, scientists worldwide are able to communicate with each other about organisms without having to understand different languages.

Attempts to classify all plants

While Linnaeus's system covered all living things, he still continued to be mostly interested in plant life. In 1751 he published a set of rules for the study and advancement of botany, *Philosophia botanica*. He also set about using his new system to classify all known plants. This work appeared in the mammoth 1753 book *Species plantarum,* in which he categorized and described more than 8,000 plant species.

Linnaeus's desire to classify all living things bordered on the obsessive (that is, he felt a nearly overwhelming urge to do it); he believed his work to be inspired by God and considered those who did not follow his system to be "heretics" (people who hold beliefs that contradict either generally accepted wisdom or the teachings of the Catholic Church). Nonetheless, he was a skilled and caring instructor who nurtured the interests of his many students, often sending them abroad to the Middle East, China, and the Pacific Islands for new specimens. In 1761 Linnaeus was recognized for his scientific achievements by the Swedish royalty and given the noble title von Linné. His popularity even caused the king of Spain to offer him a large amount of money to move to his country. But Linnaeus remained in Sweden at Uppsala until his death on January 10, 1778. He had suffered from a series of strokes that some believed were brought about by his intense pursuit of his work.

Today an international commission of scientists maintains the Linnaeus classification system and adheres to its rules when newly discovered species or subspecies need to be classified. Although the system depends on the judgments and opinions made by biologists, its concept and general organization are accepted by scientists throughout the world.

Further Readings

Asimov, Isaac, *Asimov's Biographical Dictionary of Science and Technology,* Doubleday, 1972, pp. 163-64.

Dictionary of Scientific Biography, Volume VIII, Scribner's, 1972, pp. 374-81.

The McGraw-Hill Encyclopedia of World Biography, Volume 6, McGraw-Hill, 1973, pp. 509-11.

Schiebinger, Linda, "The Loves of the Plants," *Scientific American,* February 1996, pp. 110-15.

Wangari Maathai

Born April 1, 1940
Nyeri, Kenya

Wangari Maathai is an environmentalist who has contributed greatly to preserving the natural resources of her native Kenya and done much to improve the health of her people.

Kenyan environmentalist Wangari Maathai (pronounced "wan-gar-ee ma-tie") has a long string of firsts next to her name: she was the first woman in central or eastern Africa to hold an advanced degree, the first woman to become an assistant professor at the University of Nairobi, and the first woman to head a university department in Kenya. But Maathai's best-known work has been far from the halls of the university. Since the 1970s, she has gained international support and fame for her Green Belt Movement, an environmental organization that has planted millions of trees in Africa since 1977. For her work with the Green Belt Movement, Maathai has received many honors, including the Right Livelihood Award in 1985. Yet, while Maathai's involvement with environmental and human rights issues have earned her worldwide respect, the Kenyan government has condemned her political and environmental protests as undesirable anti-government activities. A courageous and outspoken woman, Maathai blends the best of science and humanitarianism in her work (humanitarianism is the promotion of human welfare and soical reforms).

Family agrees to education

Wangari Muta Maathai was born on April 1, 1940, in Nyeri, Kenya. She was the oldest daughter of farmers who belonged to the prosperous Kikuyu tribe and was raised in the White Highlands region of Kenya. It was common among rural families there to give many of the household chores to the oldest daughter at a young age. But her older brother believed that Maathai should receive an education, and he convinced their parents to send her to school. A few years later, Maathai's teachers at the Loreto Limuru Girls School helped her obtain a scholarship that allowed her to continue her education in the United States at Mount St. Scholastica College in Kansas. She graduated with a bachelor of science degree in biology from the college in 1964 and went on to earn a master of science degree from the University of Pittsburgh in 1965.

Breaks barriers in Kenya

When she returned to her native country in 1966, Maathai's skills allowed her to secure a research associate position at the University of Nairobi in the department of veterinary medicine, even though it was very uncommon for a woman to hold such a job in Kenya at that time. In Kenyan culture, women were expected to be submissive and not seek higher education or employment—these were honors to be left for the men. For this reason, Maathai's male colleagues at first did not believe that she had achieved such a high degree of education and was qualified to work in a university department. But she slowly overcame such obstacles. By 1971 Maathai had earned her doctorate degree from the University of Nairobi. Continuing to work at the university, she went on to become a lecturer, then an assistant professor, and she was finally promoted to the head of the faculty of veterinary medicine. She was the first woman ever to reach such a level of authority at the university.

Focuses on environmental concerns

Maathai became involved in environmental and humanitarian topics when her husband, a Nairobi businessman, ran for a position in the Kenyan parliament in the early 1970s. While helping with her husband's campaign, Maathai first became aware of the poverty and unemployment that affected many people in the capital city of Nairobi. Her husband made a campaign promise to create more jobs for the city's poor. But after he won the election, it was Maathai who began working on the problem of putting people to work. Maathai opened an agency that paid poor people to plant trees and shrubs so they could earn a basic living. Although the original company went out of business, Maathai did not abandon her plan. She took the idea to a women's group called the National Council of Women of Kenya in 1977. With the group's support, Maathai was able to turn her idea into a nation-wide grass-roots (operated by people at the local level) organization known as the Green Belt Movement.

Maathai's organization was based on the idea that the quality of the natural environment was closely related to the quality of life of people in that environment. Trees, for example, played a key role in the lives of many Africans. Ninety percent of the African population depended on wood for fuel. Because so many trees were used, it was becoming harder to get enough firewood for daily needs, especially cooking. Generally women were put in charge of getting wood and cooking, and the wood shortage forced them to travel long distances to find new supplies. Another result of the firewood shortage was that even though food was available, the shortage of fuel meant that women could not cook enough food to satisfy the family's needs. Because of this, nutritional problems developed.

Trees help people and land

Maathai saw a basic solution to this cycle of deforestation (the process of cutting down all the trees in a forest) and malnutrition: Plant more trees. By encouraging people to plant trees, not only would they be providing for a new source of firewood, they would also be helping the environment. Tree roots hold soil in place, and leaves and branches protect the land from the force of the wind—two things that help prevent soil erosion (the loss of usable topsoil) and desertification—the changing of productive land to desert.

Program draws international attention

The Green Belt Movement helped local people to reforest their land by establishing nurseries that offered free seedlings for communities to plant and tend. Workers were given a small payment for every tree that was planted and preserved for more than three months by the villagers. Maathai's efforts to fight the deforestation of Kenya have been incredibly successful over the years, resulting in the planting of over ten million native trees such as acacias, cedars, baobabs, and cotton trees. In addition to conserving the soil and maintaining a well-balanced natural environment, the Green Belt movement provides employment to 80,000 workers. The success of Maathai's program has gained worldwide attention. About a dozen other African countries have started programs based on the ideas of the Green Belt Movement, and the United Nations and several European countries have contributed financial support for Maathai's program. She has been richly honored for her efforts; her awards include the Windstar Award for the Environment in 1989, the prestigious Goldman Environmental Prize in 1991, the Africa Prize for Leadership, also in 1991, and the Jane Addams International Women's Leadership Award in 1993.

IMPACT

Environmentalist Wangari Maathai has taken a simple idea—planting trees—and created a successful solution to a number of environmental and humanitarian problems in her native country of Kenya (an environmentalist is someone who is concerned with preserving and protecting nature). The organization launched by Maathai to encourage people to plant trees in rural areas, known as the Green Belt Movement, has become a model for similar programs in other African countries and has drawn attention around the world. The more than ten million trees planted by the Green Belt Movement provide people in Kenya with firewood to use when cooking—this has helped prevent malnutrition. The trees also protect the land from the forces that can cause erosion and turn productive areas into deserts.

Encounters conflict with government

Maathai's refusal to accept the traditional role of Kenyan women and her involvement with political issues have created conflict both in her personal and public life. Unhappy with her high-profile position, Maathai's husband, with whom she had three children, divorced her in the early 1980s. In 1989, Maathai angered political leaders when she led an environmental campaign to stop the construction of a 60-story office tower in Uhuru Park, one of the few natural areas in Nairobi. The publicity of Maathai's fight caused foreign investors to pull out of the project, saving the park for Nairobi's citizens.

But displeased government officials began making speeches against Maathai and her Green Belt Movement; they eventually forced the organization to leave its office in a government-owned building. Maathai moved the headquarters of the Green Belt Movement to her home, but she became determined to fight for changes in Kenya's political structure that would protect citizens from abuses by the government. In 1993, she also became involved in helping minority tribes that she believes are being driven from their homes by groups secretly funded by the Kenyan government. Her activities in these areas have brought her into many confrontations with the government and the police, and she has been arrested and jailed on a number of occasions.

Despite government opposition, however, Maathai continues her work for Green Belt and gives lectures about her environmental work around the world. Her message about the connection between people and their environment has remained the same over the years, and she firmly believes that the efforts of one person can make a difference. "The Green Belt Movement is about hope," Maathai stated in a 1992 *Chicago Tribune* article. "It tells people they are responsible for their own lives.... It raises an awareness that people can take control of their environment, which is the first step toward greater participation in society."

Further Reading

Chicago Tribune, January 5, 1992, p. VI 1.

"The Green Belt Movement," *Geographical Magazine*, April 1990, p. 51.

Hultman, Tami, "Portrait of a Grass-Roots Activist," *Utne Reader*, November-December 1992, pp. 86-87.

Maathai, Wangari, "Foresters without Diplomas," *Ms.*, March-April 1991, p. 74.

Maathai, Wangari, *The Green Belt Movement: Sharing the Approach and the Experience*, International Environmental Liaison Center, 1988.

"Protectors of Forests Take Home the Prizes," *Wall Street Journal*, May 10, 1991, p. B1.

Wallace, Aubrey, *Eco-Heroes: Twelve Tales of Environmental Victory*, Mercury House, 1993, pp. 1-21.

Maria Mitchell

Born August 1, 1818
Nantucket, Massachusetts
Died June 28, 1889
Lynn, Massachusetts

Maria Mitchell was the first American woman to work as a professional astronomer. She was also a respected educator.

Maria Mitchell became a popular figure after she discovered a comet in 1847. But she was most influential as the first woman to work as a professional astronomer in the United States and as a teacher who launched the scientific careers of many other women. Mitchell was an energetic spokesperson for women's causes; she particularly stressed the idea that women had the necessary intelligence and observational abilities to pursue scientific studies and careers.

Father's love of astronomy

Mitchell was born in Nantucket, Massachusetts, on August 1, 1818. She was the third of the ten children of William and Lydia (Coleman) Mitchell, descendants of Quakers who had emigrated from England. Mitchell came by her love of learning naturally. Since her mother worked in libraries, she became an avid reader. Her father, a teacher and banker, was also an accomplished amateur astronomer, providing Maria early exposure to that field. The island of Nantucket was an important whaling center, and William Mitchell was frequently hired by sailors to check the accuracy of their ships' chronometers—a timekeeping tool—by comparing them to observations of the stars. As Mitchell matured, she began to assist her father in his astronomy work. Another important influence on the future astronomer was the community of Nantucket itself, an environment where people knew and appreciated natural phenomena. She once stated that her stargazing practices were not unusual on the island: "In Nantucket people quite generally are in the habit of observing the heavens, and a sextant [a tool for measuring the angle or altitude of celestial bodies] will be found in almost every home."

An unusual teaching style

Mitchell attended a local girls' school for a while before entering a school run by her father, where students were encouraged to make all types of observations of the natural world. She then attended a school run by a man named Cyrus Pierce, completing her education at the age of 16 and staying on to teach for a time. At the age of seventeen she opened her own school, beginning of a lifelong interest in education. She was unconventional in her approach to teaching, sometimes starting the school day before dawn to allow students to see certain birds, or extending class time into the night to encourage astronomical observations.

Assists father in observations

In 1836 she became a librarian at the Nantucket Atheneum, a post she held for 20 years. Since the library was open only in the afternoons and Saturday evenings, she was able to spend a great deal of time studying a wide range of books and observing the sky. Some of her reading included French authors, books on mathematics, and Bodwitch's *Practical Navigator.* In the evenings she and her father would take notes on the objects in the night sky from a small observatory William Mitchell had constructed on the roof of the bank where he had become the principal officer. Their research was so detailed and accurate that

M aria Mitchell was the first woman in the United States to work as a professional astronomer. She became a well-known figure around the world, both in and out of the scientific community, after discovering a comet in 1847. She also was highly respected for her work in teaching and promoting the higher education of women; as an instructor at Vassar College she spoke out frequently about her belief that women had the necessary abilities to pursue scientific careers. While not a contributor of any major new astronomical theories, Mitchell served as an important symbol of what women in the 1800s could accomplish in the sciences.

it eventually drew the attention of a number of astronomers, including the director of the Harvard Observatory and the superintendent of the United States Coast Survey. The Mitchells' observatory was named a station of the Coast Survey, for which they provided information on movements and locations of the stars and moon.

Discovers new comet

On October 1, 1847, Mitchell discovered a comet. Her father reported her finding, but because two other scientists in Europe also had claimed to have found it, it took nearly a year to determine that Mitchell had actually spotted the comet first. Once designated the discoverer of the comet, Mitchell quickly became known around the world for her accomplishment. She was awarded a gold medal from the king of Denmark, and in 1848 she was elected to the American Academy of Arts and Sciences, the first woman to be so honored. Later in life she would break another barrier in academic organizations, becoming, in 1869, the first woman named to the American Philosophical Society. She was also the subject of numerous magazine articles and began correspondences and friendships with a number of notable people in the sciences, including Joseph Henry, a physicist and director of the Smithsonian Institution in Washington, D.C.

Works as professional astronomer

Mitchell's recognized skill as a scientist brought her other opportunities as well. In 1849 she became an analyst for the *American Ephemeris and Nautical Almanac,* a publication of astronomical tables that was primarily used for navigation by sailors. Holding this paid position for about 19 years,

Mitchell helped to make accurate calculations of time, latitude, and longitude. She was named to the American Association for the Advancement of Science in 1850.

Becomes influential professor

Mitchell was given the opportunity to travel to Europe in 1857 as the chaperon for the daughter of a wealthy Chicago businessman. In Europe she visited a number of observatories and met such famous individuals as American author Nathaniel Hawthorne (1804-1864), astronomers John Herschel (1738-1822) and Mary Somerville (1780-1872), and the philosopher and naturalist Alexander von Humboldt (1769-1859).

In 1865 Mitchell became professor of astronomy and director of the observatory at Vassar College, a newly founded women's college in New York. As she had done during her early years as an educator, Mitchell ignored the usual lecture method of instruction, stressing small classes and individual attention. At Vassar's observatory, Mitchell continued her astronomical research, studying and photographing sunspots, analyzing changes on the surface of Jupiter and Saturn, and investigating binary stars and nebulae (large cloudy bodies of dust in space). Mitchell's students worked by her side in her research, and she would take them on trips across the country to make observations on astronomical events such as eclipses. A number of her students went on to become noted astronomers themselves.

Mitchell's lasting contributions to the field of astronomy are probably more in her work as an observer and teacher than as a theoretical astronomer. As an observer, she was especially interested in the Sun, witnessing several total eclipses, and watching sunspots to try to understand their origin and changes. She believed they are rotating, gaseous storms on the solar surface. She assessed Jupiter's clouds very much as modern scientists do, arguing that they are not simply atmospheric phenomena, but part of the planet itself. She guessed that these clouds are pushing upward and moving at different rates. Like Mitchell, astronomers today believe Jupiter is a gaseous planet

Jan Oort, Dutch Astronomer

Jan Oort (1900-) made a number of advances in determining the shape, size, and features of the Milky Way galaxy, the collection of stars and planets to which our solar system belongs. In 1927, Oort demonstrated that the Milky Way was rotating. He further noted that since a galaxy is not a solid object, being made up of billions of stars, it does not rotate as a single solid object. Instead, the stars near the center of the galaxy move faster, while those farther out move slower. By studying the motion of the stars in the vicinity of our solar system, Oort was able to determine that the center of the galaxy was in the direction of the constellation Sagittarius, about 30,000 light years away—a distance still accepted by astronomers today. After World War II, Oort and his associates used radio telescopes (telescopes that gather radio waves rather than light waves) to map patterns of hydrogen gas in the galaxy; their findings showed them that the Milky Way has a spiral shape.

In addition to his work on the structure of the galaxy, Oort proposed a unique theory to account for the origin of comets. He suggested that there is a great shell of cometary material about one light year away that surrounds the solar system. Occasionally a change in gravity will occur, due to the movement of a nearby star, which disturbs the material in this "Oort cloud," and a clump of the debris is pushed into the inner solar system. As this small body encounters the Sun's radiation, the material begins to evaporate, a tail is formed, and a comet is seen.

without a solid surface. Regarding Saturn, her claim that the rings and the planet are composed of different material anticipated modern findings.

Promotes women in science

Mitchell became a leading advocate of women's rights, arguing that women were suited for mathematics and other sciences. She also strongly believed that scientific methods could be applied to solve social problems, an interest that led her to be named the vice president of the American Social Science Association in 1873. She toured Europe again that year and helped found the Association for the Advancement of

Women, a moderate feminist group that she served as president from 1875 to 1876 and as chair of the science committee until her death.

Observatory built in her honor

Mitchell taught at Vassar for twenty-three years, retiring in 1888. Although she was offered a permanent residence at the school's observatory, Mitchell returned to a family home in Lynn, Massachusetts, where she died in 1889. She was buried in a cemetery near the place of her birth on Nantucket. In Nantucket in 1902, the Maria Mitchell Association was founded by a group of women to honor Mitchell's memory and to encourage further scientific research by women. The association, which occupies the house where Mitchell was born, built an observatory next to the Mitchell House in 1908; it has since become a center for astronomical research. Mitchell was also remembered for her pioneering work as America's first female professional astronomer with a bust in the New York University Hall of Fame.

Further Readings

Bailey, Martha J., *American Women in Science: A Biographical Dictionary,* ABC-Clio, 1994, pp. 253-55.

Dictionary of Scientific Biography, Volume IX, Scribner's, 1974, pp. 421-22.

Kendall, Phoebe Mitchell, *Maria Mitchell: Life, Letters, and Journals,* [Boston], 1896.

The McGraw-Hill Encyclopedia of World Biography, Volume 7, McGraw-Hill, 1973, pp. 438-39.

Notable American Women: A Biographical Dictionary, Volume II, Belknap Press, 1971, pp. 554-56.

Ogilvie, Marilyn Bailey, *Women in Science: Antiquity through the Nineteenth Century,* MIT Press, 1986, pp. 133-39.

Opalko, Jane, "Maria Mitchell's Haunting Legacy," *Sky and Telescope,* May 1992, pp. 505-7.

Wright, Helen, *Sweeper in the Sky,* [New York], 1950.

Isaac Newton

Born December 25, 1642
Woolsthorpe, Lincolnshire, England
Died March 20, 1727
London, England

Isaac Newton formulated the law of universal gravitation and the three basic laws of motion.

Isaac Newton is considered one of the most important scientists of all time. The author of the law of universal gravitation and the laws of motion, Newton presented an entirely new way of explaining the workings of the universe. These ideas, which marked the high point of the Scientific Revolution, were presented in Newton's landmark work, *Philosophiae Naturalis Principia Mathematica,* in 1687. In addition to his work on gravity and motion, Newton also contributed to the study of light, developed a form of calculus, and built the first reflecting telescope.

Born on December 25, 1642, in Woolsthorpe, Lincolnshire, England, Newton was a premature baby who was not expected to live. His father had died three months previous to the birth, and his mother was remarried to the rector of a nearby parish three years later, leaving Newton in the care of his grandparents.

Failures at school and on farm

Newton did not distinguish himself in school, but he did enjoy constructing mechanical toys like sundials and kites. At the age of 12 he was sent to King's School in the town of Grantham. He lived in the house of a local apothecary (pharmacist) while he studied there, and he developed an interest in the chemical library in the house. Newton was removed from school by his mother in the late 1650s in order to work on the family farm, which he was expected to take over someday. But Newton proved an even worse farmer than scholar. His uncle, however, saw his potential as a student and encouraged the young man to go to Cambridge University in 1660. Five years later Newton graduated, even though he had failed a scholarship exam in 1663 due to his lack of knowledge concerning geometry.

Inspired by falling apple

Newton wanted to remain at the university to earn his master's degree, but he was forced to return to the farm to escape the bubonic plague, a deadly disease that was spreading quickly through London at the time. During his time at the farm, Newton worked independently on his studies, experimenting in the areas of gravitation and optics (the study of light) and developing a form of math known as calculus. In 1666, Newton saw an apple fall to the ground, and he began to ponder the force that was responsible for the action. While this story has often been considered to be a legend, Newton confirmed that it did in fact happen. He first thought that the apple fell because all matter attracts other matter. He then theorized that the rate of the apple's fall was directly proportional to the attractive force Earth exerted upon it.

In addition, he suggested the inverse square law: force decreases according to the square of the distance from the center of Earth. Then he made a daring hypothesis (an untested idea), suggesting the force that pulled the apple was also responsible for keeping the Moon in orbit around Earth. This

The law of universal gravitation formulated by physicist and mathematician Isaac Newton was the culmination of almost 200 years of scientific thought. Newton's work marked the high point of what became known as the Scientific Revolution—the progression of rational, scientific ideas that began when Nicolaus Copernicus argued that Earth and all the other planets revolve around the Sun, overturning the ancient idea that Earth was the center of the universe. By relying on scientific observation rather than accepting as final the thoughts of ancient Greek philosophers like Aristotle, scientists began to break down the European devotion to Greek science. Johannes Kepler observed that the planets move in elliptical (oval-shaped) orbits, not perfect circles; Galileo Galilei demonstrated that a heavy object falls at the same speed as a lighter one. All of these observations could be explained and proved correct with Newton's law, which states that a natural force—gravity—influences the movement of objects on Earth as well as in space.

was an important idea because at the time most people believed in the theory of ancient Greek philosopher Aristotle (384-322 B.C.), who had said that the heavenly bodies obeyed different physical laws than objects on Earth. Newton had suggested that all bodies responded to the same physical laws, no matter where they were.

Abandons work on gravity

When Newton made calculations of what the rate of fall for the Moon should be, he came up short of what was actually observed and was quite disappointed. The problem was two-fold. First, he needed to know the radius of Earth (the distance from the surface to the center), but this was not known with precision at the time and the figure Newton used was too small. Second, he was not certain he was correct in making his calculations based on the gravitational force at the center of Earth, as opposed to the surface. Because of these issues, he set aside his work on gravity for fifteen years.

Experiments with light

During this same time (1665-1666), a book about color written by English physicist and chemist Robert Boyle (1627-1691) captured Newton's interest and he began to experiment with light. Newton passed a beam of sunlight through a prism of glass and observed that the light was refracted, or split, into a spectrum, a display of colored light that contains all the colors of the rainbow. He passed the spectrum through a second prism, and the light was recombined into a white spot. In this way, Newton discovered that all of the colors of the spectrum existed in white light, a finding that earned him recognition in scientific circles. For an unexplained reason, Newton did not notice any of the visible dark lines in the spectrum of the Sun. It was not until over 150 years later that English physicist William Hyde Wollaston (1766-1828) and Bavarian physicist Joseph Fraunhofer (1787-1826) noticed the lines, and German physicist Gustav Kirchhoff (1824-1887) realized they revealed the types of elements and chemical compounds that made up heavenly bodies. Newton's experiments led him to conclude that light was comprised of a stream of particles that moved through an invisible substance, or ether. Although this theory was later disproved, it was kept alive by Newton's influence for nearly a century.

Builds reflecting telescope

Newton returned to Cambridge in 1667, where he earned his master's degree and conducted further research on the work he had begun on the farm. In 1668 he constructed a reflecting telescope, a device that used mirrors to reflect and magnify the light of distant objects. Newton's telescope was a major advance over other telescopes of the time because it created a clear, undistorted image, and it was many times more powerful than other scopes. The high-power telescopes used by modern astronomers are modeled after Newton's reflecting design. Newton presented his invention to the Royal Society (the oldest scientific organization in England); the members were so impressed that they elected him to their organization in 1672.

Becomes center of controversy

After being elected to the Royal Society, Newton appeared in front of the group to report on his experiments with light and its spectrum. While most members were impressed by his findings and his idea that light was composed of colors, physicist Robert Hooke, who had performed similar experiments and drawn different conclusions, dismissed Newton's findings as unimportant. In response, Newton sent an angry letter to Hooke, which was later published in the Royal Society's periodical. The feud between Hooke and Newton continued to grow, although Newton's increasing reputation in the British scientific community forced the two men to act more politely—at least in public.

The two scientists' dislike for one another reached its height in 1686 when Newton published his law of universal gravitation. Hooke, who had outlined a similar theory in a letter seven years earlier, insisted that Newton had stolen his idea. It is possible that Newton was unaware of Hooke's work, which was in any event fundamentally flawed. However, modern scientists now credit Hooke with the ideas that inspired Newton to develop his own, more accurate, theory of gravitation.

Newton became involved in yet another controversy, this time with the German mathematician Gottfried Leibniz (1646-1716). Both men had independently developed a complex system of mathematical calculation called calculus, although each used different symbols and notations. Leibniz's notation, however, was considered superior and came to be preferred over that of Newton, causing a bitter controversy between the two. Their conflict quickly became a matter of national pride, and English scientists refused to accept Leibniz's version. Unfortunately this stubbornness kept the English from significantly contributing to mathematics for nearly a century.

Returns to work on gravity

Newton became very bitter about the many arguments surrounding his work, particularly his fights with Hooke. At one point he was so frustrated that he vowed not to publish any more scientific works. In the 1680s, however, Newton was drawn into publicly presenting his work again after being encouraged by his good friend, the English astronomer Edmond Halley (1656-1742). Halley told Newton that Hooke had claimed to have discovered the laws concerning the motion of celestial objects. Newton casually told Halley that he had already come up with the answer to that problem 15 years earlier in his early days of research at the family farm.

Robert Hooke, English Physicist

Robert Hooke (1635-1703) is remembered for the wide variety of fields to which he contributed, including physics, astronomy, microscopy, biology, and architecture, among others. Although Hooke introduced many new concepts he often could not formulate his ideas into fully-reasoned arguments. Thus, although Hooke's ideas inspired many scientific breakthroughs, the credit for them is often given to scientists—such as Isaac Newton and the Dutch mathematician and astronomer Christiaan Huygens (1629-1695)—who brought the work to its full development.

While working as a laboratory assistant to English physicist and chemist Robert Boyle (1627-1691), Hooke's talent for designing scientific instruments was noticed. He constructed the improved air pump that was used to establish Boyle's gas laws. A founder of the Royal Society, Hooke served as that organization's Curator of Experiments, a position that gave him the money and resources to conduct years of wide-ranging experiments. Sometime near 1660, Hooke introduced a chronometer (a timekeeping device) design based on the use of a spring rather than a pendulum. Although his design was a good one, he was unable to find financial investors to back him and his device never became popular. In 1674, Huygens patented a spring-driven chronometer of his own; Hooke immediately claimed that the invention was based on his earlier ideas, but the dispute was never resolved. Hooke was one of the first people to conduct major research with a microscope. In his 1665 work *Micrographia,* he described the structures of insects, fossils, and plants with an amount of detail never seen before. While studying the porous structure of cork, Hooke noticed the presence of tiny rectangular holes that he called cells—a word that has been adopted as the cornerstone of microbiology.

Perhaps the best-known controversies involving Hooke were his claims to be the originator of many of the ideas made popular by Isaac Newton, including the concept of universal gravitation. Although Hooke is given credit for some early ideas relating to the law of universal gravitation, his work was radically improved on by Newton. One theory that Hooke is given full credit for deals with elasticity. While experimenting with springs, he found that the amount of weight added to a spring is proportional to the distance the spring stretches. Therefore, a four-pound weight will stretch a spring twice as far as a two-pound weight. Specifically, Hooke's law states that, in an elastic system, strain is proportional to stress.

Halley convinced Newton to retry the calculations that he had abandoned before. This time the calculations worked: a more accurate measurement of Earth's radius had been reported, giving Newton better data for his calculations. Also, from other work he had done, Newton also now knew that he should make the center, not the surface, the point of gravitational attraction of a sphere. With his friend's financial help, Newton published the results of his second effort in the most important work of his career, *Philosophiae Naturalis Principia Mathematica* ("Mathematical Principles of Natural Philosophy"), which outlined the laws of gravity and motion. This book, considered to be one of the greatest scientific works ever written, established Newton as the most important scientist in England and the world.

States law of universal gravitation

In the *Principia Mathematica,* which appeared in 1687, Newton took Italian scientist Galileo Galilei's findings about motion and the speed of falling objects and organized them into three basic laws of motion. The first law stated that a body at rest remains at rest, and a body in motion remains in motion. The second law declared that force is equal to mass times acceleration. The third law observed that for every action, there is an equal and opposite reaction. These three laws allowed Newton to calculate the gravitational force between Earth and the Moon. He asserted these laws acted upon any two objects in the universe, establishing the law of universal gravitation; he proceeded to estimate, quite accurately, the masses of Jupiter and Saturn. He also used his new laws to explain the motion of comets, the movement of the ocean tides, and the timing of the equinoxes (the two times each year when the Sun crosses the plane of Earth's equator; at these times, day and night are of equal length everywhere on Earth).

Contributes to Scientific Revolution

The *Principia Mathematica* revolutionized science by providing an explanation of the forces that controlled the regular movement of planets as described by German astronomer **Johannes Kepler**'s (1571-1630; for more information, see pp. 126-132) laws of planetary motion. It also elegantly showed how celestial bodies and earthly objects followed a single law of gravitation. This overall scheme of the workings of the universe was the crowning accomplishment of the Scientific Revolution—a trend away from the theories of ancient Greek philosophers that had been the center of scientific thought for nearly 2,000 years. From the time of Polish astronomer **Nicolaus Copernicus** (1473-1543; for more information, see pp. 48-54), who stated that Earth and the planets revolve around the Sun, a new basis of science had been developing—a scientific method of observation and calculation that gradually disproved many of the long-accepted ideas that began in ancient Greece. Newton's laws are considered the point at which the scientific method became the most important influence in science.

Weakened by work

Principia Mathematica was written in only 18 months and apparently exerted an enormous strain on Newton. His physical exhaustion combined with the continual controversy surrounding him resulted in Newton suffering a nervous breakdown in 1692. Although he recovered and still had an extraordinary mathematical ability, he was never the same. In 1696 he secured a government post, where he made a number of important changes to the English monetary system. He was elected president of the Royal Society in 1703 and was reelected to that position every year until his death. He wrote another book, *Opticks,* which covered his work on light; however, to avoid antagonizing his old rival, he waited until after Hooke's death before printing it in 1704.

Remembered for landmark work

In 1705 Queen Anne knighted him; it was the first time a scientist had been so honored. Sir Isaac Newton died on March 20, 1727, at the age of 84, and was buried alongside other English heroes in Westminster Abbey. His vast influence upon science continued after his death; the only people who have since had such an important role in science and history have been English naturalist Charles Darwin (1809-1882), who popularized the idea of evolution, and German-born physicist Albert Einstein (1879-1955), who formulated the theory of relativity. But Newton was modest about his place in history. In a letter written to Hooke, Newton once stated, "if I have seen further than other men, it is because I stood on the shoulders of giants."

Further Readings

Asimov, Isaac, *Asimov's Biographical Dictionary of Science and Technology,* Doubleday, 1972, pp. 134-41.

The McGraw-Hill Encyclopedia of World Biography, Volume 8, McGraw-Hill, 1973, pp. 106-10.

Ida Tacke Noddack

Born February 25, 1896
Lackhausen, Germany
Died 1979
Germany

orking with fellow German chemist Walter Noddack (1893-1960)—her future husband—and X-ray specialist Otto Berg, Ida Tacke discovered element 75, known as rhenium, in 1925. This finding solved one of the mysteries of the periodic table of elements introduced by Russian chemist Dmitri Ivanovich Mendeleev (1834-1907) in 1869. Tacke's study of the periodic table later led her to be the first to suggest in 1934 that American physicist **Enrico Fermi** (1901-1954; for more information, see volume 1, pp. 285-291) had not made a new element in an experiment with uranium as he thought, but instead had discovered nuclear fission—the splitting of the nucleus of an atom. Her prediction was not verified until 1939.

Searches for missing element

Ida Tacke was born in Germany on February 25, 1896. She studied at the Technical University in Berlin, where she received the first prize for chemistry and metallurgy (the sci-

Ida Tacke Noddack helped discover the element rhenium and first described the process of nuclear fission.

ence and technology of metals) in 1919. In 1921, soon after receiving her doctoral degree, she set out to isolate two of the elements that Mendeleev had predicted when he proposed the Periodic System and displayed all known elements in a format now called the periodic table. Mendeleev had left blank spaces on his table for several elements that he expected to exist but that had not been identified. Two of these, elements 43 and 75, were located in Group VII under manganese.

Discovers rhenium

Assuming that these elements would be similar in their properties to manganese, scientists had been searching for them in manganese ores. Tacke and Walter Noddack, who headed the chemical laboratory at the Physico-Technical Research Agency in Berlin, focused instead on the neighbors to the side of the missing elements—molybdenum, tungsten, osmium, and ruthenium. With the assistance of Otto Berg of the Werner-Siemens Laboratory, who provided expertise in using X-rays to identify substances, Tacke and Noddack isolated element 75 in 1925. They named it rhenium, from Rhenus, the Latin name for the Rhine, an important river in their native Germany. It took them another year to isolate a single gram of the element from 660 kilograms of molybdenite ore. They also believed they had discovered traces of element 43, which they called masurium. Later research, however, did not confirm their results. Now known as technetium, element 43 has never been found in nature, although it has been produced artificially.

In 1926, Ida Tacke married Walter Noddack. They worked together in their research until Walter Noddack's death in 1960, and together they published about one hundred scientific papers. The Noddacks were awarded the Leibig Medal of the German Chemical Society in 1934 for their discovery of rhenium.

Poses idea of nuclear fission

In 1934 Tacke challenged the conclusions of Enrico Fermi and his research group that they had produced transuranium elements, artificial elements heavier than uranium, when they bombarded uranium atoms with subatomic particles called neutrons. Although other scientists agreed with Fermi, Noddack suggested he had split uranium atoms into isotopes (a variety of an element that has the same atomic number as the original element, but a different atomic mass) of known elements rather than added to uranium atoms to produce heavier, unknown elements. She had no research to support her theory, however, and for five years her hypothesis (an untested idea) that atomic nuclei had been split was virtually ignored. "Her suggestion was so out of line with the then-accepted ideas about the atomic nucleus that it was never seriously discussed," fellow German chemist Otto Hahn (1879-1968) would later comment in his autobiography. In 1939, after much research had been done by many scientists, Hahn, working with German chemist Fritz Strassmann (1902-1980) and Austrian physicist **Lise Meitner** (1878-1968; for more information, see volume 2, pp. 639-647) discovered that Tacke had been right. They named the process she had predicted nuclear fission.

The Noddacks moved from Berlin to the University of Freiburg in 1935. They later went to the University of Strasbourg in 1943, and to the State Research Institute for Geochemistry in Bamberg in 1956. In 1960, Walter Noddack died. For her scientific achievements, Tacke received the High Service Cross of the German Federal Republic in 1966. During her life she received honorary membership in the Spanish Society of Physics and Chemistry and the International

IMPACT

Nuclear fission, the process in which the nucleus of a uranium atom is split, is the powerful force behind such developments as the atomic bomb and the commercial production of nuclear power. German chemist Ida Tacke Noddack, going against accepted scientific thought in 1934, was the first person to suggest that bombarding a uranium atom with neutrons—an experiment first carried out by Italian-born physicist Enrico Fermi (1901-1954)—resulted in the chemical alteration of the uranium atom into isotopes (related but slightly different examples) of two other known elements. Tacke was well-respected for her work in the discovery of the element rhenium in 1925, but her concept of nuclear fission was disregarded for several years until proven correct by a team of scientists. The process that other scientists had previously thought was physically impossible soon became a very real part of modern life when a group of scientists, led by Enrico Fermi, created the first "chain" nuclear fission reaction in 1942, producing the first controlled source of nuclear power.

Emilio Segrè, American Physicist

In the 1930s, Italian-born physicist Emilio Segrè (1905-1989) sought to prove the existence of element 43. Segrè believed that if he took an atom of the element with the atomic weight 42 (molybdenum) and added the weight of one neutron (a subatomic particle with weight but no charge), he would create the element with atomic weight 43. Segrè obtained a sample of molybdenum that had been treated in this way and began to look for evidence of the predicted element. At the end of 1936, Segrè and his colleague C. Perrier announced that they had successfully found chemical samples of element 43. Because this was the first new element to be produced artificially, the scientists named their discovery technetium, based on the Greek word *teknetos,* meaning "artificial."

Segrè emigrated to the United States in the late 1930s. Working at the University of California at Berkeley, he was involved in the discovery of yet another new element—plutonium—element number 94. This research, along with Segrè's previous work on neutron physics, made him an important part of the Manhattan Project—the work conducted by the United States in the 1940s to construct an atomic bomb.

In 1955, along with American physicist Owen Chamberlain (1920-), Segrè successfully proved the existence of the antiproton—a negatively charged proton. This finding helped to confirm the theory of English physicist Paul Dirac (1902-1984) that all atomic particles have "anti-" counterparts with opposite charges. For the discovery of the antiproton and its importance to the theory of antimatter, Segrè and Chamberlain were awarded the 1959 Nobel Prize in physics.

Society of Nutrition Research, as well as an honorary doctorate of science from the University of Hamburg. Ida Noddack retired in 1968 and moved to Bad Neuenahr, a small town on the Rhine. She died in 1979.

Further Reading

Hahn, Otto, *A Scientific Autobiography,* Scribner, 1966.

Weeks, Mary E., *The Discovery of the Elements,* Mack, 1954, pp. 321-22.

David Powless

Born May 29, 1943
Ottawa, Illinois

David Powless developed a method for recycling hazardous wastes from steel mills.

David Powless, an environmental scientist and businessman, began his career as a professional football player. But when he was forced to leave the game because of injuries, he turned to the business of cleaning up the toxic wastes produced by steel mills. A member of the Oneida tribe, an Iroquoian-speaking group, Powless was inspired by his Native American heritage that stressed caring for Earth. He worked with scientists to develop a process that uses heat to change dangerous substances (such as oil, zinc, lead, and cadmium) in steel mill waste into a safe, reusable form. His work was supported with a grant from the National Science Foundation in 1977—the first such grant awarded to an individual Native American.

David Allen Powless was born on May 29, 1943, in Ottawa, Illinois, the fifth of six children born to Merville and Adeline (Tucktenhagen) Powless. His father was a government employee who worked at various times for the Bureau of Indian Affairs, the Department of Navy, and the Department of Army. He was also a staunch believer in the value of education. As Powless recalled in an interview, "My father motivated us all.... When I was being raised, we were told that as Oneidas, we had a special obligation to our tribe to act well, because whatever we did, that was the way people would think all Oneida Indians acted. But we were also told that we had been given special skills and abilities with which to fulfill that duty.... We were Indian people, first. We were Indian people who were going to get a good education, second."

Plays football professionally

Powless lived up to his father's high expectations by winning a football scholarship to the University of Oklahoma. He stayed for one year before transferring to the University of Illinois, where he continued to pursue football while studying marketing and economics. After playing on a team that won the 1963 Rose Bowl, Powless graduated with a bachelor of science degree in 1966. He was drafted to play professional football for the New York Giants in 1965. He spent a season with them before being traded to the Washington Redskins, but a back injury brought an early end to his sports career.

Recycles hazardous wastes

In 1967, Powless began a nine-year career as a marketing representative for the Foseco company. His job, which involved selling chemical additives and insulation materials to steel mills, gave him a close-up view of how that industry worked. In 1976, he started his own company, convinced that the hazardous wastes generated by the steel mills represented a problem for which he could supply a practical solution. As he said in an interview, "This is when I started seeking my identity as a Native person. All of our traditions are focused on care and concern for the Earth."

Powless developed his recycling method with the aid of scientists at the Colorado School of Mines in Golden. They helped him write a proposal for the National Science Founda-

IMPACT

One of the substances that is left behind in the steel-making process is a combination of iron oxide and a mixture of environmentally-dangerous materials including oil, zinc, lead, and cadmium. Environmental businessman David Powless felt that this harmful industrial waste did not need to be left untreated. His idea was to use extremely high heat to free the toxic materials from the waste. The materials are then safely formed into small chunks that can be used again in the steel mill. Powless's imaginative solution has provided the steel industry with a way to avoid polluting the environment and to stop wasting valuable resources.

tion, and after almost half a year of negotiations he was awarded a grant from the organization. He then established a pilot plant at Kaiser Steel in California.

In Powless's recycling method, various contaminants are first removed from iron oxide wastes using an indirect fired rotary kiln—a constantly burning furnace with an outside flame hitting the shell. As materials enter the kiln, they become hot enough to ignite. But as the materials move farther into the furnace, there is less oxygen available to support the fire. In this high-temperature, low-oxygen environment, contaminants such as oil, zinc, lead, and cadmium come off of the waste material. Then the cleaned-up materials are agglomerated, or collected, into briquettes, small pieces which can later be reintroduced into the steel-making process. According to Powless: "This was a spiritual experience for me, because it involved the use of fire and flame for purification."

Works with Native American companies

Powless's company marketed this technology until 1986, when the search for his roots took Powless to the Oneida reservation in Wisconsin. There he soon became involved in the start-up of a tribally owned and managed environmental analytical testing laboratory called ORTEK. This profitable enterprise included an operating group that conducted organic and inorganic testing of soil, water, and air for contaminants. In 1992, Powless left his position as president of ORTEK and accepted a new one as vice president of marketing for the Arctic Slope Regional Corporation. There, Powless has assumed a key role in the Inuit-owned firm's expansion outside Alaska.

Powless has been recognized in many ways for his successful career. He was named American Indian Business Owner of the Year by the United Indian Development Association in 1980. The following year, he was presented with the Small Business Administration's National Innovation Advocate of the Year Award by then-Vice President George Bush at a ceremony in the White House Rose Garden. Powless has served on the board of directors of the American Indian Science and Engineering Society. He is also a popular speaker on the relationship between traditional teachings, spiritual growth, and science. Powless was married in 1968 to Carol Monson, with whom he has a son. That marriage ended in divorce, and on November 6, 1983, Powless wed Anna Kormos in Los Angeles. The couple and their daughter make their home in Corrales, New Mexico.

Further Reading

Vogel, Mike, "Native American Parley Fuses Culture, Technology—900 Expected at Conference," *Buffalo News,* November 9, 1990, p. B15.

Weidlein, Jim, "People of the Whale," *Winds of Change,* summer 1993, pp. 10-15.

Weidlein, Jim, "Sharing a Piece of the Whale," *Winds of Change,* autumn 1993, pp. 140-47.

Julia Robinson

Born December 8, 1919
St. Louis, Missouri
Died July 30, 1985

Julia Robinson helped to solve the important mathematical question known as Hilbert's tenth problem.

Excelling in the field of mathematics, Julia Robinson was instrumental in solving the mathematical puzzle known as Hilbert's tenth problem. Over a period of two decades, she developed the framework on which the solution was constructed. In recognition of her accomplishments, she became the first woman mathematician elected to the National Academy of Sciences, the first female president of the American Mathematical Society, and the first woman mathematician to receive a MacArthur Foundation Fellowship (popularly known as a "genius grant").

Robinson was born Julia Bowman on December 8, 1919, in St. Louis, Missouri. Her mother, Helen Hall Bowman, died two years later; Robinson and her older sister then went to live with their grandmother near Phoenix, Arizona. The following year their father, Ralph Bowman, retired and joined them in Arizona after becoming disinterested in his machine tool and equipment business. He expected to support his children and his new wife, Edenia Kridelbaugh Bowman, with his savings.

In 1925, Robinson's family moved to San Diego, California; three years later a third daughter was born.

Fascination with mathematics

At the age of nine, Robinson contracted scarlet fever, and the family was quarantined (kept in isolation to prevent the spread of disease) for a month. They celebrated the end of isolation by viewing their first talking motion picture. The celebration was premature, however, as Robinson soon developed rheumatic fever and was bedridden for a year. When she was well enough, she worked with a tutor for a year, covering the required material for the fifth through eighth grades. She was fascinated by the tutor's claim that it had been proven that the square root of two could not be calculated definitively. Her interest in mathematics continued at San Diego High School; when she graduated with honors in mathematics and science, her parents gave her a slide rule (a device for making complex mathematical calculations) that she treasured and named "Slippy."

At the age of sixteen, Robinson entered San Diego State College. She majored in mathematics and, because she was aware of no other careers in mathematics, she prepared to become a teacher. At the beginning of Robinson's sophomore year, her father found his savings depleted by the economic problems of the Great Depression (a period in the late 1920s and early 1930s when the United States suffered from an extremely slow economy and widespread unemployment) and committed suicide. With help from her older sister and an aunt, Robinson remained in school. She transferred to the University of California at Berkeley for her senior year and graduated in 1940.

Begins career at Berkeley

At Berkeley, Robinson found teachers and fellow students who shared her excitement about mathematics. In December of 1941, she married an assistant professor named Raphael Robin-

Driven by a natural curiosity about the workings of mathematics, Julia Robinson spent more than twenty years of her life attacking a problem that had eluded the best mathematicians before her. Known as Hilbert's tenth problem, the question was one of a list of twenty-three unsolved mathematical questions that represented the most complex issues in the field. Robinson's years of work were spent carefully piecing together the different calculations that would lead to the final answer to Hilbert's tenth. While the final solution was constructed by Russian mathematician Yuri Matijasevic, Robinson's critical earlier work earned her an important place in the mathematical and scientific community.

son. At that time she was a teaching assistant at Berkeley, having completed her master's degree earlier in 1941. The following year, however, the school's nepotism rule—which stated that married couples could not work in the same department—prevented her from teaching in the mathematics department. Instead, she worked in the Berkeley Statistical Laboratory on military projects. During this time, Robinson had an unsuccessful pregnancy; because of damage to Robinson's heart caused by the rheumatic fever, her doctor warned her not to try again to have children. Her hopes of motherhood crushed, Robinson endured a period of depression that lasted until her husband rekindled her interest in mathematics.

Investigates Hilbert's tenth problem

In 1947 Robinson embarked on a doctoral program under the direction of Polish American mathematician Alfred Tarski (1902-); she received her doctorate in mathematics in 1948. That same year, Tarski discussed an idea about complex mathematical problems with Raphael Robinson, who shared it with his wife. The problem caught Julia Robinson's interest and she began working intensely on it. Eventually she realized that what she was working on was directly related to the tenth problem on the list of 23 unsolved problems that had been drawn up by German mathematician **David Hilbert** (1862-1943; for more information, see volume 2, pp. 454-462) in 1900. Hilbert's list represented the most difficult questions in mathematics, and presenting an answer to any of them is considered a groundbreaking accomplishment. But by the time Robinson recognized the importance of the problem she was investigating, she had become too involved in the topic to be intimidated. For the next twenty-two years she attacked various aspects of the problem, building the foundation that Russian mathematician Yuri Matijasevic would later use to present an answer to Hilbert's tenth problem in 1970.

Contributes to game theory

Robinson also contributed to the area of game theory, the mathematics involved in determining the effect of a particular strategy in a competition between forces, as in a game of chess, a military battle, or in selling products. While working at the RAND Corporation in 1949 and 1950, Robinson developed a way of determining the most effective mathematical strategy for players involved in a two-person zero-sum game (a contest in which the amount gained by the winner equals the amount lost by the loser). This was her only contribution to game theory, but it is considered a fundamental theorem (a proven mathematical idea) in the field.

Robinson's heart damage was surgically repaired in 1961, but her health remained impaired. Her fame from the Hilbert problem solution resulted in her becoming a full professor at Berkeley in 1976, but, because of her health problems, she only carried one-fourth of the normal teaching load. She developed leukemia eight years later and died on July 30, 1985.

Further Reading

"Julia Bowman Robinson, 1919-1985," *Notices of the American Mathematical Society,* November 1985, pp. 738-42.

Reid, Constance, "The Autobiography of Julia Robinson," *The College Mathematics Journal,* January 1986, pp. 2-21.

Smorynski, C., "Julia Robinson, In Memoriam," *The Mathematical Intelligencer,* spring 1986, pp. 77-79.

Carl Sagan

Born November 9, 1934
Brooklyn, New York
Died December 20, 1996
Seattle, Washington

"I believe our future depends on how well we know this Cosmos in which we float like a mote of dust in the morning sky."

An astronomer as well as a best-selling author and popular television figure, Carl Sagan was one of the best-known scientists in the world during his lifetime. He was one of the first scientists to take an active interest in the possibility that life exists elsewhere in the universe. Working with the National Aeronautics and Space Administration (NASA) spacecraft missions to Venus, Mars, and the outer planets, he helped look for signs of life within our own solar system. He shared his enthusiasm for the possibility of extraterrestrial life with television viewers as a regular guest on the *Tonight Show* with host Johnny Carson, and later as the host of the television series *Cosmos,* seen in 60 countries by more than 400 million people. Sagan also drew public attention when he co-wrote a paper that predicted drastic global cooling after a nuclear war; the concept of "nuclear winter" affected not only the scientific community but also national and international policy and public opinion about nuclear weapons and the arms race.

Plans astronomy career at age five

Sagan was born in Brooklyn, New York, on November 9, 1934, the son of Samuel Sagan, a Russian immigrant and a cutter in a clothing factory, and Rachel Gruber Sagan. He became fascinated with the stars as a young child and was an avid reader of science fiction, particularly the novels by Edgar Rice Burroughs about the exploration of Mars. By the age of five he was sure he wanted to be an astronomer. As he told Henry S. F. Cooper, Jr., of the *New Yorker,* he sadly assumed it was not a paying job; he expected he would have to work at "some job I was temperamentally unsuited for, like door-to-door salesman." When he found out a few years later that astronomers actually got paid, he was ecstatic: "That was a splendid day," he told Cooper.

Important scientists support his studies

Sagan's degrees, all of which he earned at the University of Chicago, consisted of a bachelor of arts degree in 1954, a bachelor of science degree in 1955, a master of science degree in physics in 1956, and a doctorate in astronomy and astrophysics in 1960. As a graduate student, Sagan was deeply interested in the possibility of life on other planets, a discipline known as exobiology. This was an interest which at the time was not considered part of responsible scientific investigation, but he received important early support from scientists such as the Nobel Prize-winning American geneticists Hermann Joseph Muller (1890-1967) and Joshua Lederberg (1925-). He also worked with American chemist and physicist Harold C. Urey (1893-1981), who had won the 1934 Nobel Prize in chemistry and had been the thesis adviser of American chemist Stanley Lloyd Miller (1930-) when he conducted his famous experiment on the origin of life. Sagan wrote his doctoral dissertation, "Physical Studies of the Planets," under Dutch American astronomer Gerard Peter Kuiper (1905-1973), one of the few astronomers at that time who was a planetologist (a person who studies the physical bodies in the solar system, including planets and their satellites, comets, and meteorites). It was during his graduate student days that Sagan

Astronomer Carl Sagan is best known for bringing the scientific marvels and mysteries of the universe into the living rooms of millions of people with his popular television series, *Cosmos*. Sagan was well prepared for his role as the science instructor of the viewing public—he was one of the people who helped design the pioneering NASA space missions that gathered information about conditions on the other planets in our solar system. His interest and obvious enthusiasm for astronomy and other aspects of science made him a popular television host and a best-selling author—the book version of *Cosmos* was on the bestseller lists for more than a year. This kind of response to Sagan's work proved the scientist's main message—that science is a topic that can be appreciated by all people, not just scientists.

met his first wife, Lynn Alexander, who was then studying biology. They were married on June 16, 1957, and had two sons before their divorce in 1963.

From graduate school, Sagan moved to the University of California at Berkeley, where he was the Miller residential fellow in astronomy from 1960 to 1962. He then accepted a position at Harvard as an assistant professor from 1962 to 1968. On April 6, 1968, he married his second wife, the painter Linda Salzman; they had one son before divorcing. From Harvard he went to Cornell University, where he was first an associate professor of astronomy at the Center for Radiophysics and Space Research. He was then promoted to professor and associate director at the center. In 1977 he became the David Duncan Professor of Astronomy and Space Science at Cornell, a position he would hold for the rest of his life.

Ideas about Mars and Venus confirmed

Sagan's first important contributions to understanding the environments of other planets began as ideas he had while still a graduate student. Color changes on the surface of Mars had been observed by scientists for a long time, and some believed these variations were due to seasonal changes of some form of Martian plant life. Sagan, working at times with scientist James Pollack, suggested that the changing colors were instead caused by Martian dust, shifting because of the action of wind storms. This interpretation was later confirmed with photos taken by the *Mariner 9* spacecraft that orbited Mars in the early 1970s—a mission that Sagan himself contributed to. He also suggested that the surface of

Venus was incredibly hot, since the Venusian atmosphere of carbon dioxide and water vapor held in the Sun's heat, thus creating a version of the greenhouse effect. This theory was confirmed by another exploring spacecraft, the Soviet probe *Venera IV,* which transmitted data about the atmosphere of Venus back to Earth in 1967.

Although trained primarily as an astronomer, Sagan was interested in the question of how life might begin on other planets; this led him to perform chemical experiments based on the work of Stanley Lloyd Miller. In the early 1950s, Miller had conducted an experiment in which he replicated the physical conditions that were thought to have existed early in the history of Earth. His experiment resulted in the creation of amino acids, the building blocks of living things. His work gave other scientists an important clue about how life may have first started on Earth. Sagan used this information to study the production of more complex organic molecules in an atmosphere like that of primitive Earth or contemporary Jupiter. This work eventually earned him a patent (government grant for an invention that allows the inventor sole right to make or sell the invention) for a technique that used gaseous mixtures to produce amino acids.

Works on several NASA space missions

Sagan first became involved with spaceflight in 1959, when Lederberg suggested he join a committee on the Space Science Board of the National Academy of Sciences. He became increasingly involved with NASA during the 1960s and participated in many of their most important robotic, or unmanned, missions. He developed experiments for the Mariner mission to Venus and helped design the imaging system for the *Mariner 9* spacecraft that reached Mars's orbit. For *Viking 1* and *Viking 2,* the first missions to land successfully on the surface of Mars, he was part of the team that selected the landing sites. He also worked on *Pioneer 10,* launched in 1972, the first spacecraft to pass Jupiter; and on *Pioneer 11,* launched in 1973, which passed both Jupiter and Saturn. Sagan and his colleagues set their sights even further into the solar system with the *Voyager I* and *II* missions. The two spacecrafts had passed Jupiter and Saturn and reached the outer planets of Uranus and Neptune by the late 1980s, and in 1990 they sent back to Earth the first photographs taken from outside the orbit of Pluto.

Both the Pioneer and the Voyager spacecrafts left the solar system carrying plaques—which Sagan helped to design—with messages for any extraterrestrials that find them; they have pictures of two humans, a man and a woman, as well as various sounds of Earth and astronomical information about Earth's location. During the plaque project Sagan met his third wife, Ann Druyan, who was working as the creative director. Druyan is also a professional writer and served as the secretary of the Federation of American Scientists. They had two children.

Searches for extraterrestrial life

Sagan continued his involvement in space exploration in the 1980s and 1990s. The expertise he developed in biology and genetics while working with Muller, Lederberg, Urey, and others is unusual for an astronomer, and he extensively researched the possibility that Jupiter's moon, Titan, which has an atmosphere, might also have some form of life. Sagan was involved in less direct searches for life beyond Earth as well. He was one of the main supporters of NASA's establishment of a radio astronomy search program that Sagan called CETI, for Communication with Extra-Terrestrial Intelligence. CETI scans the universe for radio signals that may be created by intelligent beings.

A scientist who worked with Sagan on the Viking missions explained to Cooper of the *New Yorker* in 1976 that this desire to find extraterrestrial life was the focus of all of Sagan's various scientific works. "Sagan desperately wants to find life someplace, anyplace—on Mars, on Titan, in the solar system or outside it. I don't know why, but if you read his papers or listen to his speeches, even though they are on a wide variety of seemingly unrelated topics, there is always the question 'Is this or that phenomenon related to life?' People say, 'What a varied career he has had,' but everything he has

Sagan uses a model of the solar system to demonstrate why the orbits of the planets are stable

done has had this one underlying purpose." When Cooper asked Sagan why this was so, the scientist had a ready answer: "I think it's because human beings love to be alive, and we have an emotional resonance with something else alive, rather than with a molybdenum atom."

Cosmos captures public's interest

During the early 1970s Sagan began to make a number of brief appearances on television talk shows and news programs; Johnny Carson invited him on the *Tonight Show* for the first time in 1972, and Sagan soon was almost a regular there, returning to discuss science two or three times a year. But it was *Cosmos,* a series examining the wonders of science and the universe, which the Public Broadcasting System (PBS) began broadcasting in 1980, that made him into a media sensation. Sagan narrated the series, which he wrote with his third wife, Ann Druyan, and Steven Soter, and they used special effects to illustrate a wide range of astronomical phenomena such as black holes (regions in space that exert an extremely intense gravitational force from which nothing, including light, can escape). The series was extremely popular and widely praised both for its showmanship and its content, although some reviewers felt that Sagan tended to claim as fact what most scientists considered only hypotheses (unproven ideas).

Warns the world about nuclear winter

Sagan was active in political issues as well as science; as a graduate student he was arrested in Wisconsin for soliciting (trying to obtain) funds for the Democratic Party, and he was also involved in protests against the Vietnam War. In December 1983 his scientific and political interests were brought together when he and several other scientists published an article about the possible consequences of nuclear war on Earth's atmosphere. They proposed that even a limited number of nuclear explosions could drastically change the world's climate by starting thousands of intense fires that would throw tons of smoke and ash into the atmosphere, lowering the average temperature ten to twenty degrees and bringing on what they called a "nuclear winter." The authors had discovered this possibility by accident a few years earlier, while they were observing how dust storms on the planet Mars cooled the planet's surface and heated up the atmosphere. Their warning provoked a storm of controversy at first, but the article was then followed by a number of studies on the effects of war and other human activities on the world's climate. Later research confirmed the scientists' suspicions that even a limited nuclear war might well lead to catastrophic environmental changes.

The idea of nuclear winter gave many countries, institutions, and individuals a new picture of the results of nuclear war. It also produced great advances in research about Earth's atmosphere. In 1991, when large oil fields in Kuwait were set on fire by Iraqi forces during the Persian Gulf War, Sagan and others used their theory to calculate the effect that the smoke from these fires would have on the climate. They based their prediction on the idea of nuclear winter and they used historical examples of the effects of smoke from large volcanic eruptions. The predictions about the effect of the Kuwait fires, however, have not turned out to be accurate, although the smoke from the oil fires represented only about one percent of the volume of smoke that would be created by a full-scale nuclear war.

Honored for scientific work and writing

In 1978 Sagan won a Pulitzer Prize for his book called *The Dragons of Eden: Speculations on the Evolution of Human Intelligence.* He also received a number of awards for his scientific work, including NASA's Apollo Achievement Award, NASA's Exceptional Scientific Achievement Medal, NASA's Medal for Distinguished Public Service (twice), the Mazursky Award from the American Astronomical Association, and the Public Welfare Medal— the highest award of the National Academy of Sciences. Sagan was a member of the American Association for the Advancement of Science, the American Academy of Arts and Sciences, the American Institute for Aeronautics and Astronautics, and the American Geophysical Union. He also served as the chair of the Division for Planetary Sciences of the American Astronomical Society from 1975 to 1976 and for twelve years was editor-in-chief of *Icarus,* a journal of planetary studies.

Diagnosed with life-threatening disease

Sagan was diagnosed with myelodysplasia, a dangerous disease affecting the bone marrow, in the early 1990s. He received a bone marrow transplant in 1995 to treat the condition, but was left in a very weak condition. In March of 1996, Sagan published another book, titled *The Demon-Haunted World: Science as a Candle in the Dark.* The book outlines the philosophy that Sagan had practiced throughout his career:

science does play a role in the lives of all people, therefore all people should be interested and informed in scientific topics, not drawn to unscientific practices like astrology. In an interview in *U.S. News & World Report* after the publication of his book, Sagan reflected on the role of science in his life and in society: "We have a civilization with immense technological powers.... The lives of many of us are dependent on medical technology—certainly including me. Science has saved my life; not just that, scientific methods and discoveries *of the last five years* have saved my life. If we were to back off from science and technology, we would in fact be condemning most of the human population of Earth to death."

On December 20, 1996, Carl Sagan died of pneumonia, a complication brought on by his bone marrow illness, at the Fred Hutchinson Cancer Research Center in Seattle, Washington. He was remembered in the media and the scientific community for his many accomplishments as a scientist and popular television personality. Dave Eicher of *Astronomy* magazine remembered Sagan as "a giant in astronomy" who inspired the careers of many young astronomers. The head of the National Academy of Sciences, Bruce Alberts, in a quote in the *New York Times,* summed up the even larger role that Sagan played during his life: "Carl Sagan, more than any contemporary scientist I can think of, knew what it takes to stir passion within the public when it comes to the wonder and importance of science."

Further Readings

Baur, Stuart, "Kneedeep in the Cosmic Overwhelm with Carl Sagan," *New York,* September 1, 1975, p. 28.

Contemporary Authors: New Revision Series, Volume 11, Gale, 1984.

Cooper, Henry S. F., "A Resonance with Something Alive," *New Yorker,* June 21, 1976, pp. 38-80, and June 28, 1976, pp. 29-57.

Dicke, William, "Carl Sagan, 62, Astronomer, Popularizer of Science," *New York Times,* December 21, 1996.

Eicher, Dave, "Carl Sagan, 1934-1996," *Astronomy,* March 1997, p. 28.

Goodell, Rae, *The Visible Scientists,* Little, Brown, 1975.

Ridpath, Rian, "A Man Whose Time Has Come," *New Scientist,* Volume 63, July 4, 1974, p. 36.

Ruina, Jack, "A Path Where No Man Thought," *Nature,* August 29, 1991, p. 765.

Sagan, Carl, *Cosmos,* Random House, 1980.

Sagan, Carl, *The Demon-Haunted World: Science as a Candle in the Dark,* Random House, 1996.

Sagan, Carl, *The Dragons of Eden: Speculations on the Evolution of Human Intelligence,* Random House, 1977.

Sagan, Carl, with Stephen Budiansky, "Keeper of the Flame," *U.S. News & World Report,* March 18, 1996, p. 78.

Zimmer, Carl, "Ecowar," *Discover,* January 1992, p. 37.

Helen Brooke Taussig

Born May 24, 1898
Cambridge, Massachusetts
Died May 21, 1986
Pennsylvania

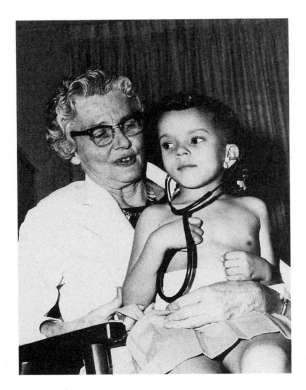

Helen Brooke Taussig investigated the deadly "blue baby" syndrome and proposed the surgical procedure that saved the lives of thousands of children with the condition.

Physician and cardiologist (heart doctor) Helen Brooke Taussig spent her career as the head of the Children's Heart Clinic at Johns Hopkins University. In the course of her work with young children, she discovered that cyanotic infants—known as "blue-babies" because of the bluish or purplish color of their skin—died of insufficient blood circulation to the lungs, not of cardiac arrest, as had previously been thought. To correct the problem, she and colleague Dr. Alfred Blalock developed a surgical procedure called the Blalock-Taussig shunt. First used in 1944, the Blalock-Taussig shunt has saved the lives of thousands of children.

In 1961, after investigating reports of numerous birth defects in Germany, Taussig determined that the cause was the use of the drug thalidomide. Her intervention prevented thalidomide from being sold in the United States. The recipient of numerous honorary degrees and awards, she was presented with the Medal of Freedom in 1964 and a National Medal of Science in 1977.

Taussig was born on May 24, 1898, in Cambridge, Massachusetts, the youngest of four children of well-known Harvard economist Frank William Taussig and Edith Gould Taussig. As a child she had severe reading problems because of a disorder known as dyslexia, yet in spite of her difficulties she became an excellent student. Taussig's mother had attended Radcliffe College in Cambridge, Massachusetts, and was interested in the natural sciences. Like her mother, Taussig was also interested in the sciences and attended Radcliffe, where she played championship tennis. Later she transferred to the University of California at Berkeley, where she earned her bachelor of arts degree in 1921.

Encounters sex discrimination

Having decided on a career in medicine, Taussig found her educational choices were limited by sex discrimination. Although she began her medical studies at Harvard University in Cambridge, Massachusetts, the medical school did not admit women to its regular curriculum. She then enrolled in Harvard's School of Public Health, where she was permitted to take courses but not allowed to work toward a degree. After studying anatomy at nearby Boston University, she was accepted into the medical school at Johns Hopkins University in Baltimore, Maryland, where she eventually specialized in heart research.

After receiving her doctor of medicine degree in 1927, Taussig became a pediatric intern, or a person who is training for a career as a children's physician. She worked as an attending physician at the university's recently established Pediatric Cardiac Clinic. Upon completion of her internship in 1930 she was appointed physician-in-charge of the Pediatric Cardiac Clinic, where she would spend her entire career until her retirement in 1963. In 1946 she was appointed associate professor of pediatrics and in 1959 she was promoted to full professor, becoming the first woman in the history of the medical school to hold that title.

Throughout her career, Helen Brooke Taussig contributed important information about children's health issues, particularly heart problems. In order to observe a patient's condition, she pioneered new medical tools and practices, including the use of X rays to view the workings of the heart and the use of electrocardiograms to monitor the heart's movements. By identifying the cause of the "blue baby" syndrome and coming up with the idea for the surgery that fixes the condition, Taussig helped to save the lives of thousands of children who would have died without treatment. The medical researcher also prevented countless children from developing birth defects when she identified thalidomide, a drug sometimes used by pregnant women, as the cause of severe deformities in babies. Because of Taussig's findings about the dangers of thalidomide, which had been widely used in Europe, it was never approved for use in the United States.

Conducts ground-breaking research

In 1930 Taussig began her studies of congenital (existing before birth) heart disease. Over the years she also examined and treated hundreds of children whose hearts were damaged by rheumatic fever, a disease that causes inflammation of body joints and heart valves. She developed innovative ways of gathering information about the heart that led to a new understanding of pediatric heart problems. Taussig learned to use the fluoroscope, a new instrument that passed X-ray beams through the body, in order to project images of the heart, lungs, and major arteries onto a florescent screen. She also developed the use of the electrocardiograph, an instrument that makes a graphic record of the heart's movements.

Does pioneering work with Blalock

As Taussig's work progressed she became interested in cyanotic children, known as "blue babies." She realized the blueness of cyanotic children was the result of insufficient oxygen in the blood. In the normal heart, bluish blood from the outer parts of the body enters the right atrium (upper receiving chamber) of the heart and then goes to the right ventricle (the lower pumping chamber) to be pumped through a major artery to the lungs. In the lungs, the blood receives a new supply of oxygen that changes its color to bright red. Then the blood returns to the heart, entering the left atrium and descending to the left ventricle, which pumps the blood to the rest of the body. The two sides of the heart are kept separate by a wall called the septum. Taussig discovered that the insufficient oxygen level of the

blood of "blue-babies" was usually the result of either a leaking septum or an overly narrow artery leading from the right ventricle to the lungs. At that time surgeons were unable to enter the heart to repair the septum surgically. But in cases where the artery to the lungs was the problem, Taussig believed it might be possible either to repair the artery or to attach a tube that would perform the same function.

Taussig persuaded Dr. Alfred Blalock, the chair of the Department of Surgery at the clinic, to work on the problem. Blalock and his assistant, Vivian Thomas, developed a procedure that was first used on a human in 1944, when the operation was performed on one of Taussig's infant patients. Blalock rerouted a branch of the aorta (the main artery of the human body that starts at the left ventricle of the heart and carries blood to all the organs except the heart) that normally went to the infant's arm and connected it to the lungs. In the years that followed, this procedure, called the Blalock-Taussig shunt, saved the lives of thousands of cyanotic children.

As the fame of the Pediatric Cardiac Clinic grew, Blalock and Taussig developed team methods for dealing with different phases of treatment. Their management techniques became the model for many cardiac, or heart treatment, centers as well as other kinds of medical care facilities. Taussig trained a whole generation of pediatric cardiologists, doctors who treat children's heart problems. She wrote the standard textbook in the field of pediatric cardiology, *Congenital Malformations of the Heart,* which was first published in 1947. She also continued her research on rheumatic fever, which was by then the leading cause of heart problems in children.

Influences U.S. policy on thalidomide

During the 1950s Taussig served on numerous national and international committees. In 1962 a German graduate of her training program told her about the alarming increase in Germany of phocomelia, a rare birth defect that causes infants to be born with severely deformed limbs. The defect was thought, but not yet proven, to be associated with a popular

Alfred Blalock, American Surgeon

After Helen Brooke Taussig discovered that the "blue baby" syndrome was caused by a congenital heart defect (that is, a defect that developed before birth), which limited the flow of blood from the heart to the lungs, she turned to her colleague Dr. Alfred Blalock (1899-1964) to help devise a surgery that would correct the problem. Blalock was a professor of surgery and chief surgeon at Johns Hopkins Hospital. Before coming to Johns Hopkins, he had achieved national prominence in the field of vascular surgery (surgery focusing on parts of the body that circulate blood) at Vanderbilt University Hospital in Nashville, Tennessee. Taussig believed that blue babies could be cured by an operation similar to the one she knew Blalock had performed on dogs while he was at Vanderbilt Hospital, and she discussed the possibility with the surgeon. When Taussig suggested increasing the blood flow to the lungs by hooking up the subclavian artery with the pulmonary artery, Blalock agreed that it might be possible. After two years of experiments with two hundred procedures on dogs, he told Taussig he was ready to save a baby, and in 1944 he performed his first "reoxygenation" surgery on a blue baby.

Although the infant that Blalock operated on improved at first and began to gain weight, he died nine months later. But this pioneering surgery did prove that the pulmonary artery could be bypassed. In 1945, after Blalock had done sixty-five blue-baby operations, he suddenly became a hero in the press when reporters discovered that he had saved 80 percent of his "doomed" patients. Patients came from all over the world; Blalock operated on suitable children after they had been thoroughly evaluated by Taussig. From 1945 to 1950 surgery was performed on more than one thousand cyanotic patients (meaning blue in color from lack of oxygen, cyanotic is pronounced 'si-in-ah-tik). With improvements in surgical technique and better selection of cases, the death rate of patients receiving the Blalock-Taussig shunt, as the new procedure was called (a shunt is a kind of detour, redirecting the flow of—in this case—blood around a damaged area), fell from 20.3 percent in 1945 to 4.7 percent in 1950. Before Blalock's pioneering surgical achievement, blue babies could only expect to live about twelve years. With the Blalock-Taussig shunt, many ill children were allowed to lead relatively normal lives.

sedative called Contergan. The drug was sold throughout Germany and other European countries and often taken by women to counteract nausea during early pregnancy. Deciding to investigate for herself, Taussig spent six weeks in Germany visiting clinics, examining babies with the abnormalities, and interviewing their doctors and mothers.

Taussig noted the absence of such birth defects in the infants of American soldiers living at U.S. military installations in Germany, where the drug was banned. But there was one exception—a baby whose mother had gone off the post to obtain Contergan was born severely deformed. Taussig immediately reported her findings to colleagues in the United States. Hearing about Taussig's discovery, Dr. Frances Oldham Kelsey, a staff physician at the U.S. Food and Drug Administration (FDA), acted on her own suspicions about Contergan, which was known as thalidomide in the United States. She urged banning the sale of the drug in the United States until its effects could be thoroughly studied. Taussig's research was thus instrumental in the FDA's rejection of the application from the William S. Merrell Company to market the drug thalidomide.

Enjoys an active retirement

Although Taussig formally retired in 1963, she remained deeply involved in causes that affected the health of children. Shortly after retiring she had operations to restore her hearing, having spent most of her career in a state of near deafness. For the first time since she was a child she was able to hear ordinary sounds without a hearing aid. She was the author of 100 major scientific publications, 41 of which she wrote after her retirement. In the late 1970s she moved to a retirement community near Philadelphia. On May 21, 1986, while driving fellow retirees to vote in a primary election, she was killed in an automobile accident at the age of 87.

Further Reading

Baldwin, Joyce, *To Heal the Heart of a Child: Helen Taussig, M.D.,* Walker, 1992.

Nuland, Sherwin B., *Doctors: The Biography of Medicine,* Knopf, 1988, pp. 422-56.

Valentina Tereshkova

Born March 6, 1937
Maslennikovo, Union of Soviet Socialist
Republics (now Russia)

Until she was 25 years old, Valentina Vladimirovna Tereshkova lived quietly as a factory worker and skydiving enthusiast in the Russian city of Yaroslavl. Her life was transformed in 1962, when she entered the Soviet cosmonaut (astronaut) training program and went on to become the first woman to fly in space. From humble beginnings, she was thrust into stardom by a quirk of fate.

Tereshkova was born on March 6, 1937, in Maslennikovo, a village near the Russian city of Yaroslavl. Her father, who was killed in action during World War II (1939-46), had been a tractor driver on a collective farm in Maslennikovo. After her father's death she moved to Yaroslavl, where her mother found work in a textile factory and where Tereshkova started school in 1945. At age 16 Tereshkova went to work in the Yaroslavl tire factory while continuing her studies at night school. In 1955 she took a job as a loom operator at the Red Canal Cotton Mill and enrolled in correspondence courses at a technical school.

Valentina Tereshkova, a Soviet cosmonaut, was the first woman to fly in space.

215

IMPACT

omen did not participate as astronauts in the early flights of the space programs of either the United States or the Soviet Union. This was probably due to the perception by some people that women were not capable of handling the physical, psychological, and technological challenges of space flight. But when the Soviet Union put cosmonaut Valentina Tereshkova into orbit in 1963, all of those misperceptions about women in space were proved wrong. Even though Tereshkova's mission was a success, however, the United States would not put its first woman into space for another twenty years.

Interest in parachuting

At this time Tereshkova became interested in parachuting as a hobby, making her first jump in May 1959 and founding a parachute club at her factory. Although she once landed in the Volga River and nearly drowned, she did not give up and ultimately accomplished 126 successful jumps. She also progressed professionally and politically. By 1961 she was a spinning machinery technician and a secretary of the local Communist Youth League. That same year she pursued her fascination with spaceflight, which had begun with the Soviet Union's first successful unmanned space launch, the *Vostok I,* in May 1960.

Tereshkova was so enthusiastic when Yury Gagarin (1934-1968) made the first manned spaceflight in April 1961 that she wrote a letter to the Soviet Space Commission asking to be considered for cosmonaut training. The commission filed her letter along with several thousand others. In early 1962, however, Soviet leader Nikita Khrushchev decided that the country could score a public relations coup against its space rival, the United States, by sending a woman into space. At that time the United States did not accept women for astronaut training and, in fact, would not initiate a program for women for another 20 years. At Khrushchev's urging, the commission reviewed the letters it had received the previous year. On February 16, 1962, Tereshkova and four other Soviet women were chosen for cosmonaut training.

First female cosmonaut

For the first woman in space, Khrushchev wanted to choose an ordinary Russian worker, not one of the many highly skilled Soviet women who worked as scientists or airplane pilots. Tereshkova, with her background as a factory worker and amateur parachutist, was the ideal candidate. When the Soviet Space Commission notified her that she had been selected, she was instructed not to tell her friends or family what she would be doing. Instead, she was to say she had been selected for a women's precision skydiving team. She immediately entered an intensive training program at the Baikonur space center, which involved working in a centrifuge and isolation chamber, functioning under weightless conditions, and making parachute jumps in a space suit. She also received jet pilot training. Since Tereshkova had no scientific experience, she reportedly had difficulty with space technology, but she applied herself to the course and eventually mastered it.

Tereshkova may not have been the initial choice for the first female cosmonaut. There is some speculation that she was originally selected as the backup pilot to another female cosmonaut who was later disqualified for medical reasons. In any case, Tereshkova was aboard the *Vostok 6* rocket when it was launched shortly after noon on June 16, 1963, as part of a joint spaceflight with the *Vostok 5* rocket. The *Vostok 5,* with Valeri Bykovsky on board, had been launched two days earlier. This was the Soviet Union's second joint spaceflight. In August 1962 cosmonauts Andriyan Nikolayev and Pavel Popovich had flown in two rockets, one trailing the other by a few miles in a single orbit. Bykovsky and Tereshkova, however, were launched into two totally separate orbits that ranged from being only three miles apart to as many as several thousand miles apart.

Conducts tests in space

Bykovsky's and Tereshkova's activities provide insight into early spaceflight. They conversed with one another and relayed television pictures back to Earth. Tereshkova carried out a series of physiological tests as part of a continuing effort to learn about the effects of weightlessness and space travel on humans. When she experienced some nausea, the European and American press reported she had been violently ill. Actually, she reacted so well that the flight, which had originally been scheduled for one day, was expanded to three days. Tereshkova landed after 2 days, 22 hours, and 50 minutes in

Sally Ride, American Astronaut

In 1977, Sally Ride (1951-) answered a newspaper ad placed by the National Aeronautics and Space Administration (NASA) requesting applications from young scientists to serve as mission specialists on future space flights. With her background in physics, Ride qualified to become one of the members of NASA's 1978 astronaut training class. In addition to her physical and technological training, Ride also became a part of the space program's technical team. Working with other engineers, she helped to design a remote-control mechanical arm that could be used to deploy and retrieve satellites in space. For two flights of the space shuttle *Columbia* in 1981 and 1982, she served as the ground-based communications officer, relaying messages back and forth between the shuttle crew and NASA managers.

In April 1982, Ride became the center of national attention when it was announced that she would be one of the crew members on the seventh space shuttle flight, making her the first American woman to be sent into space. The space shuttle *Challenger*, with Ride on board, took off on June 18, 1983, from Cape Canaveral, Florida. After the shuttle achieved Earth orbit, Ride deployed two communications satellites, conducted trials of the mechanical arm that she had helped design, and performed and monitored about 40 scientific experiments.

The shuttle mission ended on June 24, 1983. Ride flew on another space shuttle mission, on board the *Challenger* from October 5 to October 13, 1984. Following her landmark flight, a number of other women have flown on U.S. space shuttle missions.

space. In order to return to Earth, Tereshkova fired the retro-engine to brake the rocket. As the space capsule reentered the atmosphere, flames caused by atmospheric friction surrounded the capsule, which then stabilized under a small parachute. Tereshkova was ejected through the side hatch and landed in a regular aviation parachute.

Publicity tours and political career

Tereshkova's successful flight made her an immediate celebrity. Upon landing she was whisked to Moscow to deliver an address to an International Women's Peace Congress. She was then scheduled for an exhausting round of personal appearances that required her to travel around the world making speeches on spaceflight and the international role of women. Yet she had time to resume her personal life, renewing her friendship with fellow cosmonaut Andriyan Nikolayev, whom she had met during the training program. They were married on November 3, 1963, in Moscow in a nationally broadcast ceremony presided over by Khrushchev. In June 1964 Tereshkova and Nikolayev had a daughter, whom they named Valentina. Over the years, however, the couple grew apart, and in June 1983 a Soviet news service announced their divorce.

Tereshkova continued her publicity appearances and official functions. She was elected as a member from Yaroslavl to the Supreme Soviet (the country's highest legislative body) in 1967 and served until 1974. In 1974 she was elected to the presidium, or executive committee, of the Supreme Soviet, an important position that she held until 1991.

Further Reading

Gurney, Gene, and Clare Gurney, *Cosmonauts in Orbit: The Story of the Soviet Manned Space Program,* Franklin Watts, 1974.

Harvey, Brian, *Race into Space: The Soviet Space Program,* John Wiley & Sons, 1988.

Oberg, James E., *Red Star in Orbit,* Macmillan, 1977.

Riabchikov, Evgeny, *Russians in Space,* translated by Gary Daniels and edited by Nikolai Kamanin, Doubleday, 1971.

J. J. Thomson

Born December 18, 1856
Cheetham Hill, England
Died August 30, 1940
Cambridge, England

J. J. Thomson
changed scientific
thought about
the atom when
he discovered
the electron.

A scientist of diverse interests, J. J. Thomson was awarded the Nobel Prize in physics in 1906 for his theoretical and experimental research on the behavior of electricity in gases. A result of that research was Thomson's discovery of the subatomic particle known as the electron in 1897. He also was interested in a number of other topics, including optics (the study of light), magnetism, radioactivity, photoelectricity, and thermionics (a branch of physics relating to the emission of charged particles from an incandescent, or glowing, source).

Joseph John Thomson was born at Cheetham Hill, a suburb of Manchester, England, on December 18, 1856. His father was a bookseller and publisher who specialized in antique volumes. J. J., as he was widely known, originally planned to become an engineer, and arrangements were made for him to apprentice (to study a trade while working for a professional in the field) with a friend of his father's. When the senior Thomson died in 1870, however, the family could no longer afford to pay the expense of J. J.'s apprenticeship, and he enrolled at Owen's College, now the University of Manchester. Thomson studied mathematics, physics, and chemistry under a distinguished science faculty, and with the encouragement of Thomas Baker, a professor of mathematics, Thomson applied for and won a scholarship to Trinity College at Cambridge University.

Spends four decades at Cambridge

Thomson entered Trinity College in 1876 and majored in mathematics, beginning an affiliation with Cambridge University that would last the rest of his life. Although some of the most exciting and important physical and chemical research was going on within a few steps of Thomson's college, he made no attempt to find out about them. However, his single-minded attention to mathematics was rewarded when, in 1880, he earned second place in the college examination on that subject.

Investigates electromagnetism

Thomson's first published work dealt with the research of a fellow scholar at Cambridge whom he had never met, the Scottish physicist **James Clerk Maxwell** (1831-1879; for more information, see volume 2, pp. 616-621). Maxwell had only recently devised his mathematical theory of electromagnetism (the relationship between electricity and magnetism), and Thomson was curious about what this theory would mean for certain physical conditions. For instance, when Thomson analyzed the properties that might be expected of a charged sphere that is placed in motion, he discovered that the apparent mass, or weight, of the sphere would increase as it gained electrical charge. Although Thomson did not pursue this line of research, the finding was a preview of the concept of mass-energy equivalence (the idea that mass can be converted to energy and energy can be converted to mass) that would be proposed by German-born American physicist Albert Einstein (1879-1955) a decade later.

In 1881 Thomson was awarded a fellowship (position offering a grant of money for further study) that allowed him to

When mathematician and physicist J. J. Thomson discovered in 1897 that all atoms have charged subatomic particles called electrons, he not only changed people's ideas about what an atom was like, he influenced several important areas of science and technology. Electric power, and all the devices that use it, are a direct result of learning about the nature of the electron. The science of chemistry was revolutionized by the knowledge that chemical reactions involve the loss, gain, or sharing of electrons between different elements and compounds. The discovery of the electron also led to one of the most important scientific advances of the twentieth century—the principles of quantum mechanics. Quantum mechanics is important because it provides a way of predicting the behavior of microscopic particles such as atoms and electrons, which do not obey the same physical laws as larger objects.

stay at Trinity College. In his research there, he often argued that the best way to attack a problem may sometimes be to devise analogies (comparisons based on the similarities of things) or to construct models of the phenomenon under investigation. An example of this approach was an essay he wrote in 1882 for the Adams Prize competition. The subject of that competition was vortex rings, spinning cloud-like bodies somewhat similar to smoke rings. Vortex rings were of great interest to scientists toward the end of the nineteenth century because many thought that atoms might have a similar structure. Thomson's essay won the prize but, probably more important, it eventually led him into a line of research—electrical discharges in gases—that would produce his greatest accomplishments.

Named to prestigious post

In 1884, Lord Rayleigh retired as Cavendish Professor of Physics—one of the most prestigious chairs of science in the English-speaking world—and he recommended that Thomson be appointed to replace him. Word of the recommendation caused an uproar in the Cambridge scientific community; numerous well-qualified and famous scholars wanted the position for themselves and were outraged that a young man of twenty-eight was being considered for the post. Critics of Thomson's candidacy felt that his background in experimental science was weak because most of his earlier studies and research had been in mathematics or theoretical science (dealing with abstract thought or speculation rather than physical experiments). Still, the selection committee chose Thomson as

Rayleigh's replacement and director of the world-famous Cavendish Laboratory at Cambridge.

Focuses on cathode rays

The research field that Thomson turned to was one related to the topic of his Adams Prize essay—electrical discharge in gases. This was an area of study that had become extremely popular among physicists during the previous decade, largely as the result of the work of Julius Plücker, Johann Wilhelm Hittorf, William Crookes, Eugen Goldstein, and others. Most experiments followed a common model: an electrical discharge was caused to pass through a gas under very low pressure in a glass tube. Under these circumstances, a glowing beam called a cathode ray was observed to follow the electrical discharge from one end of the tube to the other.

The primary question that remained in the mid-1890s concerned the nature of cathode rays. Were they streams of charged particles, and if they were, how big were the particles? Thomson turned his attention to answering this question. A key development in his approach to the problem was the creation of better equipment; by using better vacuums to lower the pressure inside the tube, Thomson was able to obtain clearer results than other researchers. Using improved equipment, Thomson was able to deflect cathode rays with an electrical field and a magnetic field—proving that the rays did consist of particles.

Research reveals the electron

Thomson then went one step further: by measuring the angle at which the rays were deflected by such fields, he was able to calculate the ratio (relationship in quantity or size between two things) of the electrical charge to the mass (e/m) for the particles that made up the rays. He found that the value of e/m was the same for any gas used in the experiment. This led Thomson to deduce that whatever particle made up the cathode rays occurred in all gases. Therefore, the particle must be a part of all the different atoms of those gases.

Thomson also extended his research to other phenomena caused by electrical discharges, such as the discharge from a negatively charged heated wire. He found results similar to those observed in the original glass tube experiments. He concluded that some fundamental particle with a constant e/m ratio was present in all of these experiments and, therefore, was a component of all atoms. The term used by Thomson for these particles—"corpuscle"—was soon replaced by a name suggested earlier by Irish physicist G. J. Stoney (1826-1911)—"electron." Thomson's reports on his discoveries to the British Association (a scientific organization) in 1889 were so well documented that the existence of a new subatomic particle was almost immediately accepted by scientists worldwide.

Proposes "plum pudding" atomic structure

Thomson's discovery raised a number of fundamental questions about the structure of the atom. For nearly a century, scientists had thought of the atom as some kind of indivisible, uniform particle or mass of material. But Thomson had shown that this view could not be correct and that the atom must consist of at least two parts, one of which was the newly discovered electron. To account for his discovery, Thomson proposed a new model of the atom, sometimes referred to as the "plum pudding" atom. In this model, the atom was thought to consist of a positively charged sphere or cloud containing randomly scattered individual electrons, much as individual plums are embedded in the traditional English plum pudding. However, this model was never very successful, and, in the work of Thomson's successor, English physicist Ernest Rutherford (1871-1937), a better atomic picture would soon evolve.

Develops early mass spectrometer

In recognition of his research on electrical discharges in gases, Thomson was awarded the 1906 Nobel Prize in physics. Two years later, he was knighted for his accomplishments in science. By this time, however, Thomson had gone on to a new field of research, the study of the positively charged

William Crookes, English Physicist

William Crookes (1832-1919) is best remembered for his invention of the Crookes tube, a cathode-ray tube that was the forerunner to modern television and video tubes. He is also credited with the discovery of the element thallium in 1861. While trying to determine the precise atomic weight of thallium, Crookes became interested in the use of vacuum tubes, which are electric tubes from which all matter has been removed. By placing a tiny amount of thallium within a vacuum tube and weighing it there, a very accurate measurement could be made. However, he noticed that the arms of the scale would occasionally jerk unexpectedly, even though no visible force was acting upon them. Crookes later discovered that very small amounts of air had remained within the tube, and when struck by light the contents of the tube became disrupted and would move the sensitive scale. In order to demonstrate this phenomenon, Crookes invented a device called a radiometer, which measured the movement of air molecules as they were heated. This device was (and still is) mostly a science toy, but it was also used by Scottish physicist James Clerk Maxwell (1831-1879) to prove the kinetic theory of gases, which states that the particles of a gas move around very quickly, continually bumping into each other and thus changing direction and speed.

Crookes's most important work also stemmed from his experiments with vacuum tubes, particularly cathode-ray tubes. At that time, an improved vacuum tube had been developed that could be used to pass an electric current through the air in the tube and create the glowing effect known as cathode rays. Crookes made improvements to the cathode-ray tube, placing two electrodes—a cathode (a negative electrode) and an anode (a grounded cylinder)—at either end of the tube. He also made the discovery that a small device placed in the path of the cathode ray would move slightly, as if in the current of a stream. It was not known just what made up this invisible stream. Crookes himself thought that it was an ultragaseous fourth state of matter (not belonging to solid, liquid, or gas forms) that was created within the tube. It was not until 1897 that J. J. Thomson announced that a stream of electrons was created by the Crookes tube. Today, the same kind of technology in the Crookes tube exists in the electron guns used in televisions (to "shoot" the electrons at the screen where they appear as the bits of light that make up the images we see) and in electron microscopes.

"channel" rays that are also produced during electrical discharge in gases. Thomson used a method similar to that with which he discovered the electron, the deflection of channel rays with magnetic and electrical fields. The instrument he developed to accomplish the procedure was the forerunner of today's mass spectrometer, with which particles of differing e/m ratios can be separated from each other.

Thomson's use of scientific instruments eventually became so sophisticated that he was able to separate two isotopes (forms of an element with the same chemical properties but different atomic weights) of neon, neon-20 and neon-22, from each other. He was not able to completely interpret the results of this experiment, however, and he eventually turned the work over to one of his graduate students, Francis Aston (1877-1945), who would later earn the 1922 Nobel Prize for chemistry. Aston's continuation of this work resulted not only in a more refined form of the spectrometer, but also in a confirmation that he and Thomson had indeed discovered the first isotopes of a stable element.

Accomplishments in teaching and administration

The work on channel rays marked the end of Thomson's most creative years. His efforts after 1912 focused more on teaching and administration, although he did remain active in research to some extent. He was elected president of the Royal Society in 1915 and was appointed Master of Trinity College in 1918. He resigned as Cavendish professor in the following year, but was then appointed to an honorary chair at the university. Thomson was succeeded in the Cavendish chair by one of his greatest students, Ernest Rutherford.

Thomson's impact on science was just as notable for his skills as a teacher and administrator. He was responsible for the expansion of the Cavendish Laboratories (on two occasions) as well as for its efficient operation for thirty-five years. He had a talent for finding, educating, and nurturing young researchers; seven of his students eventually received Nobel Prizes in the sciences. A few years before Thomson's death, he was honored by a dinner given in his honor at Cambridge.

The list of guests contained most of the leading figures in physical research of the day. At the dinner, Thomson was given a letter of tribute signed by more than two hundred friends, students, and colleagues.

Thomson died in Cambridge on August 30, 1940, and was laid to rest in Westminster Abbey close to two other revolutionary English scientists: Isaac Newton (1642-1727), who developed the laws of motion and the universal law of gravitation, and Charles Darwin (1809-1882), who proposed the theory of evolution based on natural selection. Thomson had married a student of his, Rose Paget, in 1892. Their son, George Paget Thomson (1892-1975), carried on the family legacy of scientific achievement, becoming a renowned experimental physicist who, like his father, was awarded the Nobel Prize in physics.

Further Readings

Jaffe, Bernard, *Crucibles: The Story of Chemistry,* Simon & Schuster, 1957, chapter 12.

Rayleigh, Lord John, *The Life of J. J. Thomson,* [Cambridge], 1943.

Thomson, G. P., *J. J. Thomson and the Cavendish Laboratory in His Day,* [New York], 1965.

Thomson, J. J., *Recollections and Reflections,* [London], 1936.

Weber, Robert L., *Pioneers of Science: Nobel Prize Winners in Physics,* American Institute of Physics, 1980, pp. 29-30.

Alan Turing

Born June 23, 1912
Paddington, England
Died June 7, 1954
Wilmslow, Cheshire, England

Alan Turing described a mathematical problem-solving machine that was the model for the modern computer.

Mathematician Alan Turing is recognized as a pioneer in computer theory. His classic 1936 paper, "On Computable Numbers, with an Application to the Entscheidungs Problem," described a machine that served as a model for the first working computers. During World War II, Turing took part in the top-secret ULTRA project to decipher German military codes. His groundbreaking work at that time led to the first operational digital electronic computers. He published another notable paper in 1950 that offered what became known as the "Turing Test" to determine if a machine possessed intelligence.

Displays talent in math

Alan Mathison Turing was born on June 23, 1912, in Paddington, England, to Julius Mathison Turing and Ethel Sara Stoney. Turing's father served in the British civil service in India, and his wife generally accompanied him. Thus, for the majority of their childhood, Alan and his older brother, John, saw very little of their parents. While in elementary school, the young Turing boys were raised by a retired military couple, the Wards. At the age of 13, Turing entered Sherbourne school, a boys' boarding school in Dorset. His record at Sherbourne was not generally outstanding; he was later remembered as untidy and disinterested in scholastic learning. He did, however, distinguish himself in mathematics and science, showing a particular facility for calculus. Turing also developed an interest in competitive running while at Sherbourne.

Describes computing machine

Turing twice failed to gain entry to Trinity College in Cambridge but was accepted on a scholarship at King's College (also in Cambridge). He graduated in 1934 with a master's degree in mathematics. In 1936 Turing produced his first, and perhaps greatest, work. His paper "On Computable Numbers, with an Application to the Entscheidungs Problem," answered a logical problem staged by German mathematician **David Hilbert** (1862-1943; for more information, see volume 2, pp. 454-462). The question involved the completeness of logic—whether all mathematical problems could, in principle, be solved. Turing's paper, presented in 1937 to the London Mathematical Society, proved that some problems could not be solved. The paper also contained a footnote describing a theoretical automatic machine, which came to be known as the Turing machine, that could solve any mathematical problem— provided it was given the proper algorithms (problem-solving equations or instructions). Although it may not have been Turing's intent at the time, his Turing machine defined the modern computer.

After graduating from Cambridge, Turing was invited to spend a year in the United States studying at Princeton University. He returned to Princeton for a second year—on a Proctor Fellowship—to finish his doctorate. While there, he worked on the subject of computability with Alonso Church and other mathematicians. Turing and his associates worked

Mathematician Alan Turing laid the groundwork for the development of working computers. He first described a computer-like device, known as a "Turing machine," in a 1936 paper. Working for the British government during World War II, he applied his ideas to machines that could break secret codes and later assisted in the creation of the first working digital electronic computer. Named the Colossus, the computer used large vacuum tubes to switch electric signals, and was much larger than computers today, which use small silicon chips. Turing also devised a test to determine if a computer had artificial intelligence, or could perform independent thinking, a milestone that he believed would be reached by the end of the twentieth century.

with binary numbers (1 and 0) and Boolean Algebra, a system combining logic and math that was developed by English mathematician George Boole (1815-1864). Using these tools, they developed a system of equations called logic gates. These logic gates were useful for producing the type of problem-solving algorithms that would be needed by an automatic computing machine. From the initial paper exercise, it was a simple matter to develop logic gates into electrical hardware, using relays and switches, which could—theoretically, and in huge quantities—actually perform the work of a computing machine. As a side project, Turing put together the first three or four stages of an electric multiplier, using relays he constructed himself. After receiving his doctorate, Turing had an opportunity to remain at Princeton, but decided to accept a Cambridge fellowship (position offering a grant of money for further study) instead. He returned to England in 1938.

Helps crack German war codes

Cryptology, the making and breaking of coded messages, was greatly advanced in England after World War I (1914-18). During World War II (1939-45), however, the German military modified a device called the Enigma machine that mechanically coded messages. The English found little success in defeating this method. The original Enigma machine was not new, or even secret; a basic Enigma machine had been in operation for several years and was mostly used to produce commercial codes. The Germans' alterations, though, greatly increased the number of possible letter combinations in a message. The Allies (the countries fighting Germany, including England) were able to duplicate the modifications, but it was a continual cat-and-mouse game; each time Allied analysts figured out a message, the Germans would change the code again, making all of their work useless.

In the fall of 1939, Turing joined the British ULTRA project that was devoted to deciphering (decoding) German codes. He was placed at a top-secret installation in Bletchley, England, where he played a critical role in the development of a machine that deciphered the Enigma's messages by testing key codes until it found the correct combinations. Although this substitution method was uncomplicated, it was impractical to apply because the number of possible combinations could range into the tens of millions. Here Turing was able to put his experience at Princeton to good use; no one else had bridged the gap between abstract logic theory and electric hardware as he had with his electric multiplier. Turing helped construct relay-driven decoders (which were called Bombes, after the ticking noise of the relays) that shortened the code-breaking time from weeks to hours. The Bombes helped uncover secret communications about German military movements, particularly in the German submarine war in the Atlantic Ocean, for almost two years. Eventually, however, the Germans changed their codes and the new level of complexity was too high to be solved practically by electrical decoders. British scientists agreed that although a Bombe of sufficient size could be built for further deciphering work, the machine would be slow and impractical.

Other advances helped to increase the abilities of the decoding machine. Vacuum tubes used as switches (the British called them thermiotic valves) used no moving parts and were a thousand times faster than electrical relays. A decoder made with tubes could do in minutes what it took a Bombe several hours to accomplish. Thus work began on a device that was later named Collosus. Based on the same theoretical principles as earlier Bombes, Collosus was the first operational digital electronic computer. It used 1800 vacuum tubes and proved successful. To this day, the British government has not released much information about Collosus. Some people have claimed that Turing supervised the construction of the first machine to bear the name.

Develops reputation as an eccentric

Many stories were circulated about Turing during the war, mostly surrounding his eccentricity (odd or whimsical behavior). Andrew Hodges noted in his book *Alan Turing, the Enigma*, "With holes in his sports jacket, shiny grey flannel trousers held up with an ancient tie, and hair sticking out at the back, he became the cartoonist's 'boffin' (a scientific expert)—an impression accentuated by his manner of practical work, in which he would grunt and swear as solder failed to stick, scratch his head and make a strange squelching noise as he thought to himself." Unconvinced of England's chances to win the war, Turing converted all of his money to two silver bars, which he buried and was later unable to find. He was horrified at the sight of blood. He may also have been perceived as different than mainstream English society because of his outspoken atheism (disbelief in any deity or god) and his homosexuality. But Turing was highly respected and recognized for the major role he played in the British war effort with the Order of the British Empire, a high honor for someone who served the military in a non-combat position.

Continues to develop computer

In the final months of the war, Turing turned his thoughts back to computing machines. He conceived of a device, built with vacuum tubes, that would be able to perform any function described in mathematical terms and would carry instructions in electronic symbols in its memory. This universal machine, clearly an example of the Turing machine described in his 1936 paper, would not require separate hardware for different functions, only a change of instructions. Turing was not alone in his ambition to construct a computing machine. A group at the University of Pennsylvania had built a computer called ENIAC (Electronic Numerical Integrator and Computer) that was similar to, but more complex, than Colossus. In the process, they had concluded that a better machine was possible. Turing's design was possibly more remarkable because he was working alone out of his home while the ENIAC creators were a large university research group with the full backing of the American military. The American group published well before Turing did, but these advances in computing machines made the British government take a greater interest in Turing's work.

In June 1945 Turing joined the newly formed Mathematics Division of the National Physical Laboratory (NPL). Here he finalized plans for his Automatic Computing Engine (ACE). The rather old-fashioned term "engine" was chosen by NPL management as a tribute to the Analytical Engine proposed in the nineteenth century by English mathematician Charles Babbage (1782-1871); it also allowed for the pleasing acronym "ACE." Turing, however, was unprepared for the slowness and limitations of a government foundation. All of his previous engineering projects had been conducted during wartime, when time was of the essence and no budget limits existed. More than a year after the ACE project was approved, though, no engineering work had been completed and there was little cooperation between participants. A scaled-down version of the ACE was finally completed in 1950. But Turing had already left NPL in 1948, frustrated at the slow pace of the computer's development.

Predicts artificial intelligence

In 1950 Turing produced a widely read paper titled "Computing Machinery and Intelligence." This classic paper expanded on one of Turing's interests—whether computers could possess intelligence. He proposed a test called the "Imitation Game," still used today under the name the "Turing Test." In the test, an interrogator is connected by teletype (later, by computer keyboard) to either a human or a computer at a remote location. The interrogator is allowed to pose any questions and, based on the replies, the interrogator must decide whether a human or a computer is at the other end of the line. If the interrogator cannot distinguish between the two in a statistically significant number of cases, then artificial intelligence has been achieved. Turing predicted that within fifty years, computers could be programmed to play the game so effectively that after a five-minute question period the interrogator would have no more than a 70 percent chance of making the proper identification.

Personal troubles mount

Turing's personal life deteriorated in the early 1950s. After leaving NPL he took a position with Manchester College as deputy director of the newly formed Royal Society Computing Laboratory. But he was not involved in designing or building the computer on which they were working. By this time, Turing was no longer a world-class mathematician, having been sidetracked for too long by electronic engineering, nor was he an engineer. The scientific world seemed to be passing him by.

While at Manchester, Turing, who was homosexual, had an affair with a young man named Arnold Murray. Turing's house was subsequently burglarized by one of Murray's associates. When the investigating police learned of the relationship between Turing and Murray, which Turing did nothing to hide, he was tried and convicted of "gross indecency"— homosexuality was still considered a felony, a major crime, in England in 1952. Because of his social class and relative prominence, he was sentenced—in lieu of serving a jail term—to a year's probation and "treatments" with the female hormone estrogen.

Turing committed suicide by eating a cyanide-laced apple on June 7, 1954. His death puzzled his colleagues; he had been free of the hormone treatments for a year, and he seemed to have weathered the incident with his career intact. He left no note, nor had he given any hint that he had contemplated this act. His mother tried for years to have his death declared accidental, but the cause of death was never officially questioned.

Further Readings

Hodges, Andrew, *Alan Turing, the Enigma,* Simon & Schuster, 1983.

Shurkin, Joel, *Engines of the Mind,* W. W. Norton, 1984.

Slater, Robert, *Portraits in Silicon,* MIT Press, 1987.

Turing, Sara, *Alan M. Turing,* Heffers, 1959.

Picture Credits

Dian Fossey

The photographs appearing in *Scientists: Their Lives and Works* were received from the following sources:

On the cover (clockwise from top right): Luis Alvarez, Robert H. Goddard (**AP/Wide World Photos. Reproduced by permission.**); Margaret Mead (**The Bettmann Archive. Reproduced by permission.**). On the back cover (top to bottom): Edwin H. Land (**AP/Wide World Photos. Reproduced by permission.**); George Washington Carver (**The Bettmann Archive. Reproduced by permission.**).

©**Jerry Bauer. Reproduced by permission:** p. 1; **Archive Photos. Reproduced by permission:** pp. 4, 29; **Swedish Information Service:** p. 7; **The Library of Congress:** pp. v, ix, xxvii, xxxi, 22, 48, 66, 78, 87, 104, 110, 117, 120, 126, 138, 157, 161, 170, 176, 188, 215, 220; **Corbis-Bettman. Reproduced by permission:** pp. 27, 84, 218; © **Richard T. Nowitz/Photo Researchers, Inc. Reproduced by permission:** pp. xxv, 33; **AP/Wide World Photos. Reproduced by permission:** pp. 36, 40, 55, 59, 92, 98, 133, 136, 150,

198, 208, 211, 235; **Reproduced by permission of the Estate of Raimondo Borea:** p. 45; **Photograph by John Reeves. Reproduced by permission:** p. 97; **UPI/Corbis Bettmann. Reproduced by permission:** pp. 100, 203; **New York Public Library Picture Collection:** p. 130; **Queens Borough Public Library, Long Island Division. Reproduced by permission:** p. 145; **Photograph by Rolf Hamilton. Reuters/Archive Photos. Reproduced by permission:** p. 154; **Adrian Arbib/Corbis Media. Reproduced by permission:** p. 164; **The Granger Collection, New York:** p. 228.

Cumulative Index to Volumes 1-4

Italic *type indicates volume numbers;* **boldface** *type indicates entries and their page numbers; (ill.) indicates illustrations.*

Henry Ford

A

Absolute zero *3:* 866, 909
Acetyl coenzyme A *4:* 133, 134
Acid rain *1:* 34
Adams, John Couch *2:* 373
Adam's Ancestors 2: 578
Adamson, George *4:* 2–6
Adamson, Joy *4:* **1–6, 1** (ill.), 4 (ill.)
Addams, Jane *4:* 112, 114
Adler, Alfred *1:* 314
Aerobee *3:* 919
Aerodrome 3: 996
Aerodynamics *3:* 989
Afar Triangle, Ethiopia *2:* 517, 519
An African Odyssey 2: 410
AIDS (acquired immunodeficiency syndrome) *1:* 280, 282–84; *2:* 376–79, 471–72; *3:* 856
Aiken, Howard *3:* 924–26, 926 (ill.)

Aion 2: 542
Air-Crib *3:* 878
Aki, Keitti *1:* **1–6,** 1 (ill.); *3:* 782
Aki-Larner method *1:* 5
Allen, Clarence *3:* 783, 783 (ill.)
Allen, Paul *2:* 364–66
Allotropes *4:* 13
Alpha particles *4:* 121
Altair computer *2:* 365–66
Altman, Sidney *1:* 91
Alvarez, Luis *1:* **7–14,** 7 (ill.), 11 (ill.)
Alvarez, Walter *1:* 9, 13
Alvariño, Angeles *1:* **15–18**
American Ephemeris and Nautical Almanac 4: 172
American Red Cross *1:* 233, 235–36
American Revolution *3:* 772, 774
Ames, Bruce N. *1:* **19–23,** 19 (ill.)
Ames test *1:* 19–21
Amino acids *4:* 137, 201

Analytical engine *1:* 37, 40–42

Analytical psychology *2:* 541

And Keep Your Powder Dry: An Anthropologist Looks at America *2:* 636–37

Andrews, Thomas *2:* 655

Angus *1:* 50

Animal conservation *4:* 92, 94, 96, 98

The Animal Kingdom, Distributed According to Its Organization *1:* 206; *4:* 161

Animal psychology *4:* 3

Animals, ethical treatment of *2:* 411, 413

An Anthropologist on Mars *3:* 830

Anthropology *4:* 66

Antimatter *4:* 188

Antinuclear movement *1:* 124–26, 128

Antiproton *4:* 188

Apollo 11 *4:* 29

Apollo *4:* 14 29

Apollo space program *4:* 24, 29, 30

Apple Computer Inc. *2:* 508, 510–11

Apple I *2:* 510

Apple II *2:* 510–11

Appleton, Edward *3:* 941–42

Archimedes *4:* 101, 106

Argo-Jason system *1:* 49–50

Argonne National Laboratories *1:* 290

Aristarchus of Samos *4:* 50

Aristotle *1:* 206; *4:* 101–103, 106, 160, 178

Arkwright, Richard *1:* **24–29,** 24 (ill.)

Army Ballistic Missile Agency (ABMA) *4:* 26, 28

Arp, Halton *1:* 121

Arrhenius, Svante *1:* **30–36,** 30 (ill.)

Arrhythmias *3:* 929–31

Arrow (race car) *4:* 84

Arsenic *4:* 112, 114

Articulata *4:* 161

Artificial heart *2:* 502–05

Artificial intelligence *2:* 665–69; *4:* 229, 230, 233

Artificial radioactivity *4:* 117, 119, 122

Artificial satellites *3:* 920

Asilomar Conference *3:* 872

Assembly line *4:* 80, 82, 85

Astatine *4:* 188

Aston, Francis *4:* 226

Astronomical unit *4:* 132

Astronomy *4:* 23, 48–50, 53, 56, 100, 103, 126–128, 131, 170–173, 199–202, 206–207

Astrophysical Journal *1:* 154

Atanasoff, John Vincent *2:* 367

Atanasoff-Berry Computer *2:* 367

Atmosphere *4:* 16, 17, 19

Atmospheric motion *4:* 17, 20

Atomic bomb *1:* 10, 127 (ill.), 268; *2:* 402, 680, 683, 687–88, 689 (ill.)

Atomic number *2:* 657-58

Atomic structure *1:* 98–100; *3:* 805–06, 811; *4:* 222, 224

Atomic theory *1:* 197, 199–201; *4:* 7, 11

Atomic weight *1:* 197, 199, 202; *2:* 656–57; *4:* 7, 9, 11

Atoms *4:* 11

Audiometer *1:* 62, 67

Audion *1:* 217, 219–21

Aurora borealis *1:* 199; *3:* 919

Australopithecus *2:* 582–83

Australopithecus afarensis *2:* 516, 520, 522, 584

Australopithecus africanus *2:* 518; *4:* 66, 68, 70–72

The Autobiography of Bertrand Russell *3:* 795, 804

Automatic Computing Engine (ACE) *4:* 233

Automatic Implantable Defibrillator *3:* 929–30

Automobile *4:* 80, 82, 83, 85–87

Avery, Oswald *3:* 934

Awakenings *3:* 827–28, 830

AZT (azidothymidine) *1:* 281, 282 (ill.); *2:* 379, 471

B

Babbage, Charles *1:* **37–43,**
37 (ill.); *4:* 233
Baby and Child Care 1: 128
Bacon, Francis *3:* 953
Bacteriology *4:* 111
Bacteriophage *1:* 77
Baez, Albert *1:* **44–47**
Bakker, Robert T. *1:* 12
Bali *2:* 636
*Balinese Character: A
Photographic Analysis 2:* 636
Ballard, Robert D. *1:* **48–52,** 48
(ill.), 51 (ill.); *3:* 754
Ballistite *2:* 672
Balmer, Johann *1:* 100
Bang, Bernhard L. F. *4:* 78
Bardeen, John *3:* 864–68, 867 (ill.)
Barnard, Christiaan *2:* 506,
506 (ill.)
Barnett, Miles *3:* 942
Barrier Treaty *3:* 913
Barton, Otis *3:* 754
Basov, Nikolai *2:* 602–03
Bass, George *1:* **53–57,** 56 (ill.)
Bathyscaphe *3:* 754, 756
Bayliss, William *3:* 749
H.M.S. *Beagle 1:* 204–05
Becker, Hans *2:* 642; *4:* 121
Becquerel, Henri *1:* 186–88,
188 (ill.); *3:* 789, 807–08
Beebe, William *3:* 754
Bees *1:* 322–24
Begay, Fred *1:* **58–61**
Behavioral psychology *3:*
876–77, 879–80
Bell, Alexander Graham
1: **62–67,** 62 (ill.), 65 (ill.),
248; *2:* 557; *3:* 982–83
Bell, Alexander Melville *1:* 62
Bell Burnell, Jocelyn *1:* **69–74**
Bell Telephone Laboratories
3: 863–64, 868
Bergen cyclone model *4:* 20
Bergen Geophysical Institute
4: 15, 20, 21
Bergen school of meteorology
4: 15, 21
Bergen Weather Service *4:* 15,
19, 20

Berg, Otto *4:* 185, 186, 188
Berg, Paul *1:* **75–81,** 75 (ill.), 80
(ill.); *2:* 387, 389; *3:* 871, 874
Berliner, Emile *1:* 66
Berson, Solomon A.
3: 1006–07, 1011
Berzelius, Jöns Jacob *4:* **7–14,**
7 (ill.)
Bessemer, Henry *1:* **82–87,**
82 (ill.)
*A Better World for Our Children
1:* 128
*Beyond Freedom and Dignity
3:* 879–80
Big bang theory *1:* 117, 121,
270, 273; *2:* 382, 436,
438, 488, 494
Bikini Atoll, Marshall Islands
1: 127 (ill.)
BINAC (binary automatic com-
puter) *2:* 367
Binomial nomenclature *4:* 158, 162
Biodiversity *1:* 192–94, 257;
3: 969–70, 977
Biofeedback *4:* 55, 57–58
Biogen *2:* 384, 388
Biological Diversity Program
1: 193
A Biologist Remembers 1: 321
*The Biology of the Cell Surface
2:* 546
Biotechnology *1:* 78; *2:* 387
*Bird-flight as the Basis of
Aviation 3:* 990
Bismarck 1: 50
Bjerknes, Jacob *4:* 17–21
Bjerknes, Vilhelm *1:* 330;
4: **15–21**
Black body radiation *1:* 100;
3: 760, 762–63
Black Chronology 1: 230–31
Black Folk Then and Now 1: 230
Black holes *1:* 153, 156; *2:* 432,
434–36, 437 (ill.)
*Black Holes and Baby Universes
and Other Essays 2:* 439
Black, James *2:* 472
Blackburn, Elizabeth H.
1: **88–91**
Blake, Francis *1:* 66

Blalock, Alfred *3:* 897–903;
   4: 208, 212, 213
Blalock-Taussig shunt *3:* 901;
   4: 208, 212, 213
Bloch, Felix *1:* 9
Blodgett, Katharine Burr
   1: **92–97,** 92 (ill.), 95 (ill.)
Blood banks *1:* 233, 235
Blue babie syndrome *3:* 897–98,
   901–02; *4:* 208, 210, 213
Boas, Franz *2:* 634
Bohr, Niels *1:* **98–104,** 98 (ill.),
   153, 289; *2:* 400, 646; *3:* 739,
   809, 811, 813
Bolin, Bert *1:* 34, 34 (ill.)
Bolshevik Revolution *3:* 751
Boltzmann, Ludwig *2:* 640
Bombes *4:* 231
Borlaug, Norman *1:* **105–11,**
   105 (ill.)
*Born Free: A Lioness of Two
   Worlds 4:* 1, 3
Born, Max *2:* 400, 681
Born-Oppenheimer method
   2: 682
Bose, Amar *1:* 221
Bothe, Walther *2:* 642; *4:* 121
Boulton, Matthew *3:* 949–50
Boyer, Herbert W. *1:* 78
Boyle, Robert *2:* 573, 573 (ill.);
   4: 178, 181
Brahe, Tycho *1:* 135, 135 (ill.),
   156: *4:* 128, 129, 131, 132
Brattain, Walter *3:* 864–65,
   867–68, 867 (ill.)
Braun, Carl Ferdinand *2:* 613;
   3: 1021
Braun, Wernher von *2:* 395, 395
   (ill.) *4:* **22–32,** 22 (ill.), 27 (ill.)
Brave New World 3: 872–73, 885
Brenner, Sydney *1:* 179
Breuer, Josef *1:* 308, 310, 312
A Brief History of Time (film)
   2: 437
*A Brief History of Time: From the
   Big Bang to Black Holes
   2:* 436
Broom, Robert *2:* 518; *4:* 70,71
Brown, Joy Louise *3:* 885
Brown, Lester R. *1:* 258,
   258 (ill.)

Brown, Robert *1:* 262, 264
*Brown v. Board of Education
   4:* 42, 43–44
Brown, William L. *3:* 970
Brownian motion *1:* 260, 262–64
Bruce, David *4:* 78
Brucellosis *4:* 74, 76–78
Bruce, Mary Elizabeth Steele
   4: 78
Bubble chambers *1:* 7, 9, 11–12
Buckminsterfullerene *1:* 336
Bueker, Elmer *4:* 153
Bunsen, Robert *2:* 655
Burbank, Luther *1:* **112–16,**
   112 (ill.), 115 (ill.)
Burbidge, E. Margaret
   1: **117–23,** 117 (ill.)
Burbidge, Geoffrey *1:* **117–23**

C

Cairns, John, Jr. *3:* 735, 735 (ill.)
Calculus *4:* 176–177, 180, 229
Caldicott, Helen *1:* **124–30,**
   124 (ill.)
Calypso 1: 170
Campbell-Swinton, A. A. *3:* 1021
Camp Leakey *4:* 97
Cancer *4:* 36
Cancer research *1:* 20; *3:* 776, 778
Cannon, Annie Jump *1:*
   131–36, 131 (ill.), 134 (ill.)
Cantor, Georg *3:* 799, 803,
   803 (ill.)
Carbohydrate metabolism
   1: 163–64, 166
Carcinogens *1:* 20–22
Carnot, Nicholas *1:* 225
Carson, Benjamin *4:* **33–38,**
   33 (ill.), 36 (ill.)
Carson, Rachel *1:* **137–43,** 137
   (ill.), 141 (ill.); *2:* 597; *3:* 970
Carver, George Washington
   1: **144–49,** 144 (ill.), 149 (ill.);
   2: 535
Cassini, Giovanni Domenico
   4: 132
Cassini's Division *4:* 132
Catalysts *4:* 7, 11

Cathode rays *3:* 789–90;
  4: 223–225
Cathode-ray tubes *3:* 943,
  1018–21; *4:* 225
Catholic Church *4:* 50–53, 102,
  107–108, 127, 162
Caton-Thompson, Gertrude *2:* 577
CAT scan (computer axial
  tomography) *2:* 483–85
Cavendish Laboratory *1:* 176,
  179; *2:* 618; *3:* 806, 812, 935;
  4: 223, 227
CDC 1604 *4:* 62
CDC 6600 *4:* 59, 62
CDC 8600 *4:* 62
CD-ROMs *2:* 369
Cech, Thomas R. *1:* 91
Celsius scale *3:* 909
Cells *4:* 181
Center for the Biology of Natural
  Systems *3:* 743
Center for the Study of Multiple
  Birth *2:* 549–50
Centigrade scale *3:* 909
Cepheid *2:* 491
Ceres *2:* 371–72
Cerium *4:* 11, 12
Chadwick, James *2:* 642, 642
  (ill.); *3:* 812
Chain, Ernst *1:* 295, 297
Challenger space shuttle *4:* 218
Chamberlain, Owen *4:* 188
Chandrasekhar, Subrahmanyan
  1: **150–57,** 150 (ill.), 155 (ill.)
Channel rays *4:* 226
Chanute, Octave *3:* 989
Character displacement *3:* 970
Charcot, Jean-Martin *1:* 311
Chargaff, Erwin *1:* 177; *3:* 935
Charles, Jacques *3:* 907
Cheetahs *4:* 5
Chemical symbols *4:* 13
Child development *4:* 43–46,
  142, 143
Chimpanzees *2:* 405–10, 517;
  4: 93, 97
Chlorine *1:* 215
Chlorofluorocarbons (CFCs)
  2: 597
Chromosomes *2:* 623–26

Chronometer *4:* 181
Civil rights *4:* 43–46
Clark, Barney *2:* 502, 504–05
Clark, Kenneth B. *4:* **40–47,**
  40, (ill.), 45 (ill.)
Classification system, Linnaean
  4: 157–161, 163
Clausius, Rudolf *3:* 761, 906,
  908, 908 (ill.)
Cloning *1:* 78
Coalition for Responsible Genetic
  Research *3:* 873
Codons *4:* 137
Cohen, Stanley *1:* 78; *4:* 150, 154
  (ill.), 155
Coke, Thomas *3:* 915
Colby, Kenneth *2:* 566
Cold front *4:* 19, 20
Cold Spring Harbor, New York
  3: 934, 936
Color blindness *1:* 200
Colossus *4:* 230–232
Comets, origin of *4:* 174
Coming of Age in Samoa
  2: 633, 635
Commodore computer *2:* 366
Commoner, Barry *3:* 743,
  743 (ill.)
Communication with Extra-
  Terrestrial Intelligence (CETI)
  4: 202
Complimentarity, theory of *1:* 98,
  101; *3:* 742
Computer chips *1:* 158–59
Computer memory *3:* 924
Computers *4:* 59–64, 228–234
Computer simulation
  2: 563–64, 566
"Computing Machinery and
  Intelligence" *4:* 233
Congenital heart disease *4:* 210
*Congenital Malformations of the
  Heart* *4:* 212
Congestive heart failure *3:* 929
Conservation in Action *1:* 139
Conservation International *3:*
  766, 768
Conservation of energy *2:* 526–27
Conservation of mass *2:* 571–72
Conservation of parity *3:* 1012,
  1014–15

Conshelf Saturation Dive program *1:* 171–72

Contact 2: 418

Contergan *4:* 212, 214

Continental drift *3:* 784, 951, 953, 955–56, 957 (ill.), 958

Control Data Corporation (CDC) *4:* 61, 62

Conway, Lynn *1:* **158–60**

Cooper, Leon *3:* 866

Copernican theory *4:* 102, 107, 108

Copernicus, Nicolaus *2:* 443–44, 444 (ill.), 446– 47, 490; *4:* **48–54,** 48 (ill.) 102, 107, 127, 128, 131, 178, 183

Corbino, Orso Mario *1:* 287

Cori, Carl Ferdinand *1:* **161–67,** 161 (ill.), 165 (ill.)

Cori, Gerty T. *1:* **161–67,** 161 (ill.), 165 (ill.)

Cormack, Allan M. *2:* 485

Correlation of parts theory *4:* 161

Correspondence, principle of *1:* 98, 101

Cosmic Background Explorer (COBE) *2:* 438

The Cosmic Connection 2: 418

Cosmos 2: 418; *4:* 198, 200, 204

Cotton *1:* 298–301

Coulomb, Augustin *1:* 214

Courtois, Bernard *1:* 215

Cousteau, Jacques *1:* **168–73,** 168 (ill.), 171 (ill.), 241

Cousteau Society *1:* 172

Cowings, Patricia S. *4:* **55–58,** 55 (ill.)

Cow milk *4:* 76, 77

CRAY 1 *4:* 63

CRAY 2 *4:* 63

CRAY 3 *4:* 64

CRAY 4 *4:* 64

Cray Computers Corporation *4:* 63, 64

Cray Research Corporation *4:* 62

Cray, Seymour *2:* 512, 512 (ill.); *4:* **59- -65,** 59 (ill.)

Creation science *2:* 419

Cretaceous catastrophe *1:* 9

Crick, Francis *1:* **174–80,** 174 (ill.), 302, 304–06; *2:* 385, 469; *3:* 933, 935–37, 936 (ill.)

Critical Exposition of the Philosophy of Leibniz 3: 799

Crookes, William *3:* 790, 1020; *4:* 223, 225

Crop rotation *3:* 911–12, 915–16

Crossbreeding *2:* 623, 649–50

Cry of the Kalahari 2: 410

Cryptology *4:* 230, 231

Curie, Jacques *1:* 181–83

Curie, Marie *1:* **181–91,** 181 (ill.), 184 (ill.); *4:* 117–119, 121, 122

Curie, Pierre *1:* **181–91,** 181 (ill.), 185 (ill.); *4:* 117–119, 121

Cuvier, Georges *1:* 206, 206 (ill.); *4:* 161

Cyanotic heart disease *3:* 897–98, 901–02; *4:* 208, 210–213

Cybernetics *3:* 959–61

Cybernetics 3: 961

Cyclones *4:* 19

Cytology *2:* 623

D

Daimler, Gottlieb *1:* 227; *4:* 83, 87 (ill.)

Daimler Motor Company *4:* 87

Dallmeier, Francisco *1:* **192–96,** 192 (ill.)

Dalton, John *1:* 98, **197–202,** 197 (ill.); *4:* 7, 9, 11

Dark Ghetto: Dilemmas of Social Power 45–46

Dark matter *1:* 270, 272, 274; *2:* 382

Dart, Raymond A. *2:* 518, 518 (ill.); *4:* **66–73,** 66 (ill.)

Darwin, Charles *1:* **203–10,** 203 (ill.), 322; *2:* 518; *4:* 66, 68, 70, 161, 162, 184

Davies, J. A. V. *2:* 465

Davies-Hinton test *2:* 463, 465

Davis, Noel *3:* 914

Davy, Humphry *1:* **211–16,** 211 (ill.), 276– 78; *3:* 773; *4:* 9

Dawson, Charles *2:* 521

DDT (Dichlorodiphenyl-trichloroethane) *1:* 106, 137–38, 140, 142

Dearborn Independent 4: 89

Decimal system *4:* 106

Deep Rover 1: 240–41

Deep-sea exploration *3:* 754, 756

Deforestation *4:* 166, 167

De Forest, Lee *1:* **217–23,** 217 (ill.)

Degenerative diseases *4:* 155

Delbrück, Max *3:* 934, 936

Democritus *1:* 200, 200 (ill.)

The Demon-Haunted World: Science as a Candle in the Dark 4: 205

De Niro, Robert *3:* 828

Deoxyribonucleic acid (DNA) *1:* 75–79, 81, 88–89, 174, 176–79, 178 (ill.), 302–06; *2:* 384, 386, 389, 469, 471; *3:* 870, 933–36; *4:* 135, 137, 138

De revolutionibus orbium coelestium 4: 50, 53

The Descent of Man 1: 209

Desertification *4:* 167

Detroit Automobile Company *4:* 83

Deuterons *2:* 682–83

Devik, Olav M. *4:* 18

De Vries, Hugo *2:* 652, 652 (ill.)

DeVries, William C. *2:* 504

Dialogue Concerning the Two Chief World Systems-- Ptolemaic and Copernican 2: 446; *4:* 108

Dian Fossey Gorilla Fund *4:* 99

Dickinson, Richard *3:* 891

Didymium *4:* 12

Die Mutationstheorie ("The Mutation Theory") *2:* 652

Diesel engine *1:* 224–28, 226 (ill.)

Diesel, Rudolf *1:* **224–28,** 224 (ill.)

Difference engine *1:* 37, 39, 41 (ill.), 42

Difference method *2:* 552

Differentiation of cells *4:* 152

Digestion *3:* 746–48

Diggs, Irene *1:* **229–32**

Digit Fund *4:* 96, 98

Dinosaurs *1:* 9, 12, 14

Dirac, Paul *1:* 153, 286; *4:* 188

Displacement *4:* 106

The Diversity of Life 3: 969, 977

DNA (deoxyribonucleic acid) *1:* 75–79, 81, 88–89, 174, 176–79, 178 (ill.), 302–06; *2:* 384, 386, 389, 469, 471; *3:* 870, 933–36; *4:* 135, 137, 138

DNA technology, recombinant *1:* 75, 77, 79, 81; *3:* 871–74

Doppler, Christian Johann *1:* 122

Doppler effect *1:* 120–22

The Double Helix 1: 305, 307

Downbursts *1:* 329–30

The Dragons of Eden: Speculations on the Evolution of Human 2: 418; *4:* 205

Drake, Frank *1:* 72

Dreams, interpretation of *1:* 313; *2:* 538

Drew, Charles Richard *1:* **233–38,** 233 (ill.)

Drosophila 2: 623–24

Du Bois, W. E. B. *1:* 230

Duryea brothers *4:* 83

Dymaxion automobile *1:* 333, 335

Dymaxion Deployment Unit *1:* 336

Dymaxion house *1:* 333, 335

Dynamic Meteorology and Hydrography 4: 18

Dynamite *2:* 670, 672

E

Earle, Sylvia A. *1:* **239–43,** 239 (ill.), 242 (ill.)

Earthquakes *1:* 1–4, 3 (ill.), 328; *3:* 780–85

Easter Island *2:* 451

Eastman, George *4:* 82

Eastman Kodak *2:* 558

Eckert, J. Presper *2:* 367, 367 (ill.)

E. coli (*Escherichia coli*) *1:* 77, 79; *2:* 386

Ecology *1:* 192, 194; *3:* 977

Ecosystems *1:* 193; *2:* 598

Ectotoxicology *3:* 735

Eddington, Arthur Stanley *1:* 150, 152–53, 266–68

The Edge of the Sea 1: 140

Edgerton, Harold *1:* 172

Edison, Thomas Alva *1:* 66, **244–53,** 244 (ill.), 249 (ill.); *2:* 557, 614; *3:* 891–92, 894– 95, 983, 985; *4:* 82, 145–149

Edwards, Robert G. *3:* 883–87

E=mc² *1:* 260, 265, 269

Ego *1:* 314

The Ego and the Id 1: 314

Ehrlich, Anne H. *1:* 254 (ill.), 255

Ehrlich, Paul *1:* 296, 296 (ill.)

Ehrlich, Paul R. *1:* **254–59,** 254 (ill.)

Eight Minutes to Midnight 1: 129

Einstein, Albert *1:* **260–69,** 260 (ill.), 289; *2:* 434; *3:* 764–65, 813; *4:* 184, 221

Eisenhower, Dwight D. *2:* 690

Eldredge, Niles *2:* 417

Electra complex *1:* 312

Electrical discharges in gases *4:* 222, 223

Electricity, alternating-current *1:* 251; *3:* 889, 891–93

Electricity, direct-current *1:* 251; *3:* 890–92

Electrocardiograph *4:* 210

Electrochemical theory *4:* 10

Electrochemistry *1:* 211–13; *3:* 775

Electrodynanics *4:* 16

Electrogasdynamics (EGD) *2:* 422, 424

Electrolytes *1:* 30–34

Electromagnetic radiation *1:* 263; *2:* 610

Electromagnetic spectrum *2:* 619

Electromagnetic theory *2:* 618; *3:* 789; *4:* 221

Electromagnetism *1:* 275–76, 278; *2:* 374; *2:* 610, 619; *3:* 806; *4:* 221

Electrons *4:* 121, 220, 222, 224, 226

Electroweak force *3:* 832, 834–35

Elementary Seismology 3: 785

Elementary Theory of Nuclear Shell Structure 2: 403

Elementary Treatise on Chemistry 2: 572

The Elements 2: 374

Elion, Gertrude Belle *2:* **468–73,** 468 (ill.)

ELIZA *2:* 566

Elliot Smith, Grafton *4:* 67–70

Ellis, G. F. R. *2:* 435

El Niño *4:* 19

The Emperor's New Mind: Concerning Computers, Minds, and the Laws of Physics 2: 436

Encephalitis lethargica (sleeping sickness) *3:* 829

Endangered species *4:* 5

Enders, John F. *3:* 818, 840, 843

Endocrine system *3:* 847–48, 1009

Engineering Research Associates *4:* 60

ENIAC (electronic numerical integrator and computer) *2:* 367, 676; *4:* 232

Enigma machine *4:* 230

Environmental activism *4:* 2, 6, 164–169, 190–193

Environmental Protection Agency *1:* 138

Eötvös force *3:* 955–56

Epidermal growth factor (EGF) *4:* 154

Epps, Maeve *2:* 584

Erbium *4:* 12

Erosion *4:* 167

Estés, Clarissa Pinkola *2:* 540

Ethology *1:* 320–21; *2:* 405–06, 588, 590

Euclid *2:* 373–74, 374 (ill.), 456

Euclidean geometry *2:* 374; *3:* 795

European Center for Nuclear Research (CERN) *3:* 835

Evans, Alice *3:* 731; *4:* **74–79**

Evans, David *2:* 563

Ever Since Darwin: Reflections in Natural History *2:* 418

Evolution, theory of *1:* 203–04, 207, 209; *2:* 415–16, 419–20; *3:* 747, 907; *4:* 66, 68, 71, 161, 162

Exner, Sigmund *1:* 321

Exobiology *4:* 199

Experimental Researches in Electricity *1:* 279

Experiments With Plant Hybrids *2:* 653

Explorer I *3:* 920; *4:* 28

Explorer III *3:* 920

Explorer space program *4:* 28

Exploring the Dangerous Trades *4:* 116

Exploring the Deep Frontier *1:* 243

Ex-Prodigy *3:* 963

Extraterrestrial intelligence *1:* 72

Extraterrestrial life *4:* 198, 199, 202

F

Faber, Sandra M. *1:* **270–74**

Faber-Jackson relation *1:* 270–72

Faraday, Michael *1:* 31, 216, 246, **275–79,** 275 (ill.); *2:* 557, 618

Farnsworth, Philo T. *3:* 1021

Fauci, Anthony S. *1:* **280–84,** 280 (ill.)

Fermat, Pierre *2:* 460

Fermentation *3:* 723, 726–27, 729

Fermi, Enrico *1:* **285–91,** 285 (ill.); *2:* 399, 401–02, 644, 683, 688; *3:* 1013; *4:* 185–188

Fermi-Dirac statistical mechanics *1:* 285–86

Fertilization *2:* 545–47

Fessenden, Reginald *1:* 219

Fitzgerald, George Francis *1:* 263

The Flamingo's Smile *2:* 420–21

Flamsteed, John *2:* 447

Fleming, Alexander *1:* **292–97,** 292 (ill.)

Fleming, John Ambrose *1:* 220

Fleming, Williamina P. *1:* 133

Florey, Howard W. *1:* 295, 297

Fluoroscope *4:* 210

FNRS 2 *3:* 756

FNRS 3 *3:* 756

Folklore *3:* 718–19

Food preservation *2:* 427, 429–30

Ford Foundation *4:* 90

Ford, Henry *1:* 28, 28 (ill.); *4:* **80–91,** 80 (ill.), 84 (ill.)

Ford Motor Company *4:* 84–86, 89, 90

Ford Quadricycle *4:* 83

Forever Free *4:* 5

Formalism *2:* 461

Fossey, Dian *2:* 408, 408 (ill.); *4:* **92– 99,** 92 (ill.), 98 (ill.)

Foucault, Jean-Bernard-Léon *4:* 52

Foucault's pendulum *4* 52

Foundational analysis *2:* 459

The Foundations of Ethology *2:* 592

Fowler, Ralph H. *1:* 153

Fowler, William A. *1:* 119

Fox, Sally *1:* **298–301**

FoxFibre *1:* 298–301

Francis, Thomas, Jr. *3:* 839

Franklin, Rosalind *1:* 176–77, **302–07;** *3:* 935

Fraunhofer, Joseph *4:* 179

Freedom 7 *4:* 29

Freemartin *2:* 547

French Revolution *2:* 574; *3:* 772, 775

Freon *4:* 62

Freud, Anna *1:* 314

Freud, Sigmund *1:* **308–15,** 308 (ill.), 313 (ill.); *2:* 536, 538–41; *3:* 750

Frey, Gerhard *2:* 460

Friend, Charlotte *1:* **316–19,** 316 (ill.)

Frisch, Karl von *1:* **320–25,** 320 (ill.)

Frisch, Otto *1:* 288; *2:* 639, 644–46

Frost, Edwin B. *2:* 489

Fujita, Tetsuya Theodore *1:* **326–32,** 326 (ill.)

Fuller, R. Buckminster *1:* **333–37,** 333 (ill.), 335 (ill.)

G

Gadolin, Johan *4:* 12
Gagarin, Yury *4:* 216
Gaia: A New Look at Life on Earth *2:* 599
Gaia hypothesis *2:* 596, 598–99
Galápagos Islands *2:* 450
Galaxies *1:* 119, 270–74, 273 (ill.); *2:* 380–82, 487–88, 491–92
Galdikas, Birutė *4:* 97 (ill.)
Galileo Galilei *1:* 267; *2:* 444–46, 490; *3:* 789; *4:* **100–109,** 100 (ill.), 104 (ill.), 128, 178, 182
Gallagher, John *1:* 272
Galle, Johann Gottfried *2:* 373
Gallium arsenide circuits *4:* 63
Game theory *3:* 962; *4:* 197
Gasoline engine *4:* 87
Gates, Bill *2:* 363–70, 363 (ill.)
Gauss, Carl Friedrich *2:* **371–75,** 371 (ill.)
Gayle, Helene D. *2:* **376–79,** 376 (ill.)
Gay-Lussac, Joseph *1:* 215
Geiger counter *3:* 808; *3:* 920
Geiger, Hans *3:* 808–11, 810 (ill.)
Geissler, Heinrich *3:* 1020
Gelfond, A. O. *2:* 458
Geller, Margaret *2:* **380–83,** 380 (ill.)
Gene, artificial *4:* 133, 139
General Motors *4:* 90
Genes and Genomes: A Changing Perspective *3:* 874
Genes, Mind and Culture *3:* 977
Genes *4:* 135
Genetic code *1:* 78, 179, 209
Genetic engineering *1:* 76–78, 80; *3:* 870, 873–74
Genetic transposition *2:* 622, 624–25, 627
Geodesic dome *1:* 333–34, 336–37
Geophysics *4:* 18
George C. Marshall Space Flight Center *4:* 28

George III (of England) *2:* 443–47
German Society for Space Travel *4:* 23
Germ theory *3:* 726
Gifted Hands: The Ben Carson Story *4:* 38
Gilbert, Walter *1:* 81; *2:* **384–91,** 384 (ill.)
Glaser, Donald *1:* 11
Glashow, Sheldon L. *3:* 832, 835, 836 (ill.)
Glass, nonreflecting *1:* 92, 94
Glaucoma *2:* 531
Gliders *3:* 989–93
Global warming *2:* 597
Goddard, Robert H. *2:* **392–98,** 392 (ill.), 397 (ill.)
Gödel, Kurt *2:* 372, 461
Goeppert-Mayer, Maria *2:* **399–404,** 399 (ill.)
Gold, Lois Swirsky *1:* 21–22
Gold, Thomas *1:* 71
Golka, Robert *3:* 891
Gombe Stream Reserve, Tanzania *2:* 405, 407, 409
Gondwanaland *3:* 956
Goodall, Jane *2:* **405–14,** 405 (ill.), 412 (ill.); *4:* 93, 94, 97
Gorillas in the Mist *2:* 408; *4:* 93, 94, 96
Gosling, Raymond *1:* 304–06
Gough, John *1:* 198
Gould, Gordon *2:* 601, 604, 604 (ill.)
Gould, Stephen Jay *2:* **415–21,** 415 (ill.); *3:* 976
Gourdine, Meredith *2:* **422–26,** 422 (ill.), 425 (ill.)
Grand unification theory *2:* 435
Graphophone *1:* 62, 67
Gray, Elisha *1:* 64, 66, 66 (ill.)
The Great Train Robbery *1:* 250
Green Belt Movement *4:* 164, 166–168
Greenhouse effect *1:* 30, 33–35
The Greenhouse Effect, Climate Change, and Ecosystems *1:* 34
Green Revolution *1:* 105, 107–09
Greylag geese *2:* 589
Grissom, Virgil I. "Gus" *4:* 26

Growing Up in New Guinea
    2: 636
Growth factors *4:* 154
Guillemin, Roger *3:* 1009, 1010
    (ill.)
Gutenberg, Beno *3:* 781, 784
Guyots *3:* 954
Gypsum *2:* 569
Gyroscope *4:* 52

H

Hadar, Ethiopia *2:* 519–20, 523
Hadrons *2:* 500
Hahn, Otto *1:* 289; *2:* 401,
    641–42, 644–45, 647
Hale, George E. *2:* 489
Half-life, radioactive *3:* 807, 809
Halley, Edmond *4:* 180
Hall, Lloyd A. *2:* **427–31,**
    427 (ill.)
Hamburger, Viktor *4:* 152, 153
Hamilton, Alice *4:* **110–116**
Hardy, G. H. *3:* 960
Hardy-Weinberg law *2:* 552
Hargreaves, James *1:* 24–25
Harlem Youth Opportunities
    Unlimited (HARYOU) *4:*
    44–46
Harrar, George *1:* 107
Harris, Geoffrey W. *3:* 1009
Harvard University *4:* 110, 115
Hawkes, Graham *1:* 239–41
Hawking, Stephen *2:* **432–40,**
    432 (ill.)
Hazardous waste *4:* 190–192
Head Start *4:* 143
Hektoen, Ludwig *4:* 112–113
Heliocentric theory *4:* 48, 50, 51,
    53, 102, 107
Helmholtz, Hermann von *1:* 63;
    2: 527–28, 527 (ill.); *3:* 760
Hemispherectomy *4:* 36
Henry Ford Company *4:* 84
Henry, Joseph *1:* 64; *2:* 374;
    3: 984
Henslow, John *1:* 204
Heredity *2:* 625–26, 648,
    650–52; *4:* 135

Herschel, Caroline *2:* 442, 447
Herschel, John *2:* 447
Herschel, William *2:* **441–47,**
    441 (ill.)
Hertz, Heinrich *1:* 262; *2:* 610;
    4: 16
Herzfeld, Karl *2:* 401
Hesselberg, Theodor *4:* 18
Hess, Harry Hammond
    3: 954, 958
Hevesy, Georg von *4:* 123
Hewish, Antony *1:* 69–71
Hewlett-Packard *2:* 509
Heyerdahl, Thor *2:* **448–53,**
    448 (ill.)
Hidden hunger *4:* 142
High-energy physics *3:* 805
High-speed flash photography
    1: 172
Hilbert, David *2:* **454–62,** 454
    (ill.); *3:* 803; *4:* 196–197, 229
Hilbert's tenth problem *4:* 194,
    196
Hinton test *2:* 463, 465
Hinton, William Augustus
    2: **463–67,** 463 (ill.)
Hipparchus *2:* 443
Hiroshima, Japan *2:* 688
Hisinger, Wilhelm *4:* 9, 11, 12
*The History of the Corruption of
    Christianity* *3:* 775
History of Western Philosophy
    3: 802
Hitchcock, Dian *2:* 598
Hitchings, George H. *2:* **468–73,**
    468 (ill.)
Hitler, Adolf *1:* 268; *2:* 461;
    3: 765, 849
Hittorf, Johann *3:* 1020
HIV (human immunodeficiency
    virus) *1:* 81, 280, 283–84;
    2: 376, 378, 378 (ill.)
Hodgkin, Dorothy *2:* **474–79,**
    474 (ill.)
Høiland, Einar *4:* 21
Holldobler, Bert *3:* 977
Holley, Robert W. *4:* 137, 138
Home economics *4:* 142
Hominids *2:* 516–17, 519–20, 522
Homo erectus *2:* 583

Homo habilis 2: 516, 520, 522, 580, 583, 586
Homo sapiens 2: 580
Homosexuality 3: 973
Hooke, Robert 4: 179–181, 183
Hooke's law 4: 181
Hormones 3: 848, 853
Horowitz, Paul 1: 72, 72 (ill.)
Horseless carriage 4: 82, 83, 85
Hounsfield, Godfrey 2: **483–86,** 480 (ill.)
Houssay, Bernardo A. 1: 161
How to Know the Butterflies 1: 255
Hoyle, Fred 1: 119, 121
Hubbard, Gardiner 1: 63–64
Hubble, Edwin 2: **487–97,** 487 (ill.), 495 (ill.)
Hubble Space Telescope 1: 117, 122, 274; 2: 493, 493 (ill.)
Huchra, John P. 2: 381–82
Hull House 4: 112–114
Human ecology 4: 141
Human evolution 4: 66, 68, 71
Human genome project 2: 384, 387–88; 3: 933, 937
The Human Mind 2: 663
Human Use of Human Beings 3: 963
Huntsman, Benjamin 1: 84
Hutton, James 2: 599, 599 (ill.)
Huxley, Aldous 3: 885
Huygens, Christiaan 4: 101, 132, 181
Hybridization, plant 1: 112–14, 116
Hydraulics 4: 106
Hydrodynamics 4: 15, 16
Hydrogen bomb 2: 686, 690
Hydroponics 3: 914
Hydrostatic balance 4: 101
Hydrostatics 4: 101, 106
Hydrothermal vents 1: 51

I

I Am a Mathematician 3: 963
IBM 2: 368, 511, 514
Iconoscope 3: 1019

Id 1: 314
Idealism 3: 796, 798
If You Love This Planet: A Plan to Heal the Earth 1: 129
Illinois Commission on Occupational Diseases 4: 113
Industrial disease 4: 113, 114
Industrial hygiene 4: 112, 114, 115
Industrial medicine 4: 113–115
Industrial poisons 4: 110, 114, 115
Industrial Poisons in the United States 4: 115
Industrial Revolution 1: 82, 84; 3: 946, 949, 983
Infectious diseases 3: 723, 728, 855, 858
Information superhighway 2: 370
Ingram, Vernon 1: 178
Inheritance, patterns of 2: 651 (ill.)
Inquisition 4: 108
Instant camera 2: 556, 559–60
Institute of Cell Biology of the Italian National Research Council 4: 155
Institute for Theoretical Physics 1: 98, 100–01
Institute of Food Technologists 2: 427
Institute of Nautical Archaeology 1: 57
Insulin 2: 479; 3: 1008
Integrated circuit 2: 674, 676–77
Intel Corporation 2: 674, 677
Internal-combustion engine 1: 224–25; 4: 81, 82
International Center for Maize and Wheat Improvement 1: 110
International Geophysical Year 3: 920
International Rice Research Institute 1: 108–10
The Interpretation of Dreams 1: 313–14
In the Shadow of Man 2: 405, 410
Introduction to Mathematical Philosophy 3: 802

An Introduction to the Study of Stellar Structure *1:* 153
Invariant theory *2:* 454, 456
Inverse square law *4:* 177
In vitro fertilization *3:* 882, 884, 887
Ionosphere *3:* 941–42
Iron lungs *3:* 819 (ill.)
Iroquois Confederacy *3:* 718
Isomers *4:* 7, 11
Isotopes *4:* 226
Is Peace Possible? *2:* 478

J

Jackson, Robert *1:* 272
Jackson, Shirley Ann *2:* **498–501,** 498 (ill.)
Jacob, Francois *2:* 386
Janzen, Daniel H. *3:* 769, 769 (ill.)
Jarvik, Robert K. *2:* **503–07,** 502 (ill.)
Jarvik-7 *2:* 502, 504–05
Jefferson, Thomas *3:* 775
Jensen, J. Hans D. *2:* 399, 403
Jobs, Steven *2:* **508–14,** 508 (ill.)
Johanson, Donald *2:* **515–23,** 515 (ill.), 584; *4:* 68
Johns Hopkins University *3:* 823, 898, 900, 903
Joliot-Curie, Frédéric *1:* 288; *2:* 642; *4:* **117–125,** 117 (ill.)
Joliot-Curie, Irène *1:* 166, 185, 288; *2:* 642, 644–45; *4:* **117–125,** 117 (ill.), 120 (ill.)
Juno I *4:* 28
Juno II *4:* 28
Juno launch vehicle *4:* 22, 28
Joule, James Prescott *2:* **524–28,** 524 (ill.); *3:* 907
Joule-Thomson effect *2:* 528; *3:* 907
Julian, Percy L. *2:* **529–35,** 529 (ill.), 533 (ill.)
Jung, C. G. *1:* 314; *2:* **536–42,** 536 (ill.)
Jupiter *4:* 173
Jupiter C launch vehicle *4:* 22, 28

Jupiter missile *4:* 22, 26
Jupiter, moons of *4:* 105
Just, Ernest Everett *2:* **543–48,** 543 (ill.)

K

Kahn, Reuben Leon *2:* 465
Kapitsa, Pyotr *3:* 891
Karisoke Research Center *2:* 408; *4:* 94, 96, 98
Karl Menninger School of Psychiatry *2:* 662
Karroo deposits *4:* 71
Keith, Arthur *2:* 521; *4:* 70
Keith, Louis *2:* **549–55,** 549 (ill.)
Kekulé, Friedrich *3:* 741
K-electron capture *1:* 9
Kelley, William *1:* 84
Kelsey, Frances Oldham *4:* 214
Kelvin, Lord. *See* **Thomson, William, Lord Kelvin**
Kelvin scale *3:* 905-906, 909
Kenya Department of Wildlife Services *2:* 584
Kenyapithecus *2:* 580
Kepler, Johannes *1:* 156, 267; *2:* 490, 490 (ill.); *4:* 51, 53, 105, **126–132,** 126 (ill.), 130 (ill.), 178, 183
Khorana, Har Gobind *4:* **133–140,** 133 (ill.), 136 (ill.)
Khush, Gurdev S. *1:* 108
Kieselguhr *2:* 671–72
Kimeu, Kamoya *2:* 585 (ill.)
A Kind of Alaska *3:* 828
Kinescope *3:* 1019, 1021
King Solomon's Ring *2:* 592
Kipfer, Paul *3:* 755
Kirchhoff, Gustav *3:* 760–61; *4:* 179
Kittrell, Flemmie Pansy *4:* **141–144**
Kitty Hawk, North Carolina *3:* 991–93
Klaproth, Martin *4:* 11, 12
Kleew *2:* 591
K-meson *3:* 1002, 1012, 1014–15
Knorr *1:* 48, 50

Koch, Robert *3:* 858–60, 858 (ill.)
Kolff, William *2:* 503, 505
Kon-Tiki 2: 448, 450, 451 (ill.)
Kon-Tiki: Across the Pacific by Raft 2: 450
Krueger, Myron *2:* 563
Kuiper, Gerard Peter *4:* 199
Kundt, August *3:* 788–89
Kurzweil, Raymond *2:* 668, 668 (ill.)
Kwann-Gett heart *2:* 504

L

Lac repressor *2:* 386
Lacroix, Sylvestre *1:* 38
Laetoli, Tanzania *2:* 584
Lake Turkana, Kenya *2:* 575–576, 582–83
Lamarck, Jean Baptiste *1:* 208, 208 (ill.)
Lamb, Willis E. *2:* 602
Land, Edwin H. *2:* **556–61,** 556 (ill.)
Langen, Eugen *1:* 227
Langevin, Paul *3:* 1018–19
Langley Aerodrome *3:* 996
Langley, Samuel P. *1:* 67; *3:* 989, 992, 996, 996 (ill.)
Langmuir, Irving *1:* 93–94, 96 (ill.)
Lanier, Jaron *2:* **562–67,** 562 (ill.)
Lanthanum *4:* 12
The Large Scale Structure of Space-Time 2: 435
Laser *1:* 60; *2:* 601–02, 604–05
Latimer, Lewis H. *4:* **145–149,** 145 (ill.)
Lavoisier, Antoine *1:* 212; *2:* **568– 74,** 568 (ill.); *3:* 774
Law of inclined planes *4:* 106
Law of uniform acceleration *4:* 103
Law of universal gravitation *4:* 176, 178, 180–183
Laws of gravity *4:* 128
Laws of motion *4:* 102, 176, 182
Laws of planetary motion *4:* 128, 129, 131

Lawrence, Ernest Orlando *1:* 8; *2:* 688; *3:* 1001
L-dopa *3:* 830
Lead *4:* 112, 114
Lead poisoning *4:* 114
Lead-210 *4:* 123
Leakey, Jonathan *2:* 578, 586
Leakey, Louis S. B. *2:* 406–07, 516, 522, **575– 87,** 575 (ill.), 578 (ill.); *4:* 93, 94, 97
Leakey, Mary *2:* 517, 522, **575–87,** 575 (ill.), 578 (ill.)
Leakey, Philip *2:* 578, 585–86
Leakey, Richard *2:* 517, 522, **575–87,** 581 (ill.), 585 (ill.)
Least squares, statistical method of *2:* 371–72
Lederberg, Joshua *4:* 199
Lee, Tsung-Dao *3:* 999, 1002, **1012–16**
Leeman, Susan E. *3:* 851, 851 (ill.)
Legendre, Adrien-Marie *2:* 372
Legge, Thomas *4:* 115
A Leg to Stand On 3: 830
Leibniz, Gottfried *1:* 41; *4:* 180
Lenin, Vladimir *3:* 751
Lenoir, Jean-Joseph-Étienne *1:* 227
Leopards *4:* 5
Lessons in Comparative Anatomy 4: 161
Letters on Sunspots 4: 107
Leukemia *1:* 316–18
LeVay, Simon *3:* 973, 973 (ill.)
Leverrier, Jean Urbain *2:* 373
Levi, Giuseppe *4:* 151, 153
Levi-Montalcini, Rita *4:* **150–156,** 150 (ill.)
Liddel, Dorothy *2:* 577
Life Itself 1: 177
Light, polarized *2:* 557
Lightbulb, incandescent *1:* 244, 248–51
Lilienthal, Otto *3:* 989–90, 990 (ill.)
Lillie, Frank Rattray *2:* 545, 547
Lindbergh, Charles *2:* 396
Link, Edwin A. *2:* 563
Linnaeus, Carl *1:* 206, 206 (ill.), 208; *4:* **157–163,** 157 (ill.)

Lions *4:* 1, 3, 4
Lippershey, Hans *4:* 103
Lister, Joseph *3:* 726, 726 (ill.)
Lithium *4:* 11
Living Free 4: 5
Loeb, Jacques *2:* 545–46
Logic gates *4:* 230
Long, Esmond R. *3:* 857
Lonsdale, Kathleen *2:* 478, 478 (ill.)
Lorentz, Hendrik *1:* 263
Lorenz, Konrad *1:* 325; *2:* **588–95,** 588 (ill.), 593 (ill.)
Los Alamos National Laboratory *1:* 58–59; *2:* 680, 684–85, 688
Lovelace, Ada *1:* 40, 42, 42 (ill.)
Lovelock, James E. *2:* **596–600,** 596 (ill.)
Lubricating cup *2:* 629–30, 632
Lucy *2:* 515, 520, 522, 584, 586
Lumsden, Charles *3:* 977
Luria, Salvador *3:* 934
Lusitania 1: 50
Lymphatic system *3:* 822–24
Lysozyme *1:* 294

M

Maathai, Wangari *4:* **164–169,** 164 (ill.)
MacArthur, Robert H. *3:* 971
Macrophage *1:* 284
Magic numbers *2:* 403
Magnetic core memory *3:* 923, 925
Magnetohydrodynamics *2:* 424
Maiman, Theodore *2:* **601–06,** 601 (ill.)
Mall, Franklin P. *3:* 823
Malnutrition *4:* 166, 167
Malta fever *4:* 77, 78
Mammals, origin of *4:* 71
Manhattan Project *1:* 7, 10, 103, 268–69, 285, 289–91; *2:* 399, 402; *2:* 680, 683–85; *3:* 779, 1002
Manus (people) *2:* 635, 635 (ill.)
The Man Who Mistook His Wife for a Hat 3: 827, 830

Marconi, Guglielmo *1:* 218–19; *2:* **607– 15,** 607 (ill.), 609 (ill.); *3:* 806, 896
Mariner 9 4: 200, 201
Mark I *3:* 924, 926
Marriage and Morals 3: 802
Mars *4:* 129, 132, 200, 201, 204
Marsden, Ernest *3:* 809, 811
Martin, Pierre-Emile *1:* 86
Marx, Karl *3:* 797
Maser *2:* 602
Mass production *4:* 80, 82, 86, 90
Mass spectrometer *4:* 224, 226
Mass-energy equivalence *4:* 221
A Matter of Consequences 3: 880
Mauchly, John William *2:* 367, 367 (ill.)
Maury, Antonia *1:* 133
Maxam, Allan *2:* 387
Max Planck Society *3:* 765
Maxwell, James Clerk *2:* 610, **616–21,** 616 (ill.); *3:* 789, 906, 908; *4:* 221, 225
Maybach, Wilhelm *1:* 227; *4:* 87
Mayer, Joseph E. *2:* 400–01
Mayer, Julius *2:* 527
McCarthy, Senator Joseph *2:* 690
McClintock, Barbara *2:* **622–27,** 622 (ill.)
McCormick, Cyrus *4:* 82
McCoy, Elijah *2:* **628–32,** 628 (ill.)
Mead, Margaret *2:* **633–38,** 633 (ill.), 635 (ill.)
Meaning of Evolution 2: 416
The Mechanism of Mendelian Heredity 2: 626
Meiosis *2:* 624–25
Meitner, Lise *1:* 288; *2:* 401, **639– 47,** 639 (ill.); *4:* 187
Meltdown, nuclear *1:* 127
Memorial Institute for Infectious Diseases *4:* 112
Mendel, Gregor *1:* 209; *2:* 626, **648– 53,** 648 (ill.)
Mendel, Lafayette B. *3:* 857
Mendeleev, Dmitry *2:* **654–59,** 654 (ill.); *4:* 185, 186
Meningitis *4:* 76
Menlo Park, New Jersey *1:* 248

Menninger, Charles *2:* 660
Menninger Clinic *2:* 660–61
Menninger, Karl *2:* **660–64,**
   660 (ill.)
Menninger, William *2:* 661
Mental illness *2:* 660–62;
   3: 827, 830
Mercalli scale *1:* 3; *3:* 781–82
Mercedes (automobile) *4:* 87
Mercedes-Benz automobile com-
   pany *4:* 87
Mercury *4:* 112, 114
Mercury space program *4:* 29
Mesometeorology *1:* 331
Mesoscaphe *3:* 758
Messenger RNA *2:* 384–85;
   4: 137, 138
Meteorology *4:* 15, 16, 18, 19, 21
Metric system *2:* 569
Metropolitan Applied Research
   Center (Marc Corp) *4:* 46
Michelson, Albert *2:* 620–21,
   620 (ill.)
Microbursts *1:* 326, 328, 331
Microchips *2:* 674, 676-77
Microsoft *2:* 363–64, 368
Microwaves *2:* 603, 614; *3:* 943
Mid-oceanic ridges *3:* 954
Migraine *3:* 829
Milky Way *2:* 445, 447;
   4: 104, 174
Miller, Stanley Lloyd *4:* 199, 201
Minkowski, Hermann *2:* 455
Minsky, Marvin *2:* **665–69,**
   665 (ill.)
Mirowski, Michel *3:* 931
The Mismeasure of Man *2:* 419
Miss Goodall and the Wild
   Chimpanzees *2:* 410
Missile Envy: The Arms Race and
   Nuclear War *1:* 129
Missing link *4:* 70
Mitchell, Edgar *4:* 29
Mitchell, Maria *4:* **170–175,**
   170 (ill.)
Mittelwerk rocket factory *4:* 25
Model B automobile *4:* 84
Model N automobile *4:* 85
Model T automobile *4:* 82, 85, 86,
   88, 90
Moffat, John G. *4:* 134

Moi, Daniel Arap *2:* 585
The Molecular Biology of the
   Gene *3:* 937
Mollusca 4: 161
Molybdenum *4:* 188
Monod, Jacques Lucien *2:* 386
Monterey One *1:* 335 (ill.)
Morgan, Lewis Henry *3:* 719
Morgan, Thomas Hunt *2:* 626
Morgenstern, Oskar *3:* 962
Morley, Edward *2:* 620–21,
   620 (ill.)
Morse code *2:* 611; *3:* 983–84
Morse, Samuel F. B. *2:* 375;
   3: 984
Mosander, Carl Gustaf *4:* 12
Moseley, Henry *2:* 656–58
Motion of celestial objects *4:* 180
Motion sickness *4:* 55, 57–58
Motorcycle *4:* 87
The Mountain Gorilla: Ecology
   and Behavior 4: 93
Mountain gorillas *4:* 92–95,
   97, 98
Mount Palomar Observatory
   2: 495 (ill.), 496
Mount Wilson Observatory
   2: 487, 489
Moving assembly line *4:* 85, 90
mRNA (messenger ribonucleic
   acid) *2:* 384–85; *4:* 137, 138
MS-DOS (Microsoft Disk
   Operating System) *2:* 368
Muller, Hermann *3:* 934; *4:* 199
Multiple births *2:* 549–54
Myers-Briggs personality assess-
   ment *2:* 538
Mysterium Coniunctionis *2:* 542
Mysterium Cosmographicum
   4: 127

N

Nagama *4:* 78
Nagasaki, Japan *2:* 688
National Aeronautics and Space
   Administration (NASA) *1:* 59;
   2: 598; *4:* 28–31, 55–58, 198,
   200–202, 205, 218

National Earthquake Information
Center *1:* 4
National Foundation for Infantile
Paralysis *3:* 841
National Labor Relations Act
4: 90
National Oceanic and
Atmospheric Administration
1: 239
National Recovery Act *4:* 90
National Space Institute *4:* 31
Natural History 2: 417
*Natural History of Invertebrates
1:* 208
Natural philosophy *1:* 245
Natural selection, theory of
1: 203–04, 207; *2:* 589–90,
653; *3:* 747; *4:* 162
*The Nature of the Chemical Bond
and the Structure of Molecules
and Crystals 3:* 740
Navajo (people) *1:* 58, 60
Nazism (National Socialism)
1: 268; *2:* 461, 593
Nebulae *2:* 441–42, 444, 446
Neddermeyer, Seth *2:* 685, 687
Neon *4:* 226
Neptune *2:* 373
Nereis 2: 545
Nerve growth factor (NGF)
4: 150, 152, 154-156
Nervous system *3:* 847–48;
4: 151, 152
Neuroendocrinology *3:* 847–48,
851–52, 1009
Neuroendocrinology 3: 852
Neurohormones *3:* 849
Neurons *3:* 848, 852
Neurosecretion *3:* 847–50, 853
Neurosurgery *4:* 33, 35
Neutrino *1:* 285, 287
Neutron stars *1:* 71, 153
New Guinea *2:* 635
The New Science 3: 764
*A New System of Chemical
Philosophy 1:* 202
New York State Archeological
Association *3:* 721
Newcomen, Thomas *3:* 947
Newlands, J. A. R. *2:* 656
Newton, Isaac *1:* 38, 41, 246,

266, 267, 267 (ill.); *2:* 435;
3: 764; *4:* **176–184,** 176 (ill.)
NeXT Company *2:* 513–14
Nez Percé (people) *3:* 721
Night vision *3:* 1022
999 (race car) *4:* 84
Nipkow, Paul *3:* 1018
Nirenberg, Marshall Warren
4: 137
Nitroglycerin *2:* 671
Nitrous oxide *1:* 211, 213; *3:* 773
Nobel, Alfred *2:* **670–73,** 670 (ill.)
Nobel Foundation *2:* 672–73
Nobel Peace Prize *1:* 105, 109,
129; *2:* 684, 686; *3:* 738,
740, 744
Nobel Prize for chemistry *1:* 30,
33, 75, 81, 91, 96, 189, 251;
2: 389, 474, 477, 639, 647,
654; *3:* 738, 740, 805–06,
809, 895–96
Nobel Prize for literature *3:* 802
Nobel Prize for physics *1:* 7, 13,
98, 101, 150, 153, 156, 181,
187–88, 260, 263, 285, 288;
2: 399, 403, 607, 613; *3:* 759,
764, 787, 792, 832, 834–35,
862, 865–66, 868, 1003, 1012,
1016
Nobel Prize for physiology or
medicine *1:* 161, 166, 178,
297, 302, 304, 306, 320, 325;
2: 468, 472, 483, 486, 588,
594, 622, 627; *3:* 746, 749,
841, 843, 933, 1004, 1006,
1009, 1011
Nobel's Extra Dynamite *2:* 672
No-Conscription Fellowship
3: 800–01
Noddack, Ida Tacke *4:* **185–189**
Noddack, Walter *4:* 185–188
Noether, Emmy *2:* 459
No More War! 3: 744
Non-Euclidean geometry
2: 371, 373
Norrish, Ronald G. W. *1:* 303
Noyce, Robert *2:* **674–79,**
674 (ill.)
Nuclear chain reaction *1:* 289
(ill.), 289–90

Nuclear disarmament *2:* 684;
    3: 742, 744, 803
Nuclear fission *1:* 288; *2:* 402,
    639–40, 646, 683- -84; *4:* 117,
    119, 124, 185, 187
Nuclear fusion *1:* 59–60
*Nuclear Madness: What You
    Can Do! 1:* 128
Nuclear medicine *3:* 778
Nuclear winter *4:* 198, 204, 205
Nucleic acids *4:* 134, 137
Nucleotides *4:* 135, 137, 138
Nutrition *4:* 141

O

O., Anna (Bertha Pappenheim)
    1: 310
Oberth, Hermann *4:* 23
Occluded front *4:* 19
Occupational safety laws
    4: 113, 114
Ocean *4:* 17
Ocean Everest *1:* 240, 243
O'Connor, Daniel Basil *3:* 840
Oedipus complex *1:* 312
Oersted, Hans Christian *1:* 278
Olduvai Gorge, Tanzania *2:* 406,
    516, 575-76, 579-80
Olitsky, Peter K. *3:* 816
Oliver, Thomas *4:* 113
On Aggression 2: 592, 594
"On Computable Numbers, with
    an Application to the
    Entscheidungs Problem"
    4: 228, 229
On Human Nature 3: 977
*On the Economy of Manufactures
    and Machinery 1:* 40
Oort cloud *4:* 174
Oort, Jan *4:* 174
Oppenheimer, J. Robert
    2: **680–91,** 680 (ill.)
Opticks 4: 183
Oral history *3:* 718, 720
Orangutans *4:* 97
Orgel, Leslie *1:* 177

*The Origin and Development of
    the Lymphatic System 3:* 824
*The Origin of Continents and
    Oceans 3:* 953, 956
*The Origin of Species by Means of
    Natural Selection
    1:* 203–04, 207
Ortiz, Fernando *1:* 230
Osiander, Andreas *4:* 51–52
Osteodontokeratic culture *4:* 72
Ostwald, Friedrich Wilhelm *1:* 33
Otto, Nikolaus August *1:* 227
*Our Knowledge of the External
    World 3:* 800
Overpopulation *1:* 254, 256–58
Owens, Delia *2:* 410
Owens, Mark *2:* 410
Ozone layer, depletion of *2:* 597

P

Paleoanthropology *4:* 66, 68, 69
Paleontology *4:* 161
Palermo, Gianpiero *3:* 887
The Panda's Thumb 2: 419
Pangaea *3:* 953, 956
Parallel processing *4:* 64
Parc National des Virungas,
    Zaire *4:* 94
Parity, principle of *3:* 999,
    1002–03
Parker, Arthur C. *3:* **717–22**
Parthenogenesis *2:* 543, 545
Particle accelerator *1:* 10; *2:* 499;
    3: 812
Particle physics *2:* 682; *3:* 805
Particulars of My Life 3: 880
*Passages from the Life of a
    Philosopher 1:* 43
Pasteur Institute *3:* 724, 732
Pasteur, Louis *2:* 468; *3:*
    723–32, 723 (ill.)
Pasteurization *3:* 730–31; *4:* 74,
    76–79
Patent system *1:* 244, 247–48;
    3: 982; *4:* 146–149, 201
Pathology *4:* 111, 112
Patrick, Ruth *3:* **733–37,** 733
    (ill.), 737 (ill.)

Pauli, Wolfgang *1:* 153, 286–87; *2:* 403

Pauli's Exclusion Principle *1:* 286

Pauling, Linus *1:* 176, 305; *3:* **738– 45,** 738 (ill.), 935

Pavlov, Ivan *3:* **746–52,** 746 (ill.), 750 (ill.)

Peano, Guiseppe *3:* 798–99

Pendulum *4:* 101

Penicillin *1:* 292, 294–97; *2:* 474, 477

Penrose, Roger *2:* 434, 436

Pergament, Eugene *3:* 887

Periodic law *2:* 655–56, 658

Periodic table of the elements *2:* 654, 656–59, 658 (ill.): *4:* 185, 186

Perrin, Jean Baptiste *1:* 262

Pershing missile *4:* 22, 28

Person, Waverly *1:* 4

Personal computers *2:* 363–64, 368–69, 508, 510–11, 513

Pesticides *1:* 106, 137–38, 140

Petty, William, Earl of Shelburne *3:* 774

Phages *3:* 934

Pheromones *3:* 969, 971

Philosophia botanica 4: 162

Philosophiae naturalis principia mathematica 1: 267; *4:* 176, 182, 183

Philosophical Society of Albany *3:* 721

Phinney, Archie *3:* 721

Phlogiston *2:* 570; *3:* 774

Phocomelia *4:* 212

Photoelectric effect *1:* 260, 262–63; *3:* 764

Photography *1:* 251; *2:* 556

Phylon: A Review of Race and Culture 1: 230

Physical Foundations of Radiology 3: 779

Physical hydrodynamics, theory of *1:* 330; *4:* 17

Physicians for Social Responsibility *1:* 124, 127, 129

Physostigmine *2:* 529, 531

PhytoFarm *3:* 914

Piazzi, Guiseppe *2:* 372

Piccard, Auguste *3:* **753–58,** 753 (ill.), 755 (ill.)

Piccard, Jacques *3:* **753–58,** 753 (ill.)

Piccard, Jean *3:* 753

Pickering, Edward *1:* 132

Piezoelectricity *1:* 181, 183

Piltdown Man *2:* 521

The Piltdown Men 2: 521

Pioneer IV 4: 28

Pioneer space program *4:* 28, 201, 202

Pippa's Challenge 4: 5

Pixar Animation Studios *2:* 513–14

Planck, Max *1:* 99–100, 262; *2:* 640–41, 643; *3:* **759–65,** 759 (ill.), 813

Planck's constant *3:* 759–60, 763

Planetary motion *4:* 129

Planetology *4:* 199

Plant sexuality *4:* 158

Plasma *1:* 234–35

Plasma physics *1:* 59; *2:* 424; *3:* 891

Plate tectonics *1:* 51; *3:* 784, 951, 957

Plesst v. Ferguson 4: 42, 43–44

Plotkin, Mark *3:* **766–71,** 767 (ill.)

Plucker, Julius *3:* 1020

"Plum pudding" atomic structure *4:* 224

Plutonium *4:* 188

Pohlflucht 3: 955–56

Poincare, Jules Henri *1:* 263; *4:* 16

Polonium *4:* 119, 121

Polarized glass *2:* 558–59

Polarized light *2:* 557; *3:* 725

Polaroid Corporation *2:* 556, 558–59

Polio (poliomyelitis) *2:* 480–82; *3:* 815–17, 820, 838, 840–44

Polio vaccine *3:* 814, 816–18, 820, 838, 840, 842

Polonium *1:* 181, 186, 189

Polynesia, settlement of *2:* 448–50, 452

Positive reinforcement *3:* 877

PowerGlove *2:* 564
Powless, David *4:* **190–193**
PPD (purified protein derivative)
  3: 856, 860–61
Pregnancy, high-risk *2:* 552
Priestley, Joseph *2:* 571; *3:*
  772– 75, 772 (ill.)
Primate behavior *2:* 406–07, 409
Primatology *4:* 92, 94, 97
Principia Mathematica *3:* 797,
  800–01
"The Principles of Arithmetic,
  Presented by a New Method"
  3: 798
The Principles of Mathematics
  3: 799, 801
*Principles of Social
  Reconstruction* *3:* 800
Prison system *2:* 663
The Problems of Philosophy
  3: 800
Proconsul africanus *2:* 579
Progesterone *2:* 530, 532
Project Paperclip *4:* 26
Project Phoenix *1:* 72
Prokhorov, Aleksandr *2:* 602–03
Promethean Fire *3:* 977
Proteins *4:* 138
Protons *4:* 121
Protoplasm *2:* 546–47
Psychoanalysis *1:* 308, 310,
  312–14; *2:* 536, 538
Psychological Types *2:* 541
*The Psychology of the
  Unconscious* *2:* 540
Psycho-neuroimmunology *3:* 853
Pterodactyl *4:* 161
Ptolemaic system *2:* 443–44,
  446; *4:* 108
Ptolemy *2:* 443; *4:* 50, 51, 53,
  102, 107
Public health *4:* 112, 114
Pugwash Conferences on Science
  and World Affairs *2:* 684
Pulsars *1:* 69, 71, 73
Punctuated equilibrium *2:* 417
Putnam, Frederick Ward *3:* 719
Pyramids *1:* 13
 Pyroelectricity *1:* 183
Pythagoras *2:* 458, 458 (ill.), 460
Pythagorean theorem *2:* 460

Q

Quantum mechanics *1:* 101, 262;
  2: 680–82; *3:* 739–40; *4:* 222
Quantum theory *1:* 99–100;
  3: 759–60, 763–64
Quarks *3:* 835
Quarterman, Lloyd Albert *1:* 290
Quasars *1:* 70, 117, 119–22,
  121 (ill.)
Quasi-Stellar Objects *1:* 120
Queen of Shaba *4:* 5
Quimby, Edith H. *3:* **776–79,**
  776 (ill.)

R

Ra *2:* 452
Ra II *2:* 452
Rabies *3:* 731
Radar *1:* 7, 9; *3:* 939–41, 943
Radiata *4:* 161
Radiation *1:* 125–26; *3:* 776–79,
  790, 807–09
Radiation sickness *1:* 187; *2:* 688
Radio *1:* 217, 222; *2:* 614
Radioactive elements *4:* 121
Radioactive fallout *2:* 688
Radioactive tracer analysis
  4: 122, 123
Radioactive isotopes *3:* 776;
  4: 121
Radioactivity *1:* 181, 186–88;
  3: 789, 805, 807– 09; *4:* 119,
  121
Radioimmunoassay (RIA)
  3: 1004, 1006–09, 1011
Radiological Research Laboratory
  3: 778
Radiometer *4:* 225
Radio waves *2:* 607–08, 610–12;
  3: 893–94
Radium *1:* 181, 186, 189; *4:* 112,
  114, 118, 119
Radium Institute *4:* 118, 120, 124
Radium-D *4:* 123
Rain forests *1:* 257; *3:* 766,
  768–70
Raman, Chandrasekhar V. *1:* 151
Ramart-Lucas, Pauline *2:* 643

Randall, John T. *1:* 303
Rare earth elements *4:* 10, 12
Rayleigh, John *3:* 763
The Realm of the Nebulae 2: 496
Recycling *4:* 192
Redshifting *1:* 120–21, 266, 268;
  2: 381, 492
Redstone missile *4:* 22, 26, 28
Reflecting telescope *4:* 176, 179
*Reflections on the Decline of
  Science in England and on
  Some of Its Causes 1:* 43
Reflex, conditioned *3:* 746,
  749–50, 752
Reflex, unconditioned *3:* 749
Reifenstein, Edward *1:* 73
Relativity, theory of *1:* 260,
  263–67, 269; *3:* 764
Repression *1:* 310, 312
Reuleaux, Franz *1:* 227
Revelle, Roger *1:* 17
*Revolution of the Heavenly
  Spheres 2:* 444
Rhenium *4:* 185-187
Rheticus, Georg *4:* 51
Rheumatic fever *4:* 210, 212
Rheumatoid arthritis *2:* 530
Ribet, Kenneth *2:* 460
Ribosomes *4:* 137
Rice *1:* 108–10
Richer, Jean *4:* 132
Richter, Charles F. *1:* 1, 4, 328;
  3: **780–86,** 780 (ill.), 783 (ill.)
Richter scale *1:* 1, 4, 328; *3:*
  780, 782
Ride, Sally *4:* 218
RNA (ribonucleic acid) *1:* 76,
  90–91, 304, 306
The Road Ahead 2: 370
*Roads to Freedom: Socialism,
  Anarchism and Syndicalism
  3:* 802
Road to Survival 1: 255
Robbins, Frederick *3:* 818,
  841, 843
Roberts, Ed *2:* 365–66
Robinson, Julia *4:* **194–197**
Rockets *2:* 393–94, 396; *4:* 24
Rockoon *3:* 920

Röntgen, Wilhelm *1:* 132;
  3: **787–93,** 787 (ill.)
Roosevelt, Franklin D. *1:* 268
Rosenwald, Julius *2:* 546
Rosing, Boris *3:* 1018
Rotation of Earth *4:* 52
Rotblat, Joseph *2:* 684
Royal Society *1:* 39–40
Rudolphine Tables 4: 129, 131
Russell, Bertrand *3:* **794–804,**
  794 (ill.), 801 (ill.), 960
Russell, Frederick Stratten *1:* 17
Rutherford, Ernest *1:* 99, 102;
  2: 400, 641; *3:* **805–13,** 805
  (ill.), 810 (ill.); *4:* 226

S

Sabin, Albert *3:* **814–21,** 814
  (ill.), 841, 843, 845
Sabin Committee *3:* 826
Sabin, Florence R. *3:* **822–25,**
  822 (ill.), 825 (ill.)
Sacks, Oliver Wolf *3:* **827–31,**
  827 (ill.)
Sagan, Carl *2:* 418, 418 (ill.);
  4: **198– 207.** 198 (ill.), 203 (ill.)
Sakharov, Andrei *2:* 686, 686 (ill.)
Salam, Abdus *2:* 385; *3:*
  832–37, 832 (ill.), 836 (ill.)
Salam-Weinberg theory *3:* 835
Salk Institute for Biological
  Research *1:* 177, 179; *3:* 846
Salk, Jonas *3:* 818, **838–46,** 838
  (ill.), 845 (ill.)
Salts, decomposition of *4:* 9
Salvarsan *1:* 296
Samoa *2:* 634–35, 638
Sanders, Thomas *1:* 63, 65
Sandström, Johann Wilhelm *4:* 18
Sanger, Frederick *2:* 387, 389,
  389 (ill.)
Santa Rosa National Park, Costa
  Rica *3:* 769
Sarnoff, David *3:* 1021
Saturn *4:* 132, 173, 174
Saturn rockets *4:* 22, 24, 28, 29, 30
Savitch, Pavle *2:* 644
Sayer, Malcolm *3:* 828

The Sceptical Chymist 2: 573
Schaller, George *4:* 93, 94
Schally, Andrew V. *3:* 1009,
   1010 (ill.)
Scharrer, Berta *3:* **847–54**
Scharrer, Ernst *3:* 847, 849–50,
   852
Schawlow, A. L. *2:* 602–604
Scheele, Carl Wilhelm *3:* 774
Scheutz, Georg *1:* 42
Schrieffer, J. Robert *3:* 866
Schrödinger, Erwin *3:* 739
Science and the Modern World
   3: 797
Scientific method *3:* 789; *4:* 183
Scientific Revolution *4:* 178, 183
Scripps Institute of Oceanography
   1: 17
Scuba (self-contained underwater
   breathing apparatus)
   1: 239, 241
The Sea Around Us *1:* 139
Sea Cliff *1:* 243
 Seafloor spreading *3:* 954, 958
Seaman, Gary *2:* 411
*Seeing Voices: A Journey Into the
   World of the Deaf* *3:* 831
Segrè, Emilio *3:* 1001; *4:* 188 (ill.)
Segregation, hereditary law of
   2: 650, 652
Segregation of public schools
   4: 40, 43–44
Seibert, Florence *3:* **855–61,**
   855 (ill.)
Seismicity of the Earth *3:* 782
Seismic tomography *1:* 5
Seismograph *1:* 4; *3:* 780, 782
Seizures *4:* 37
Selenium *4:* 11
Selfridge, Thomas *3:* 995
Semiconductors *2:* 675; *3:* 862,
   864–65; *4:* 59
Serengeti National Park *4:* 5
Serengeti Plain, Tanzania *2:* 584
Set theory *3:* 803
Seven Samurai project *1:* 272
Sex and Temperament *2:* 636
The Shaping of a Behaviorist
   3: 880
Shepard, Alan *4:* 26, 29 (ill.)

Shockley, William *2:* 675; *3:*
   862– 69, 862 (ill.), 867 (ill.)
Shoemaker-Levy 9 *2:* 493
Shute, Nevil *1:* 125
Siamese twins *4:* 33, 36, 37
Sibling rivalry *1:* 313
Sickle-cell anemia *3:* 742
Sidereus nuncius *4:* 105
Siderostat *4:* 52
Siemens, Friedrich *1:* 86
Siemens, Wilhelm *1:* 86
Silent Spring *1:* 137–38, 140–41;
   2: 597; *3:* 970
The Silent World *1:* 168, 171
Silicon *2:* 675–77; *3:* 864
Silicon Valley *2:* 676, 678;
   3: 868
Silicosis *4:* 116
Simberloff, Daniel *3:* 972
Simpson, George Gaylord *2:* 416
Singer, Maxine *3:* **870–75,**
   870 (ill.)
Sirius B *1:* 268
6-mercaptopurine (6MP)
   2: 471–72
Skinner, B. F. *2:* 666; *3:* **876–81,**
   876 (ill.)
Skinner Box *3:* 876–78
 Sleeping sickness *4:* 78
Slipher, Vesto M. *2:* 489
Smalley, Richard *1:* 336
Smithsonian Institution *3:* 989
Smoot, George F. *2:* 438,
   438 (ill.)
Snarc *2:* 666
The Society of Mind *2:* 665, 667
Society of Women Engineers
   1: 160
Sociobiology: The New Synthesis
   3: 972, 975–76
Soddy, Frederick *3:* 807–09
Software *2:* 363–64, 368
Soil conservation *4:* 167
Solar energy *3:* 964–67
Solar system *4:* 127, 128, 131
Solar system, size of *4:* 132
Solberg, Halvor *4:* 18–20
Solid-state electronics *3:* 863
Solid-state physics *3:* 863
Somerville, Mary *2:* 447

Sommerfield, Arnold *3:* 739
Sonar *3:* 811
Southern California Seismic
    Array *3:* 785
Southey, Robert *1:* 213
Soya beans *2:* 531–32, 534
Spaceship Earth *1:* 254, 333
Space-time continuum *1:* 266
Space-time singularities *2:* 434
Species plantarum 4: 162
Spectral analysis *1:* 267
Spectrum of light *4:*178, 179
Speed of light *4:* 52
Spinning jenny *1:* 24–25
Spock, Benjamin *1:* 128, 128
    (ill.); *2:* 636
Spontaneous abortion, in cows
    4: 76
Spontaneous generation *3:* 729–30
The Spotted Sphinx 4: 5
Sputnik 1: 45–46
SRC Computers *4:* 64
Staelin, David *1:* 73
Stakman, Elvin Charles *1:* 106
Star clusters *2:* 441–42
Stars, variable *1:* 132–33
Star Trek: The Next Generation
    2: 439
Statics *4:* 106
Statistical Mechanics 2: 401
Steam engine *3:* 945–47, 949;
    4: 81
Steelmaking *1:* 82, 84; *4:* 191
Stellar spectroscopy *1:* 132–33
Steptoe, Patrick *3:* 882–88,
    882 (ill.)
Sterols *2:* 534
Stevin, Simon *4:* 102, 106
Stoney, G. J. *4:* 224
Strassmann, Fritz *1:* 289; *2:* 401,
    644–45, 647; *4:* 187
"A Structure for Deoxyribose
    Nucleic Acid" *1:* 305
Studies in Hysteria 1: 312
Sun, rotation of *4:* 105
Sunspots *4:* 105, 173
Supercomputer *2:* 512; *4:* 59, 61,
    62, 64

Superconductivity *3:* 866
Superego *1:* 314
Supernova *1:* 69, 71, 73, 119, 156
Sutherland, van *2:* 563
Sverdrup, Harald Ulrik *4:* 18, 21
Svedberg, Theodor *3:* 860
Swaminathan, M. S. *1:* 110
Swan, Joseph Wilson *1:* 248–49,
    251, 251 (ill.)
Swedish Academy of Science
    4: 9, 10
Synthesizer, electronic *2:* 668
Syphilis *1:* 296; *2:* 463–65,
    466 (ill.)
Syphilis and Its Treatment 2: 465
Systema Naturae 4: 159
Szilard, Leo *1:* 268

T

Taieb, Maurice *2:* 517, 519
The Tale of John Sickle 2: 591
Tales of a Shaman's Apprentice:
    An Ethnobotanist Searches for
    New Medicines in the Amazon
    Rain Forest 3: 768, 770
Taniyama, Yutaka *2:* 460
Tanjung Puting reserve, Indonesia
    4: 97
Taphonomy *4:* 72
Taussig, Helen Brooke
    3: 900–01, 901 (ill.);
    ***4:* 208–214,** 208 (ill.), 211 (ill.)
Technetium *4:* 186, 188
Tektite II project *1:* 241
Telegraph *1:* 246, 248; *3:* 980,
    983–85
Telephone *1:* 62, 64, 66; *3:* 982
Telepresence *1:* 49–50
Telescope *4:* 103
Telescope, reflector *2:* 442, 489;
    4: 176, 179
Television *3:* 1017, 1019, 1021
Telkes, Maria *3:* 967
Teller, Edward *2:* 399, 401–02
Telomerase *1:* 90
Tensegrity dome *1:* 336
Terbium *4:* 12

Tereshkova, Valentina
4: **215–219,** 215 (ill.)
Tesla coil *3:* 894
Tesla, Nikola *1:* 251; *3:* **889–96,**
889 (ill.), 893 (ill.)
Testosterone *2:* 530, 532
Test tube babies *3:* 882, 884–85
Thalidomide *4:* 208, 210, 214
Thallium *4:* 225
Thenard, Louis *1:* 215
Thermodynamics *4:* 15
Thermometer *4:* 102
The Starry Messenger 4: 105
*The Theory of Games and
Economic Behavior 3:* 962
Theory of the Earth 2: 599
Thomas, Vivien *3:* **897–904,** 897
(ill.); *4:* 212
Thomson, J. J. *1:* 99, 102, 102
(ill.); *3:* 806, 1021; *4:* **220–227,**
220 (ill.)
**Thomson, William,
Lord Kelvin** *2:* 526, 611;
3: **905–10,** 905 (ill.)
Thorium *3:* 807–08; *4:* 10
Thorium-X *3:* 808
Three Mile Island nuclear reactor
1: 127
Throckmorton, Peter *1:* 54–55
Through a Window 2: 411
Tiling *2:* 436
Tinbergen, Nikolaas *1:* 325;
2: 590–91, 591 (ill.)
Tirio (people) *3:* 769
Titanic 1: 48, 50
Tobacco mosaic virus (TMV)
1: 306
Todd, Alexander *4:* 134
Topeka Institute for
Psychoanalysis *2:* 662
Tornadoes *1:* 328–31, 329 (ill.)
Townes, Charles H. *2:* 602–04,
603 (ill.)
Townshend, Charles *3:* **911–16,**
911 (ill.)
Toy Story 2: 513–14
Transfer ribonucleic acid (tRNA)
4: 137, 138
Transistor *2:* 675–76; *3:* 862,
864–67; *4:* 59, 62

Trefusis-Forbes, Katherine
3: 944
Treponema pallidum 2: 466 (ill.)
Trieste 3: 757, 757 (ill.)
Trounson, Alan *3:* 887
Truman, Harry S *2:* 688
Trypanosome *4:* 78
Tsetse flies *4:* 78
Tuberculosis *3:* 824, 855–56,
858–61
Tuck, James *2:* 687
Tull, Jethro *3:* 915
Turing, Alan *4:* **228–234,**
228 (ill.)
Turing machine *4:* 230, 232
The Turing Option 2: 669
"Turing Test" *4:* 228, 233
Tuskegee Institute *1:* 146–48
Two New Sciences 4: 108
Tychonic System *4:* 128
Typhoid fever *4:* 113

U

ULTRA project *4:* 228, 231
*The Undersea Odyssey of the
"Calypso" 1:* 173
*The Undersea World of Jacques
Cousteau 1:* 168
Under the Sea-Wind 1: 139
Underwater archaeology
1: 53–55
Undulant fever *4:* 74, 76, 77
Unification theory *3:* 834
United Auto Workers (UAW)
4: 90
United States Coast Survey *4:* 172
UNIVAC (universal automatic
computer) *2:* 367; *4:* 61
Uranium *1:* 126, 185–86; *2:* 683,
687; *3:* 807–08
Uranium-235 (U-235)
2: 683, 685
Uranus *2:* 441–42
Urban VIII *4:* 108
Urey, Harold *2:* 402; *4:* 199

V

V-2 rocket *4:* 22, 24-26, 28
Vaccine, killed-virus *3:* 818, 838–39, 841
Vaccine, live-virus *3:* 817, 840–41, 845
Vacuum tubes *4:* 231
Valadium *4:* 11
Van Allen belts *3:* 917–18, 921, 921 (ill.)
Van Allen, James *3:* **917–22,** 917 (ill.)
Veblen, Oswald *3:* 960
Venera IV *4:* 201
Venus *4:* 201
Venus, phases of *4:* 105
Vertebrata *4:* 161
Viking space missions *4:* 201
Virtual reality *2:* 562–64, 565 (ill.), 566–67
Virus, computer *2:* 365
Viscose rayon industry *4:* 116
The Vitalizer *2:* 431
Vitamin B^{12} *2:* 474, 477
Vitamin C *3:* 745
Vitamin C and the Common Cold *3:* 745
Vivamos Mejor/USA *1:* 47
Volta, Alessandro *1:* 213–14, 214 (ill.)
Voltaic pile *1:* 214; *4:* 9
Von Braun, Wernher *2:* 395, 395 (ill.); *4:* 22–32, 22 (ill.), 27 (ill.)
Von Neumann, John *3:* 962–63, 962 (ill.)
Vorlesungen über Thermodynamik *3:* 761
Vortex rings *4:* 222
Vostok I *4:* 216
Vostok 5 *4:* 217
Vostok 6 *4:* 217
Voyager space missions *4:* 202
Vries, Hugo de *2:* 626, 653
V-2 rocket *2:* 395; *3:* 919

W

Walden Two *3:* 878–79
Wang, An *3:* **923–28,** 923 (ill.)

Wang Laboratories *3:* 923–25, 927
War Crimes Tribunal *3:* 804
Warm front *4:* 19, 20
War of the Worlds *2:* 393
Washkansky, Louis *2:* 506
Wassermann, August von *2:* 465
Water frame *1:* 25, 27 (ill.)
Water pollution *3:* 734–36
Watkins, Levi, Jr. *3:* **929–32,** 929 (ill.)
Watson, James D. *1:* 174, 176, 178, 180, 302, 304– 06; *2:* 384–85, 469; *3:* **933–38,** 933 (ill.), 936 (ill.)
Watson, Thomas A. *1:* 63–65
Watson-Watt, Robert *3:* **939–44**
Watt, James *3:* **945–50,** 945 (ill.)
Weak force *1:* 287; *3:* 833
Weather forecasting *4:* 15–17, 19, 20
Weber, Wilhelm *2:* 373
Webster, Arthur Gordon *2:* 393
Wegener, Alfred *3:* **951–58,** 951 (ill.)
Wegener's granulomatosis *1:* 281
Weinberg, Steven *3:* 832, 834–35, 836 (ill.)
Weinberg, Wilhelm *2:* 552
Weizenbaum, Joseph *2:* 566
Weller, Thomas *3:* 818, 841, 843
Wells, H. Gideon *3:* 857
Westinghouse, George *3:* 892; *3:* 1020
What Mad Pursuit: A Personal View of Scientific Discovery *1:* 179–80
Wheat *1:* 107–09
Wheatstone, Charles *2:* 375
Wheelwright, George *2:* 558
Whitehead, Alfred North *3:* 796–97, 797 (ill.), 799
Whitehouse, E. O. W. *3:* 909
Whiting, Sarah Frances *1:* 132
Whitney, Eli *4:* 82
Why Men Fight: A Method of Abolishing the International Duel *3:* 800
Wien, Wilhelm *3:* 762–63
Wiener, Norbert *3:* **959–63,** 959 (ill.)

Wigner, Eugene Paul *2:* 403
Wildlife conservation *4:* 5
Wiles, Andrew J. *2:* 460
Wilkins, A. F. *3:* 941
Wilkins, Maurice *1:* 176–77, 302, 304, 306; *3:* 933–36
Williams, Robin *3:* 828
Williamson, James S. *3:* **964–68**
Wilson cloud chamber *4:* 120
Wilson, Edward O. *3:* **969–79,** 969 (ill.)
Wilson, Woodrow *3:* 801
Wind shear *1:* 326, 330–31
Winton, Alexander *4:* 83
Wireless receiver *2:* 609, 609 (ill.)
Wollaston, William Hyde *4:* 179
Woman's Medical School of Northwestern University *4:* 112
Women Who Run with the Wolves *2:* 540
Wonderful Life: The Burgess Shale and the Nature of History *2:* 420
Wong-Staal, Flossie *1:* 283, 283 (ill.)
Woods, Granville T. *3:* **980–86,** 980 (ill.)
Woods Hole Oceanographic Institute *1:* 49; *2:* 544, 547
Woodwell, George M. *1:* 142, 142 (ill.)
Worlds in the Making *1:* 35
Worldwatch Institute *1:* 258
Wozniak, Stephen *2:* 508–11, 513
Wright, Almroth *1:* 293
Wright Flyer I *3:* 993
Wright Flyer III *3:* 994
Wright, Orville *3:* **987–98,** 987 (ill.), 992 (ill.)
Wright, Wilbur *3:* **987–98,** 987 (ill.), 995 (ill.)
Wu, Chien-Shiung *3:* **999–1003,** 999 (ill.), 1012, 1015

X

X-ray crystallography *1:* 177; *2:* 474–76, 478
X-ray diffraction *1:* 175–76, 303–04, 306
X-ray imaging *1:* 44–45, 47
X-ray photograph *3:* 791 (ill.)
X rays *2:* 483; *3:* 776–77, 779, 787, 789–93, 807
X-ray spectroscopy *2:* 657
X-ray telescope *1:* 45

Y

Yalow, Rosalyn Sussman *3:* **1004–11,** 1010 (ill.), 1004 (ill.)
Yang, Chen Ning *3:* 999, 1002, **1012–16,** 1012 (ill.)
The Year of the Greylag Goose *2:* 592
Yerkes Observatory (University of Chicago) *2:* 489
Young, Thomas *2:* 617
Ytterite *4:* 12
Yttria *4:* 12
Yukuna (people) *3:* 768

Z

Zero Population Growth *1:* 257
Zinjanthropus *2:* 579–80
Zion, Élie de *3:* 747
Zionist movement *1:* 269
Zoological Institute, University of Munich *1:* 321, 324
Zoological Philosophy *1:* 208
Zooplankton *1:* 15, 17–18
Zwicky, Fritz *1:* 156
Zworykin, Vladimir *3:* **1017–22,** 1017 (ill.)